Dad

from Lenore

Christmas, 1978

General Pope
and U.S. Indian Policy

RICHARD N. ELLIS

General Pope
and U.S. Indian Policy

ALBUQUERQUE
UNIVERSITY OF NEW MEXICO PRESS

TO ROBERT G. ATHEARN
Scholar, Teacher, Friend

Acknowledgments

John Pope was a prolific letter writer, and his personality was such that he undoubtedly kept copies of his correspondence. His personal papers, however, have not been discovered, and as a result, this study is based upon his official correspondence and is supplemented by other records from the War and Interior Departments and by the papers of contemporaries and superiors such as William T. Sherman and Philip Sheridan. Although the records of the Adjutant General's Office were closed for microfilming when this book was researched, Robert Bahmer, former Archivist of the United States kindly granted permission to use these records for the 1880s because of the lack of material from the Division of the Pacific which was Pope's last command.

I wish to thank Robert Kvasnicka of the Social and Economic Branch of the National Archives, Jack Brennan of the Western History Collection at the University of Colorado, and staff members of the Library of Congress, Yale University Library, University of Colorado Library, and the Henry E. Huntington Library for their assistance. Faculty research grants from Murray State University and the University of New Mexico provided funds for research and typing. Portions of this book previously appeared in the *Southwestern Historical Quarterly* and *Minnesota History*.

Special thanks are due to Robert G. Athearn of the University of Colorado to whom this book is dedicated and to Mrs. Sara D. Jackson who is now with the National Historical Publications Commission. Sara Jackson, formerly of the National Archives provided invaluable assistance during my research. Professor Athearn was a constant source of guidance and encouragement.

Preface

The American public has been captivated by Indian wars and Indian fighters, and although there are numerous treatments of various campaign and field commanders, little attention has been given to the departmental and divisional commanders who formulated the plans, issued the orders, and directed the campaigns. For example, not until the publication of Professor Robert G. Athearn's *William Tecumseh Sherman and the Settlement of the West* in 1956 did that key officer's western career receive more than passing comment by historians. General John Pope is one of the administrative generals who has been ignored by historians, yet following his banishment to the West in 1862 he played an important role in the government's relations with the western tribes.

Born in 1822, Pope grew up in Illinois but spent much of his military career in the West. After graduating from West Point in 1842, he served in the Corps of Topographical Engineers. In 1846 he was attached to Zachary Taylor's army in Texas and remained with it throughout the war with Mexico, receiving brevet ranks of first lieutenant and captain. Following the war he returned to the corps and continued as a surveyor in Minnesota and then in New Mexico and Texas where he participated in the survey for the transcontinental railroad along the 32nd parallel. With the outbreak of the Civil War in 1861 Pope jumped in rank from captain in the regular army to brigadier general of the volunteers and assumed command of units in the Mississippi Valley. After initial success at New Madrid and Island No. 10 he was called East where he was defeated by Robert E. Lee at Bull Run. As a result, he was sent to Minnesota to fight Indians.

With the exception of a brief period in the late 1860s Pope spent the remainder of his military career in the West as a departmental and divisional commander, directing campaigns against hostile Indians when necessary. Although he talked of extermination at first, he was an able and thorough administrator and carefully studied his foes. Close scrutiny of the Indian problem caused a growing concern for the welfare of the red men, and throughout the latter part of his career he used his influence to prevent bloodshed and secure adequate treatment for the tribes. Glory and fame from fighting Indians were elusive. Although there were opportunities for conflict, as well as authorization and encouragement from the Interior Department, Pope at times demurred. He had no desire for a reputation as an Indian fighter or exterminator. Moreover, he was a humane man with a sincere interest in the welfare of an unfortunate minority. Firm but fair, he was more realistic than most officials connected with the Indian Bureau.

Contents

Illustrations

CHAPTER ONE

"The Sioux Indians
. . . have risen"

In June 1862 victory-starved Northerners eagerly scanned press dispatches for signs of improvement in the military situation. The war had not gone well, but a new general—John Pope, a westerner—had arrived in Washington to command the recently created Army of Virginia. And he promised action. His headquarters would be in the saddle; "attack and not defense" would be the order of the day; the Army of Virginia would look ahead and not behind. In the West, he said, "we have always seen the backs of our enemies."

Pope was not an unknown in the summer of 1862. The reading public, following the course of the conflict, was familiar with the West Point graduate who had brought victories in the West. New Madrid and Island No. 10 were common topics of conversation, and he promised to do the same in the East where victory was still uncertain. He would march to New Orleans, he said, and Unionists hoped that he would fulfill his promise to "bag the whole crowd" in one swoop.[1]

The boasting and the promises pleased the Radical Republicans and members of the Committee on the Conduct of the War. Eager to be rid of Democratic George McClellan, they warmly supported the newcomer. McClellan had provided little action and even less in the form of victories. A good organizer, he had what President Lincoln described as a bad case of the "slows." Advancing on Richmond from the East, he had bogged down on the York Peninsula, causing Lincoln to call in John Pope.

Americans from Maine to Minnesota who were intently following the maneuvers in the rolling countryside south and west of Washington were suddenly startled by newspaper reports of bloodshed in the valley of the Minnesota River. Federal officials were as surprised as the rest of the nation when the Santee Sioux went on the warpath. With the attention of the country centered on the conflict with the Confederacy, warnings of trouble with the Indians had gone unheeded.

Indian troubles had occurred on the plains during the 1850s but had been so minor that the Forty-Niners and Fifty-Niners had crossed the plains country to California and Colorado with little difficulty. The tiny, 16,000-man U.S. Army, stationed primarily at the frontier, had begun to establish posts along the major lines of travel, and Forts Kearny and Laramie on the Platte Route and Fort Pierre on the Upper Missouri were important way stations.

The inception of travel to the Pacific Coast and the Rocky Mountains also brought the government into contact with the horse Indians of the Great Plains, and in the Fort Laramie Treaty of 1851 these tribes had acknowledged the right of travel through their domain. Some disturbances followed, however, and in 1855 Colonel William Harney punished the Brulé Sioux, but in general the 1850s were relatively peaceful in the western country. When the Civil War erupted, the regular army was called eastward, but Indian troubles did not increase appreciably.

Although the Fort Laramie Treaty had brought the government into contact with the powerful Teton Sioux—the

Brulé, Miniconjou, Oglala, Hunkpapa, and other sub-tribes—there had been a long period of peaceful relations with the Minnesota or Santee Sioux. Traders with the American Fur Company had been in the region for years, and peace was maintained even when settlers moved into the Upper Mississippi Valley. In 1851, two years after the creation of the Territory of Minnesota, treaties were made with the Santee Sioux clearing title to about 24 million acres of land; and seven years later an additional 1 million acres was ceded to the government. The Santee Sioux were placed on a reservation, roughly ten miles wide, in the valley of the Minnesota River. Agencies were established and attempts made to civilize and Christianize the Indians. The Sisseton and Wahpeton were placed at the Upper Agency on the Yellow Medicine River, while the Wah-pekute and Mdewakanton were located at the Lower or Redwood Agency about fourteen miles from Fort Ridgely.[2]

By 1862 there were over 6,500 Santee Sioux on the reservation, and trouble was brewing. Although Minnesota, still a frontier state, had only five towns of over 2,000 people, the Indians felt the increasing pressure of white settlement and understood the insecurity of their position. Discontented with the activities of the traders (who had exacted an agreement that debts be paid by Indians out of their annuity monies) and aware of the Civil War and the absence of troops in the state, the Indians were becoming troublesome. Often wronged in the past and presently under the control of Agent Thomas Galbraith, an inexperienced political appointee, the Minnesota Sioux were near starvation; their annuities had not arrived, and Galbraith refused to issue provisions although he had them on hand. Traders added to the Indians' discontent by refusing to extend credit, and one trader, Andrew J. Myrick, callously

3

remarked, "if they are hungry, let them eat grass."[3]

Conflict almost broke out on August 4, when the hungry Indians broke into the agency warehouse for provisions, and then on August 17 a small party of Sioux hunters suddenly decided to commit murder. Five whites were shot, and, fearing repercussions, the reservation Sioux decided on war. The uprising began on August 18 with attacks on the Upper and Lower Sioux agencies and were quickly followed by attacks on Fort Ridgely and the nearby town of New Ulm. Agency employees and citizens in the vicinity, including Andrew Myrick, were the first to die. Myrick's corpse was found with his mouth stuffed with grass.

Citizens in the Union states of the North were shocked when news of the bloodshed circulated throughout the country. Their attention was momentarily diverted from the events in Virginia and Tennessee to the full-scale Indian war that had broken out on the thinly settled Minnesota frontier. Panic spread as hundreds of settlers fell under the tomahawks and scalping knives of the Santee Sioux. Farms and towns were abandoned, and rumors traveled like wildfire throughout the upper Northwest. Frantic calls for help went out as Minnesota prepared to defend herself. Governor Alexander Ramsey hastily made his old political opponent, Henry H. Sibley, colonel of the militia, and placed him in charge of the defense of Minnesota. Sibley, a fur trader and politician, had been the state's first governor and was one of her leading citizens. His long experience with the Indians made him an ideal man for the crisis.[4]

Ramsey, who had been the first governor to offer troops to the Federal government after the firing on Fort Sumter, now appealed to President Lincoln for assistance. Draft quotas for the Union Army could not be filled, he told the

President, because half the population had left their homes, and the men were needed on the Minnesota frontier.[5]

All along the Minnesota-Dakota-Iowa frontier settlers were fleeing for safety. Sioux Falls in Dakota Territory was abandoned by the inhabitants and burned soon after by the Indians. Dakotans fled to Yankton, the capital, or left the territory entirely, and Governor William Jayne, a close friend of President Lincoln and his former family physician, called the population to arms.

As panic spread, officials in adjacent states and territories echoed the demands from Minnesota. Settlers in northern Iowa, remembering the Spirit Lake massacre of 1857, were abandoning their homes and Governor Samuel Kirkwood, fearing that the other tribes of the great Sioux nation were becoming involved, requested permission to retain regiments that were then being enlisted in Iowa for service in the South. The needs of Iowa were preeminent, he said, warning Washington that "something must be done at once." His words were repeated in Nebraska. Rumors that the entire Sioux nation had taken up arms brought panic there, and Acting Governor A. S. Paddock telegraphed to Secretary of War Edwin Stanton: "Instant action demanded."

Governor Edward Salomon of Wisconsin added to the chorus of demands, and the reports from the Northwest were verified by Lincoln's secretary, John G. Nicolay, who was in Minnesota for negotiations with the Chippewa Indians. Nicolay warned that the Chippewa and Winnebago tribes were threatening as well, and he called for a war of extermination against the Sioux. On September 6, Governor Ramsey of Minnesota requested immediate assistance. This was no mere local outbreak, he said; it was a "national war."[6]

At first the cries for help were ignored as Washington officials concentrated on the maneuvers of Generals John Pope and Robert E. Lee in the vicinity of Manassas Junction, less than thirty miles west of Washington, D.C. But the situation required action. The government could not permit the Northwest to be overrun by bloodthirsty Indians. It was an important source of fighting men and food, and Minnesota politicians such as William Windom of the House Committee on Indian Affairs and Henry Rice of the Senate Committee on Military Affairs were in positions to exert pressure on the War Department. Nor were Dakota leaders William Jayne, brother-in-law of Senator Lyman Trumbull, and John B. S. Todd, cousin of Mrs. Lincoln, without influence. There was also the belief expressed by some officials that Confederate agents were involved in the Indian troubles, and this could not be discounted since it was also believed that Confederate agents were working with the tribes of the south-central plains. Confederate interest in the western mining regions was strong, and an attempt had already been made to seize control of Colorado Territory and the Southwest. It is understandable that many people credited the Confederacy with stirring up Indian troubles, if only to distract and torment the Federal government.

The situation in the Northwest was so serious that something had to be done, and President Lincoln responded to Governor Ramsey's request of September 6. Just a week before, on August 30, the second Battle of Bull Run had ended in such inglorious defeat that John Pope had been replaced by George McClellan;[7] and Lincoln had a major general without a job, just the man, perhaps, to unify and direct the defensive operations required in the northwestern states and territories.

On September 6, Pope received orders to return to the

West. A new department had been created—the Department of the Northwest—embracing the states of Wisconsin, Iowa, and Minnesota and the territories of Nebraska and Dakota. Headquarters were no longer "in the saddle." Pope would direct the Indian war from St. Paul, Minnesota.

Orders emphasized that a major Indian war was in progress in the area covered by the new department, but they also hinted at Lincoln's dilemma: what to do with a high-ranking general who had suddenly fallen into disgrace. The orders stated that the Indian war required "the attention of some military officer of high rank, in whose ability and vigor the Government has confidence." This was an important command, Pope was told, but he understood its relative unimportance because the War Department had no detailed information regarding the outbreak or the forces engaged. The measures to be taken were left to his "judgment and discretion," and he was instructed to "employ whatever force may be necessary to suppress the hostilities."[8]

When General Pope arrived in St. Paul on September 17, he found himself in the midst of one of the most serious Indian uprisings in American history. He quickly assessed the situation and concluded that unless immediate measures were taken one-half of the population of Minnesota and Wisconsin would be gone by winter. He acted quickly. Four regiments were ordered into the field from Wisconsin; munitions and supplies were collected; and 2,500 horses were ordered for the troops. "I will push forward everything to your assistance as fast as possible," he informed Colonel Sibley.[9]

Although Sibley was plagued by inexperienced troops, lack of cavalry, ancient weapons, and ammunition of the wrong size, he had already engaged the Santee Sioux. On

7

September 2, he had gone to the relief of a party of 170 soldiers and settlers who had been surrounded and almost exterminated at Birch Coulee near the Lower Agency. At the time Pope assumed command, Sibley was camped near the battlefield making his final preparations to advance against the warriors under the Santee chief, Little Crow.

Pope sent forward what little assistance he had available and ordered Sibley to push forward into the Sioux country to defeat the enemy and destroy their crops and property. Offense was the order of the day. The Indians must be punished before a settlement was made. He warned Sibley that no arrangements should be made until the Indians were "badly punished," for he was convinced that the best way to end the Indian troubles was "by exterminating or ruining all the Indians engaged in the late outbreak."[10] Pope wanted the Indian war terminated, and he wanted it done quickly. He did not intend to remain outside the mainstream of events any longer than necessary. He would crush the Indian rebellion and restore his reputation; then he would once again hold the important command in the main event, the Civil War, that he believed he deserved.

The aggressiveness of the new commander pleased Colonel Sibley. "I am glad to perceive that you have so just an appreciation of the magnitude of the war in which we are engaged with the Sioux or Dakota, the most warlike and powerful of the tribes on this continent." This attitude was not shared by others, however. Brigadier General John M. Schofield of the Department of the Missouri complained to General-in-Chief Henry Halleck that Pope was detaining the Iowa regiments which had been ordered to St. Louis. "I beg of you do not let him take them from me," he wrote.[11]

Halleck, ignorant of the situation of the Northwest, believed that the Indians could not be very numerous, and he ordered Pope to release the Iowa troops. At the same time Pope was protesting that he had little to work with and needed more men and material. His plan was to pursue and exterminate the Indians, and more troops were required. But this time Pope's requisitions for troops, animals, and supplies had begun to alarm Secretary of War Edwin Stanton who was more concerned with the Civil War than the Indian war on the northern plains. Stanton instructed General Halleck to define the extent of operations in the Northwest and to limit Pope's expenditures and bluntly informed Pope that he could not have the men and material requested because they were needed in Kentucky. Halleck also informed Pope that the development of a large force for an Indian campaign was not deemed necessary and was not approved by the War Department.[12]

The telegraph wires between St. Paul and Washington began to hum with a debate on the extent of the Indian war. Pope and his superiors were in obvious disagreement about the necessity for a quick and decisive victory. Pope understood the impact of the outbreak in the Northwest and was in part swept up in the panic, but he was also determined to make his new command one of importance. He was not happy with his exile to the frontier, and the tarnished reputation needed refurbishing. He had no desire to become a forgotten general, or one remembered only for failure. Victory in the Northwest, he thought, would serve as a stepping-stone to a more prominent position.

However unconcerned Minnesotans, such as Henry Rice of the Senate Committee on Military Affairs, may have been with the career of John Pope, they did agree that action was needed. Half-way measures would not suffice; the Sioux must be defeated and driven from the state. Pope, therefore, continued to request troops and supplies. The outbreak was serious; the Secretary of War must be made to realize this. "Universal panic prevails along the whole frontier," he wrote Stanton, and the settlers west of the Missouri are abandoning everything in their flight. The Sioux, he wrote, were believed to number 2,600 warriors. He reported that the frontier in Minnesota and the territories of Nebraska and Dakota were "nearly depopulated;" more than 50,000 citizens had abandoned their property, and over 500 people had been murdered in Minnesota alone.

"You have no idea of the wide, universal, and uncontrollable panic everywhere in this country," Pope wrote Halleck. Influenced by the wild rumors which had spread across the Northwest, Pope reported that the Chippewa and Winnebago of Minnesota and all the tribes of the northern plains were on the verge of joining the war. The situation was so serious and the panic so widespread that a larger force was needed to quiet the fears of the people. He did not have the means to fight, he said, for "there is positively nothing here."[13]

Although he accepted the reports regarding the extent of hostilities, Pope was attempting to make more of the conflict than the War Department was willing to accept. The military situation in Kentucky and Virginia was far from encouraging. During July and August, Nathan Bedford Forrest and John H. Morgan struck savagely at Union outposts and supply lines in Kentucky and Tennessee, and in September Braxton Bragg was threatening Louisville and Lexington. In the East, George McClellan, who had regained command of Union forces in Virginia when Pope was sent westward, had blocked Lee's drive to the North at Antietam, but Lee still maintained the initiative. For this reason Pope was ordered to limit the scope of his operations and to keep expenses at a minimum. It was hoped, however, that paroled Union soldiers could be sent to Pope to protect the frontiers and replace troops that were needed in the South.[14]

While Pope was struggling to get more men and supplies, Colonel Sibley was rapidly bringing the Indian war in Minnesota to a close. On September 19 he left camp near the Lower Agency and moved up the Minnesota River with about 1,450 men. On the 22nd he camped by Lone Tree Lake, unaware that any Indians were near. But there were from 700 to 1,200 hostiles in the vicinity, and during the night they moved near the camp planning to attack as the troops began their march the next morning. As the camp came to life that morning, however, a party of men from the veteran Third Minnesota went foraging and rode directly into the waiting Indians. The battle began abruptly, but Sibley quickly cleared the field and dealt the Sioux a decisive defeat. Deeply concerned with the fate of the captives, Sibley did not pursue the fleeing warriors, but the victory divided the Indians. The hostiles retreated toward the Dakota prairie, while a peace faction protected the captives and awaited the approach of the victorious army. On September 26, the 269 captives were recovered at a place Sibley named "Camp Release."[15]

Following the battle large numbers of Santee Sioux began to surrender. Although troops were still chasing the scattered hostiles, and a $500 reward was offered for Little Crow, Pope announced on October 9, "The Sioux war may be considered at an end."[16] Despite the fears and protests of the Minnesota settlers, the war in that state was ended. There were to be some small raids in following years, but the hostile Minnesota Sioux had been driven onto the plains, and settlers returned safely to their farms.

On September 26, approximately 1,200 Indians were taken into custody, and the number increased rapidly as small parties of Sioux continued to surrender. On September 28, Pope informed Sibley that no treaties would be made with the Minnesota Sioux and urged him to complete the punishment of the hostiles. Pope wrote, "The horrible massacres of [white] women and children and the outrageous abuse of female prisoners, still alive, call for punishment beyond human power to inflict." It was his aim to "utterly exterminate the Sioux" if he had the power to do so, and he instructed Sibley to destroy their property and drive them onto the plains if he could not capture them. "They are to be treated as maniacs or wild beasts," he said "and by no means as people with whom treaties or compromises can be made."[17]

On the same day Colonel Sibley began preparations for the extermination of at least some of the Sioux by convening a five-man military commission to try those who had participated in the outbreak. While the commission was in session, Pope wrote to Halleck that the convicted Indians should be hung. By November 5 the commission had completed its work, and on November 8 Pope forwarded a list of 303 Indians to President Lincoln requesting his approval for their immediate execution. Pope believed that this would have a profound effect on both the remaining Indians and the settlers, and he was concerned that the people of Minnesota might take matters into their own hands if the government did not take stern measures. The people of the state were demanding action, and the troops guarding the prisoners were not only Minnesota men and in full sympathy with the people but were also mostly raw recruits and could not be relied on in case of trouble.[18] Pope feared that all the prisoners, approximately 1,800 Indians, would be slaughtered.

The urgings of General Pope and Governor Ramsey had little effect, however, for Lincoln refused to be hurried. Humanitarians, who were begging the President to be lenient, were joined by Commissioner of Indian Affairs William Dole who believed that the Indians were savages, far beneath the whites, and should not be judged by the standards of white morality. While Lincoln studied the matter, the people of Minnesota made their views known. The Minnesota congressmen urged the execution, while Governor Ramsey suggested that if Lincoln did not wish to order the executions, the condemned prisoners should be turned over to the state. He was more than willing to put them to death.[19]

The residents of St. Paul protested against a presidential pardon and in a memorial demanded the removal of all Sioux from Minnesota: "The blood of hundreds of our murdered fellow-citizens cries from the ground for vengeance. 'Vengeance is mine, I will repay saith the Lord,' and the authorities of the United States are, we believe, the chosen instruments to execute that vengeance. Let them not neglect their plain duty." The memorialists continued by demanding security for the future. The Sioux must not be allowed to remain within the state. "The Indian's nature can no more be trusted than the wolf's. Tame him, cultivate him, strive to Christianize him, as you will, and the sight of blood will in an instant call out the savage, wolfish, devilish instincts of the race," they said. "It is notorious that among the earliest and most murderous of the Sioux, in perpetrating their late massacre, were many of the 'civilized Indians,' so called, with their hair cut short, wearing white men's clothes, and dwelling in brick houses built for them by the government." The Federal government must act, they demanded. Unless it did, the people would.[20]

The editor of the *Yankton Dakotian* was angered by the work of eastern humanitarians, for he learned that a group of Philadelphia Quakers had requested clemency. "This," he wrote, "illustrates the extent of cupidity to which people are sometimes driven by what may be termed religious fanaticism." The editor was outraged that these eastern Quakers, "imbued with peace and surrounded by comfort and ease" favored clemency for criminals who had been convicted of "the most cold-blooded, heartless and wanton butchery of men, women and children." He was confident that even if President Lincoln pardoned the condemned prisoners, "those Indians will die, and that right speedily," for some Minnesotans had "taken a sacred and solemn oath to devote the remainder of their lives to killing Indians" and would not allow the butchery to go unavenged.[21]

The threat of vengeance was more than mere words, for even innocent Indians were attacked during their removal to Fort Snelling; and the condemned Indians were attacked while they were being marched under guard to Camp Lincoln near South Bend. The citizens of New Ulm were reburying their dead when the prisoners were marched through town, and with the memory of the fighting still fresh, they attacked the Indians. Fifteen natives and several guards were severely wounded before a bayonet charge drove back the enraged whites. On December 4 a group of citizens from Mankato decided to murder the captives, but they were dispersed by troops under the command of Colonel Stephen A. Miller of the Seventh Minnesota Infantry.[22]

On December 6, Lincoln approved the death sentence of those Indians who had been convicted of rape and murder, and on December 26, 1862, thirty-eight Sioux warriors sang their death song and were hanged. But the disposition of the other prisoners remained the subject of lively discussion. The warriors who escaped execution through the benevolence of President Lincoln were confined at Man-

14

kato while the remainder of the prisoners, some 1,600, were placed in a camp near Fort Snelling as military prisoners.

If the people of Minnesota had had their way, the entire group would have been exterminated, but they were content with attempts to have the rest of the group permanently removed from the state. In September, Governor Ramsey demanded that either they be exterminated or driven from the state, and Pope conceded that removal was necessary. He found the prisoners embarrassing to the military because they were expensive to maintain and tied up troops that were needed in the field. He wrote to General Halleck with some justification that the care of these Indians was the responsibility of the Indian Bureau and that it should accept its responsibility and put the Indians in some place of confinement outside the state of Minnesota. Such efforts were to no avail, however, for although the question became the subject of cabinet discussion, Halleck regretfully informed Pope that the Department of the Interior disclaimed any responsibility for them and that the army had no alternative but to guard and feed them.[2 3]

While Pope was urging the Interior Department to act, other plans were being proposed. Colonel Sibley suggested that the Indians be settled near Devil's Lake in the northeastern part of Dakota Territory, implying that they should remain under the full control of the War Department. Indian Agent Thomas Galbraith agreed that they must be removed from Minnesota and that they should be isolated from any contact with white settlers and traders. He suggested placing them on the Coteau des Prairies in the eastern portion of Dakota Territory, surrounding them with a military reservation to isolate them from the whites, and forcing them to become agriculturists. But the most unusual proposal was one made by James W. Taylor of St.

Paul who suggested that all the Indians of Minnesota be placed on Isle Royal in Lake Superior to live or die as nature saw fit.[24]

Removal was the issue of the day and while Minnesotans talked, Congress acted. On January 1, 1863, the House of Representatives adopted a resolution by William Windom of Minnesota to have the Commissioner of Indian Affairs select the location of a new reservation for the Santee Sioux. A few months later the Sioux prisoners and the guiltless Winnebago were moved to a new reservation at Crow Creek on the Missouri River above Fort Randall.[25]

During the long discussions regarding the disposition of the Sioux prisoners, General Pope was considering plans for the future protection of the Minnesota frontier. Even before he announced that the war was over in that state, he had suggested that a spring campaign would be necessary to settle the Indian problem in the Northwest. Governor Ramsey thought that the war was over, but there were many who did not agree.

The *St. Paul Pioneer* informed the governor that if he allowed "a soldier of this state to be withdrawn until this matter is satisfactorily settled, the blood of his thousand murdered constituents" would "cry out against him, and the arms of their living kin be raised for his destruction."[26] The *St. Paul Press* echoed similar sentiments in an editorial entitled, "THE SIOUX WAR: WHAT SHALL WE DO WITH IT?" The editorial proclaimed, in the lurid language so typical of frontier editors, "It is not ended! The blood of our brethren cries to us from the ground! What the people of Minnesota demand is—not that the enemy shall retire towards the Missouri to boast in Teton lodges that five whites to one Indian had been slain, and while parading their plunder, to instigate another attack with tenfold the numbers on the settlements of the Minnesota and the Missouri; but that the war shall now be *offensive.*" As the captives had been recovered, all obstacles to just retribution had been removed. "Now in God's name let the columns of vengeance move on," the paper announced. There should be no peace "until the whole accursed are crushed—crushed as no band of these North American Sepoys have ever been punished by military force." With these sentiments the Dakota press was in full accord. [27]

All the clamor was unnecessary, for Pope was planning a spring campaign. In October when he announced that the Indian war in Minnesota was over, he suggested that a military movement into Dakota Territory was necessary. While the hostile Santee Sioux had been driven onto the plains, they must not be allowed to escape. It was also evident that the Teton Sioux along the Upper Missouri River were showing increased signs of hostility, and now that they had been joined by the fugitive Santee trouble was almost assured.

All reports from the Upper Missouri during 1862 indicated that the Teton Sioux were hostile. Angered by increased travel through their country, they announced that they would allow no whites to pass through their domain, either by land or river. In July, nine Hunkpapa chiefs bluntly told their agent, Samuel Latta, that no travel would be permitted. "The whites in this country have been threatening us with soldiers," they said. "All we ask of you is to bring men, and not women dressed in soldier's clothes . . . " Having thrown down the gauntlet, they continued: "You may get this and tear it up, and tell your Father that we are all quiet and receive your present, and by this means keep your place and fill your pockets with money . . . Tell our Great Father what we say, and tell him the truth." [28]

Samuel Latta was convinced of the sincerity of the Teton Sioux. He reported that two-thirds of them were hostile. They wanted no more annuities from the government and warned him that if he returned next year he would do so at the risk of his life. One trader reported that these Sioux were acting "more as a people at war with us than otherwise," and as if to emphasize his words, they attacked the river steamer *Shreveport* in August.[29]

Conditions in the Indian country caused grave concern, and in both Minnesota and Dakota Territory the whites feared that the Santee and their brethren would once again descend on the frontier in the spring. In late December, Governor William Jayne and other Dakota officials warned President Lincoln that the Sioux were organizing a campaign for the early spring. Traders along the river forwarded similar reports and petitioned the Commissioner of Indian Affairs for protection. There was not, they said, a single solder along the 1,800-mile length of the Missouri River between Fort Randall and Fort Benton. Taking up the cry for protection, the Territorial Council and Legislative Assembly of Dakota Territory petitioned both President Lincoln and Secretary of War Edwin Stanton for assistance and threw their support behind General Pope and his plans for a spring campaign. The editor of the *Yankton Dakotian* criticized the indifference to the Indian question manifested by those who were far from the scenes of bloodshed. Action was demanded by citizens of the frontier who have "seen their wives and husbands, fathers, mothers and children, butchered before their eyes, ravished, crucified or roasted, by these demented monsters in human form."[30]

Pope, in his new headquarters in Milwaukee, was convinced that something must be done. Disappointed with Washington's failure to recognize his accomplishments and

18

realizing its apparent intent to leave him in the Northwest, he determined to continue the Indian war. Although the hostiles had been driven out of Minnesota, they were still at war and were stirring up the disenchanted Teton Sioux. All reports indicated increased Indian hostilities in the spring, and Pope decided that a spring campaign was in order. Minnesotans and Dakotans supported his plans.

As spring approached and a new growth of grass appeared, a giant pincer movement would begin. Three columns would scour the plains of Dakota Territory and force the hostile Sioux into battle. One column under General Sibley would move westward from Minnesota; a second would travel up the Missouri River from Fort Randall, and a third would advance northward from Iowa by way of the Big Sioux River. Attacked from three directions, the Sioux would be unable to escape, and the Indian problem in the Northwest would be solved.[31]

Henry Sibley, now a brigadier general of the volunteers by appointment of President Lincoln, was not at all pleased with Pope's plans and began to exhibit the caution that was to become so characteristic of him. Fearing that the frontier would be left undefended and subject to massive attack, he requested more troops for the protection of Minnesota. As a leading politician, Sibley could not ignore the demands of the Minnesotans, but Pope did, and Sibley's views brought an immediate rebuke from the departmental commander. Pope informed him that over six and one-half regiments were more than adequate and that never before had such a force been organized to fight Indians.[32] He pointed out that garrisons had been left in the frontier villages only to restore the confidence of the panic-stricken population and that it would be unnecessary for them to remain there once the campaign began. "I shall not refer your letter to Washington, where I am sure it will occasion as much surprise as it did me. . ." he went on.

While Pope castigated Sibley for his excessive caution, he himself received a sharp rebuke for becoming involved in U.S. foreign policy. Canada offered a convenient haven for harried Indians, and Pope believed that this sanctuary must be destroyed if military operations were to succeed. He informed Washington that all Indians who had committed depredations or who made their homes in the United States would be pursued wherever they went, regardless of international boundary lines. These orders, he said, would stand unless overruled.[33]

Concerned with the immediate needs of the military campaign, Pope did not see the implications of such a move. He had raised a serious question, one which had far greater significance than the successful prosecution of an Indian war, and it was inconceivable that the President could allow the activities of a military commander to influence relations with a foreign power, especially a neutral power of the strength and importance of Great Britain. The direction of American foreign policy remained in the hands of the President, not of army officers. Pope had overstepped his authority; he had attempted to dictate a new and dangerous policy; and General-in-Chief Henry Halleck quickly warned Pope that no troops could cross into British territory without presidential authorization.[34]

The original plans for the spring campaign called for the Missouri River column to initiate the attack with a northward movement by mid-May, but it was not until June 1 that final plans were made. The campaign now consisted of two columns rather than the original three. General Sibley would move toward Devil's Lake, and the Missouri River column, commanded by Brigadier General Alfred Sully— 2,000 cavalrymen—would advance northward along the river. The Sioux would be trapped between two strong forces. About 3,000 additional soldiers would remain to protect the Minnesota frontier, and although this seemed more than adequate, Pope expected much criticism and complaint. He was confident that as soon as one Indian appeared on the frontier he would be deluged with demands for additional protection.

On June 16, after months of preparation, Sibley led approximately 3,300 men from Camp Pope on the Minnesota River and moved in a northwesterly direction toward Devil's Lake. Leaving the supply train at a temporary depot called "Camp Atchison," some forty miles southeast of the lake, his column turned southwest under the blazing Dakota summer sun. On July 24 the scouts discovered a large body of Indians, and Sibley quickly corralled his train and prepared for battle. The Sisseton, Wahpeton, Yanktonai, Cut Heads, Blackfeet, and Hunkpapa Sioux were hunting buffalo and were oblivious of the approaching troops. Finally one Indian discovered the troops and fled to the camp crying that "all the Americans in the land are right here." [35]

Taken by surprise, the Sioux warriors rushed to defend their camp. Conversations were begun between the hostiles and Sibley's scouts. Sibley had been warned by Gabriel Renville, his half-breed scout, not to parley because it was a trap, but Surgeon Joseph Weiser rode out to join the scouts and was unexpectedly shot. The battle of Big Mound was thus begun, and Sibley's troops quickly drove the hostiles from the field and continued in pursuit until dark. Sibley maintained the chase, skirmishing briefly with the Sioux at Dead Buffalo Lake on July 26. Two days later the hostiles attacked as the troops were breaking camp at Stony Lake, but they were driven from the field and fled across the Missouri River.

Sibley, in bringing the fight to the Indians in their own

country, had taken them by surprise; and although he punished them by destroying vast amounts of supplies and equipage, they were still defiant. The strategy that had looked so good on paper had failed, for the Sully expedition was nowhere in the area. After waiting several days for Sully to arrive at the rendezvous, Sibley began the return march on August 1.[36] While Sibley was fighting, Brigadier General Alfred Sully was still making preparations to advance up the Missouri River.

Command of the Missouri River column had changed several times during the spring. Brigadier General John Cook, the original commander, had been replaced by Brigadier General Benjamin Roberts, who was in turn replaced by Brigadier General Alfred Sully, despite Pope's objections. Sully, a West Point graduate and an experienced Indian fighter, had fought the Seminole in Florida and the Rogue River Indians of Oregon in the 1840s. He had also served in Minnesota and Dakota and campaigned with General William Harney in 1855.

Ideally suited to command the expedition, Sully was delayed by lack of supplies. The extreme low level of the Missouri River caused further delays because Sully depended on the river steamers for supplies, and it was not until August 13, nearly two weeks after General Sibley had begun his return march, that the expedition left camp near Fort Pierre.

In the meantime, Pope was becoming increasingly impatient. Delay jeopardized the entire campaign, and Pope had purposely planned a cavalry expedition. Speed and mobility were the objectives, and as the delays continued, Pope became angry. On August 5 he prodded Sully: "I never had the slightest idea you could delay thus along the river, nor do I realize the necessity of such delay." When Pope learned that the Sioux had escaped the trap by fleeing westward across the Missouri River, Sully was made to feel his displeasure. The criticism was harsh and bitter. Sully was informed that if he had reached the rendezvous point in time, the Sioux would have been crushed, and Pope believed "that with energy this much at least could have been accomplished." Pope made it very plain that while Sully had moved only 160 miles with a cavalry column, Sibley's infantrymen had covered 600 miles and fought three engagements with the hostiles. Pope wrote: "It is painful for me to find fault . . . but I feel bound to tell you frankly that your movements have greatly disappointed me, and I can find no satisfactory explanation of them."[37]

Annoyed by these criticisms, Sully finally left Fort Pierre on August 13 and moved up the Missouri River. After a week's travel he turned eastward and ascended the Little Cheyenne River looking for Indians. On September 3 an advance party of 300 men under Major Albert House of the Sixth Iowa Cavalry was suddenly surrounded by Indians. While the taunting warriors prepared for a ceremonial massacre, the guide, Frank LaFramboise, rode for help. Sully was ten miles distant, but he galloped to the rescue and struck the hostile camp near White Stone Hill. The battle was short, and the Indians fled, but Sully took 156 prisoners and destroyed tons of buffalo meat and supplies. About 100 soldiers spent two days in burning the camp and the meat.[38]

General Sully estimated that 150 hostiles were killed and described the conflict as "one of the most severe punishments that the Indians had ever received." But so many had escaped that the Sioux had not been crushed. More important, however, than the number killed or escaping was the destruction of the camp and the winter meat supply. Coming late in the summer, this was a hard blow to the hostiles, for it would mean suffering and privation during the bitter Dakota winter.

While Generals Sibley and Sully were fighting the hostiles, Pope was engaged with enemies close at hand. During the spring and summer of 1863 Pope's strategy of offensive movements against the Indians was subjected to mounting criticism, and Pope had to ward off these attacks while attempting to deal with the Indians. Political considerations and rivalries were very much a part of attacks on military men in the Department of the Northwest.

During the autumn of 1862, for instance, there had been a movement to have Henry Sibley removed as colonel of the Minnesota militia and as field commander in the Indian war, and when President Lincoln had proposed Sibley as brigadier general of the volunteers, Congress delayed confirmation of the appointment. Apparently this was the work of Henry Rice, Democratic senator from Minnesota. Rice, a member of the influential Committee on Military Affairs, had long been a rival and enemy of Sibley. Rice, briefly associated with Sibley in the Minnesota fur trade, had quickly become a bitter competitor. The animosity between the two men continued and deepened as Minnesota became first a territory and then a state. Both men became involved in politics, and although both were members of the Democratic Party, that bond did nothing to heal their differences. Sibley, the most influential citizen in Minnesota, led the struggle for territorial status and served as territorial delegate and when Minnesota became a state in 1858, he was elected governor.[39]

Eager to thwart and discredit his rival in any way, Rice worked first for the removal of Sibley; when that failed, he attempted to replace General Pope as commander of the Department of the Northwest. As a Democrat Rice's chances for reelection to the Senate were slim, and the command of the Department of the Northwest would not only keep him in the public eye but would also place Sibley under his control.

Late in 1862 Pope first heard about the movement to replace him and asked his old friend and commander, General Halleck, for more information. Hallack had also learned of the plot and promised his friend to oppose it. Pope was not at all averse to moving on to a new command, but he was distrustful of all Democrats and did not wish General Sibley to be destroyed by Rice, who was one of the leading critics of military affairs in the Northwest. Pope warned Halleck that "unscrupulous speculators and traders" would use every means to have one of their members appointed to command the department. The appointment of Rice, he said, would result in many years of border wars and "ruinous Indian treaties and frauds." He called Rice "a reckless and ruined speculator and old Indian trader" and a representative of "this band of Malays" who wished to control military affairs in the department. "His appointment will be based upon a knowledge of Indians and Indian character, acquired during many years of unlimited concubinage with Indian women. . . . Politically he is ruined, and he looks to this position to restore his broken political and material fortunes." Pope was more than willing to be promoted to more important commands, but if and when this happened, Sibley, and not Rice, should be his replacement.[40]

Rice failed in his plotting, but he and the maverick Republican Senator, Morton Wilkinson, continued to interfere with military operations and maintained a constant barrage of criticism. They loudly predicted the failure of the 1863 campaign and claimed that the frontier would be visited with hordes of howling savages throughout the summer. The troops should be kept in Minnesota. On this presumption they engineered the authorization to raise a battalion of cavalry under Major Edwin Hatch, an old friend of Rice, who, although he had once been an Indian agent, had no military experience. The creation of this independent battalion was clearly a usurpation of Pope's power, and Pope demanded a copy of Hatch's orders and information on the extent of his authority. He could not believe that an independent command would be authorized for his department, but this was exactly what Rice had in mind.[41]

Pope was sure that "Hatch is but an instrument of Rice," and while he was unable to block the formation of the battalion, it was put under his control. To have allowed an independent military force to operate within an established military command would have been ridiculous. Sibley effectively dealt with Hatch by sending him to Pembina near the Canadian boundary to establish a post in mid-winter.

Wilkinson and Rice continued to meddle in department affairs by working behind the scenes in Washington. They claimed that Sibley's force was too large, that one-third of the number would be more effective because no probability existed in meeting any large groups of Indians, and that naturally it would be better to keep most of the troops stationed in Minnesota. Pope immediately jumped to Sibley's defense, pointing out that all reports showed the Indians still concentrated at Devil's Lake. Sibley, Pope said, was a man of long experience with the Indians and had fought them successfully the year before "in the midst of the same carping and fault-finding. It may be fairly presumed that General Sibley understands his business as well at least as anybody else does."[42]

The critics refused to remain silent, however, and the

press took up the charges. Pope, becoming increasingly irate, castigated his enemies: "I think my opportunities for knowing the condition of affairs in this department are as good, if not better, than those of any one not connected with the military service." It was clear, Pope felt, that "there are not troops enough in our whole armies to satisfy the people of Minnesota," for they wanted a regiment or at least a company "in the front door of every settler's house in the country."[43]

Pope was concerned when the victories of Generals Sibley and Sully did not silence his opponents, and he lashed out at them in self-defense. There would be attempts to keep all the troops in Minnesota, he predicted, but the men who were already voicing this demand were the same people who claimed that Sibley's force was too large. The angry departmental commander also turned his fire on the Interior Department, claiming that Indian agents profited from their position and charging collusion between his critics and members of the Indian Bureau.[44]

Colonel Stephen Miller, a friend of General Sibley and an opponent of the Rice-Wilkinson faction, agreed with this assessment. He wrote to Pope that he was glad to see that the general properly appreciated "the trading, corrupt Indian politicians of Minnesota. They are selfish and heartless as Satan," he said, "and, were it not for the encouragements held out to them at Washington, we should consign the whole tribe to merited infamy."[45]

The demands for permanent military protection rather than offensive movements were typical of frontier regions. As long as any danger existed, the troops would be retained, and the economic benefit to the frontier regions would be considerable. Westerners were continually demanding new posts and more troops for economic reasons, and Pope realized this. It would take five times as many troops if a defensive posture were maintained, and the protection could never be effective. "No one knows better than yourself," he wrote Halleck, "how difficult it is to get troops away from any frontier settlement where momentary necessity has occasioned their being posted."[46]

By the end of August, Pope reported that Minnesota was secure against any further Indian troubles and that he could begin to send troops south. The Sully-Sibley campaign had not sent many Indians to the happy hunting ground, nor had it ended the Sioux trouble on the northern plains. But it had brought the war to their homeland, and the destruction of vast quantities of supplies had proved effective. The prospect of suffering and starvation during the frigid Dakota winter brought reports that many bands desired peace. Rather than make a hasty and inconclusive peace, however, Pope preferred to wait until spring and again send an expedition into the heart of the Sioux country to convince all the bands of the Upper Missouri that peace was indeed desirable.

Dakotans agreed that the Sioux were still hostile and that another campaign was needed. "The Sioux Nation is still hostile, and until every nose on each of its many heads is tweaked, and they bear the humiliation without a murmur, we shall not admit that the Indian war is ended," the *Yankton Dakotian* announced. "They must be conquered, and when they are, and our benevolent old Uncle gets them under his capacious thumb, we trust our Indian affairs will be managed with more wisdom and sagacity than heretofore."[47]

Some were more critical of the military. Henry Boller, who had traveled up the Missouri River on the steamboat, *Robert Campbell,* had observed Sully's army prepare to take the field. He sarcastically commented, "The army took the field—the bugles were blown, the antelope badly frightened . . . while from the distant bluffs 'the d———d redskins' defiantly waved their breechclouts. Some few squaws were captured, and the army went into winter-quarters, the Indians having gone out of sight, and the safety of the frontiers thus being assured."[48]

The Indian campaign of 1863 did not fulfill Pope's expectations. Sibley and Sully won victories, but each time the Indians escaped to fight again. If General Sully, however, had been on the Missouri as planned, the Indians in fleeing from Sibley, would have run right into Sully's cavalrymen, and the results might have been different.

General Pope was more successful in fighting off his critics than in conquering the Sioux. He found himself in a political struggle in Minnesota that affected the affairs of his department. Henry Rice and the renegade Republican, Morton Wilkinson, were involved in machinations against Sibley and then Pope, but they failed to discredit either officer. In the autumn of 1863, Rice lost his senate seat to Alexander Ramsey, a friendly political rival of Henry Sibley, and Colonel Stephen Miller, a subordinate of Sibley and an enemy of Rice, was elected governor.

Although Rice had fallen from power and the political influence of the critics had been weakened, there was little chance that they would cease their efforts to harass Pope and his subordinates. Like the Indians, they would continue to be a problem, and Pope would engage them in battle again. He could make plans, however, for dealing with the Indians, and he was already thinking of a new campaign. Dakotans, too, demanded that the Sioux be pacified by force, but General Halleck was more concerned with events in Kentucky and Virginia and wanted peace made with the Indians if at all possible. He added confidently, "If we want war in the spring a few traders can get one up on the shortest notice."[49] In time, however, he gave his approval to Pope's plans.

CHAPTER TWO

"The present Indian policy
has been
a woeful failure"

As he battled Indians with one hand and warded off critics with the other, General Pope was engaged by a third opponent, the Interior Department. As commander of the Department of the Northwest, Pope was necessarily concerned with Indian affairs and Indian policy. On arrival in Minnesota following the massacre of 1862, he had voiced opinions about the frontier and had talked of extermination, but as he became more familiar with the Indian problem, he modified this position. He continued to believe that Indians should be punished for their crimes, but after studying the causes of the outbreak of 1862 and observing Federal Indian policy, he made suggestions which envisioned a full-scale revision of the management of Indian affairs and would have revolutionized the government's attitude toward the Indians.

By the 1860s, American Indian policy included several key principles, such as the treaty system with its recognition of the red man's rights to his land, regulation of trade through various Indian Trade and Intercourse Acts, and promotion of civilization and education. Control of Indian affairs had originally been the task of the War Department. The Bureau of Indian Affairs, created in 1824, and the office of the Commissioner of Indian Affairs, which followed in 1832, were still responsible to the Secretary of War. In 1849, however, the Indian Bureau was transferred to the newly created Department of the Interior, which meant that the Interior Department maintained control in time of peace and that the Army would take over when bloodshed occurred.

Inheriting ideas and precedents from the colonial period, the Federal government gradually attempted to clear title to Indian lands through treaties. Government officials envisioned a gradual and orderly advance of the frontier, but the frontiersmen had other ideas and continued their search for land with little regard for treaties. During the 1830s the "removal" policy was carried out. Suggested by Thomas Jefferson and later espoused by Secretary of War John C. Calhoun and President James Monroe, the idea of removal was written into law in 1830. The Indians were to be transported to the prairie region west of the states of Arkansas and Missouri, and a permanent Indian frontier was to be established on the edge of the Great Plains. But events were taking place which would lead to the immediate destruction of this frontier: the Santa Fe trade (opened by William Becknell in 1821), the Forty-Niners, the Mormon migration, and the Fifty-Niners opened major roads through the permanent frontier; and the creation of Kansas and Nebraska territories meant that the Indians would again have to be moved out of the way. White settlers were eager for their land. And so by the 1860s the policy of establishing a permanent Indian frontier had proved a failure. However commendable the principles involved may have been, they had not produced concrete results.[1]

When Pope arrived in Minnesota, he decided that something new and practical was required. He approached the problem of the treatment of the Indians, from the viewpoint of a military commander and was not overly concerned with the theoretical basis of policy. His job was to defeat the Indians and achieve a lasting peace.

Despite his seeming relish for engaging the Indian Bureau in verbal duels, Pope was forced to deal with the existing Indian policy and what he wanted was something workable that would end wars and eventually assimilate the Indian into white society. The hostiles, harried by constant military activity during the summer months, along with the destruction of their winter supplies, appeared willing to make peace in increasing numbers. Pope realized that the government must decide what to do with them. How were they to be treated? Where were they to be located? Should treaties be made? Although other government officials apparently ignored this problem, Pope did not. He conducted a searching investigation of Federal Indian policy as it related to and affected his military operations. He was determined that the government should have the best possible policy. The Army had fought the Indians to bring peace, and Pope was resolved that once peace had been made it would be maintained.

The more Pope studied the current policy, the less workable he found it. It was susceptible to wholesale fraud, he believed, and was the cause of Indian wars. He gradually developed a set of counter proposals for maintaining peace with the natives, and at the same time he voiced major criticisms of the old policy and suggested ways to correct it. Although many of his suggestions were valuable and were used by others at a later date, Pope made them at an inopportune time. Officials in Washington could not spare the time from the struggle with the Confederacy to consider radical changes in a policy which seemingly affected only the frontier region of the West. War and reconstruction were issues of greater magnitude.

Pope's numerous confrontations with the Indian Bureau only strengthened his conviction that change was needed. The treatment of the Winnebago is a case in point. They had taken no part in the outbreak of 1862, but they were as guilty in the minds of the frontier Minnesotans as were the Santee Sioux; and it was evident that they, too, would be removed. In February 1863 Congress rejected Pope's recommendations that both tribes be disarmed and placed under military control. All treaties with the Santee were abrogated and a new reservation was created for the Santee Sioux and the Winnebago at Crow Creek on the Missouri River about eighty miles above Fort Randall.[2]

The Crow Creek Reservation was a failure from the beginning. The Indians were brought to their new home in the early summer of 1863, too late to plant crops. A severe drouth followed, and by autumn they were in a serious condition. Pope was concerned because starvation might force the Santee to join the hostiles. He reported their "deplorable condition" to the Indian Bureau in hopes of alleviating suffering and starvation, but he was not at all happy with the manner in which Indian Superintendent Clark Thompson of the Northern Superintendency chose to act. Rather than contract for Indian supplies in St. Louis or Sioux City and transport them by steamboat, Thompson contracted for them in Minnesota. Someone of influence in that state had on hand large quantities of condemned pork and flour, and Superintendent Thompson was soon convinced that they should be purchased for the Indians. It was claimed that these were Winnebago supplies that had been left in Minnesota during the removal, and it was also proclaimed that the journey would open a new road to the agencies on the Missouri.[3]

Senator Morton Wilkinson threw his support behind the project, but Pope was unimpressed. He complied with the request for a military escort because he did not wish the military to be blamed for the failure of the Crow Creek Reservation. The soldiers of the escort were even less impressed. They had to march across an uninhabited region in late November and December through wind, snow, and temperatures of thirty-five degrees below zero. It is not surprising that the affair became known as the "Expedition to Moscow." Although some of the soldiers attempted to sabotage the freight wagons and suffering was intense, the journey was completed.[4]

Huddled by the fire on the night of December 31, with nearly frozen hands, Private Charles W. Johnson of the Sixth Minnesota Infantry recorded his thoughts:

Ugh! it snows, and blows, and freezes,
Ugh! the cold northwestern breezes!
How they blow without your leave
On this stormy New Years eve.[5]

A successful buffalo hunt rather than spoiled supplies allowed the Indians to survive the winter, but a crop failure in 1864 brought them face to face with starvation for a second year; and this time they left the reservation and wandered among the settlements begging for food. General Sully indignantly announced that they had been "actually starved out of it."[6] Moreover Superintendent Thompson again decided to haul supplies from Minnesota during the late autumn and requested an escort. Pope could not understand why the Indian Bureau had waited until cold weather set in before sending supplies, but there was little he could do except complain.

35

The Minnesota Winnebago worried military men with their opposition to removal to the Crow Creek Reservation and their refusal to remain there and starve, but the Wisconsin branch of the tribe caused even more concern. During the summer of 1863, Pope had learned that there were about 1,000 Winnebago Indians in the vicinity of Juneau County who were becoming troublesome and causing uneasiness. With no desire to have another Indian threat added to his burdens, Pope requested that the Interior Department send an Indian agent to take charge of them and transport them to Crow Creek. When the Interior Department refused to act, he appealed to the War Department. "I offered to collect them together for shipment to the Upper Missouri," he explained, "but the Indian Department declined to have anything to do with them, and informs me if I collect them they will be 'on my hands,' by which I suppose is meant all the expenses of moving and feeding them will be thrown on the War Department." Unwilling to accept this arrangement, he said, "If these Indians are not the proper subjects for the Indian Department, I have been mistaken as to the duties of that Department."[7]

Governor Edward Salomon of Wisconsin joined Pope in demanding the removal of the wandering Winnebago. It had originally been believed that they had escaped when the Minnesota Winnebago were being removed to Crow Creek, but it was now discovered that they were old residents of Wisconsin who had no reservation and no title to land in the state. Governor Salomon could "perceive nothing in that fact which can in any manner shift from the government the responsibility of controlling them," but the Interior Department claimed lack of funds and refused to act. The outright disavowal of this legal responsibility by the Interior Department was incomprehensible to the exasperated Pope, and he was unable "to understand how the Indian Bureau can so readily disavow all concern about a tribe of Indians now occasioning alarm and difficulty on the frontier of this state."[8]

Petitions from Juneau and Monroe counties and the threat, "We shall be compelled, in self-defense, to exterminate them," finally aroused Washington. Walter D. McIndoe, Republican congressman from Wisconsin, was dispatched to investigate, but nothing came of the investigation, and the Indians continued to annoy the settlers. During 1864 and 1865, protests and petitions poured from Wisconsin, but the Interior Department refused to acknowledge any responsibility for the homeless Indians.[9]

Of greater significance than his occasional battles with the Indian Bureau over immediate issues was the development of General Pope's own Indian policy during 1862-64. In September 1862, General Pope began his attack on the treaty system and instructed Colonel Sibley that no treaties were to be made with the Santee Sioux. By 1863 he was arguing that the treaty system was unworkable and was urging that when the Sioux surrendered they be placed under the supervision of the military commanders.

The practice of making treaties with the Indians had come under attack before. President Andrew Jackson had announced it as an "absurdity" and a "farce." Indian tribes were treated as independent nations, and treaties required the consent of two-thirds of the Senate. It was an anachronism, and Jackson and others knew it. By the 1860s the Secretary of the Interior was also calling for a change. The Indians, he said, should be treated as wards of the government rather than as members of independent nations.[10]

President Jackson and others complained because it was incongruous to have an independent nation within a nation, but Pope was unconcerned with the constitutionality of this issue. He was concerned because the treaty system had failed and should be scrapped. After observing the treaty system in operation, he said that when the government desired a treaty, they gathered the Indian chiefs together to listen to an emissary from Washington, and presents were distributed to encourage the chiefs to accept the wishes of the government. It was often found convenient to misinform them regarding the contents of the treaty, as in the Treaty of 1851 when the Santee Sioux unknowingly agreed that their debts to the traders would be taken out of their treaty payments. The government also ignored the fact that in most cases the chiefs were powerless to ensure that the remainder of the tribe would accept the treaty.

Treaty payments in the form of annuities were regarded by the Indians as a sign of weakness on the part of the government. The Indians understood that they were being paid to be peaceful and believed that a few well-timed depredations would lead to increased benefits. As a result, Pope said, annuities "lead necessarily to the very hostilities they are intended to prevent." They produced other evils as well. "The cupidity of unscrupulous men" was stimulated and led to "that system of swindling and wrong to the Indian in which have originated nearly all of our Indian difficulties." The general was adamant. Such wrongs must be corrected, for it was impossible for the army to maintain peace on the frontier under this system. "Cease to pay money to the Indians, and the temptation of the whites to go amongst them and cheat them is nearly altogether taken away." That the Indians desired peace was enough; there was no reason to purchase peace.[11]

Other prominent persons agreed with Pope. Bishop Henry Whipple of Minnesota, the leading civilian critic of

Federal Indian policy, described one attempt at treaty making with the Chippewa of Minnesota in which the natives were too smart and too determined to fall for the words of the emissary from Washington. The negotiator, who had no knowledge of Indians, said to the assembled chiefs at Crow Wing, Minnesota: "My red brothers, the winds of fifty-five winters have blown over my head and have silvered it with gray. In all that time I have never done wrong to a single human being." Speaking as the representative of the "Great Father in Washington" and as their "friend," he urged them to sign the treaty at once. But the Indians were determined to keep their land, and Sha-bosh-kung, chief of the Mille Lacs band, sprang to his feet and replied: "My father, look at me! The winds of fifty-five winters have blown over my head and silvered it with gray. But—they haven't blown my brains away!" [12] That ended these negotiations, but rarely did the government fail to have its way, for usually some minor chief could be bribed to sign, and the treaty would then be regarded as binding by the government.

Federal Indian policy, Pope charged, was the result of temporary expedients rather than careful thought and planning, and a policy was needed that was adaptable to different conditions as well as to the needs of the government and the Indians. Pope recognized that there were two classes of Indians: (1) the wild tribes, such as the Teton Sioux or the Comanche; and (2) the semi-civilized tribes, of which the Winnebago or Ponca were examples. He believed that different policies were needed for each group.

Because the present policies of the government had been ill-conceived, Pope charged, the semi-civilized tribes suffered under them. White pressure for land had so reduced the reservations that the Indians could no longer support themselves by hunting. Surrounded by settlements, they

39

were brought into contact with the worst elements of white society and soon became "idle vagabonds." Annuity payments attracted a horde of low-class citizens to the reservation: white gamblers, whiskey sellers, and unprincipled Indian traders who robbed and debauched the red men. Surrounded by such corrupt influences, the Indians became gamblers, drunkards, and vagabonds "plundered and wronged on all sides."

For the Indians there was no escape; speculators and land-hungry frontiersmen would demand reservation lands; a new treaty would be made requiring reservation land, and the hapless savages would again be moved to a new location. This process was repeated so often that some of the tribes had almost disappeared, and all were on the road to extermination. The condition of the once powerful Shawnee and Cherokee supported Pope's contention, but the Delaware or Lenni-Lenape provided the best example. They were moved step by step from their homeland on the eastern seaboard to Indian Territory. For short periods they had lived in western Pennsylvania, Ohio, Indiana, Missouri, and Kansas and they had ceased to exist as a tribe by the 1860s.

General Pope also sharply criticized the permanent Indian frontier and the practice of locating reservations on the edge of the frontier line. The permanent Indian frontier was an example of the absence of long-range planning and a lack of awareness of changing conditions. Forces were building to make this policy untenable even at the very time it was being implemented, and by the 1860s it existed only as an idea. Rapidly increasing travel to the western regions ripped large holes in this frontier line, but the Indian Bureau persisted in locating reservations along it. Friction was unavoidable, and clashes between the two races occurred.

Every aspect of Federal Indian policy seemed to bring

war rather than peace. Eager to secure the right of way across the plains, the government also paid the wild tribes to leave travelers alone, but the money quickly passed into the hands of unscrupulous traders and whiskey dealers who assembled on annuity day. In time the warriors retaliated by attacking the first passerby, and war followed. Many times, Pope explained, the Indians, "goaded by swindling and wrong and maddened by drink," indiscriminately attacked white settlers.[13]

Pope and other critics argued that Federal Indian policy with its recurring wars was an expensive failure. "Both in an economic and a humane view," he wrote, "the present Indian policy has been a woeful failure." It caused rather than prevented wars, and he predicted repeated outbreaks until revisions were made.[14] If this policy were continued, he explained, it was possible that the entire race would soon be exterminated, but even if some Indians survived, their condition would not improve. They would continue to suffer; they would not be civilized and assimilated into white culture. "I think," Pope wrote, "that it will not be disputed by those familiar with the subject that our Indian policy has totally failed of any humanizing influence over the Indian, has worked him a cruel wrong, and has entailed a very great and useless expense upon the Government." He believed that the Indians were better off both morally and physically in their wild state than under the existing system.[15]

Although Pope condemned the entire system, he offered suggestions to correct its failings. The semi-civilized tribes should be disarmed and moved to some point far in the rear of the frontier settlements. Force should be used if necessary, but persuasion should be tried first. Instead of doling out annuities, the government should spend the money on buildings, tools, and subsistence. Fed and cared for by the government, surrounded by American farmers, and freed from the debasing influence of unscrupulous frontiersmen, the Indians would be in a better position to receive instruction in Christianity and to adapt to civilization.

The objective of this policy was the assimilation of the native race into American civilization. Leaving them under the care of civilian agents and sending teachers and missionaries among them would prepare them to take their place in white society. Pope realized that assimilation would be a long and tedious project. Hunters would have to be transformed into farmers. Schooling would have to be provided. Tribal organization would have to be destroyed and the Indians treated as individuals. Pope was not sure that assimilation was possible, but he regarded it as the only hope for the Indians. If it failed, it would at least have turned the semi-civilized tribes into harmless members of the community.

The wild tribes, however, required different treatment. Civilian agents could take care of the semi-civilized tribes, but they were not qualified to control the blanket Indians. This was a job for the army, and Pope insisted that he be given authority to handle it. The wild tribes should be put under the exclusive jurisdiction of the War Department. Broken treaties should be discarded, and no new treaties made. No money should be paid directly to the Indian if the exploitation of the Indian by the traders and their associates was to be controlled and their evil influence broken. Military supervision of the wild tribes was the answer. Trade laws would be enforced, eliminating a major abuse, and gradually the Indians would be collected near military posts where missionaries could begin to prepare them for assimilation.

Pope insisted that these suggestions be carried out. If

they were not, the wild tribes should be left alone. "I am convinced," he wrote, "that the condition of the Indian in his wild state is far better than his status under present Indian policy. . . . In his wild condition the Indian possesses at least many noble qualities," and was easier to manage than the semi-wild tribes. With the knowledge of the barren and treeless high plains region gained from his earlier career as an army explorer, Pope believed that the home of the blanket Indians was a desert, unsuitable for white exploitation. He was incorrect in his belief which was common at that time, and it colored his thinking on the Indian problem. White settlement, he believed, had reached the westernmost limits of the fertile belt, and he predicted that the plains would never attract the white population. While it was true that the plains would have to be crossed to reach the mining regions of the Rocky Mountain West, peace could be maintained with the wild tribes if they allowed travelers to pass unmolested.

Pope believed that the adoption of his policy would bring the United States a step closer to the solution of the Indian problem. It would at least be an improvement over the haphazard and unworkable policy then in effect. Once the Indian wars ceased, the barrier to immigration and travel would be removed. In making these proposals Pope questioned one of the cardinal principles of American Indian policy. Why, he asked, must the government recognize the Indian's title to the land? Certainly it was honorable and just to do so, but it was also unrealistic. Acknowledgment of this right checked the advance of civilization. History has shown, he wrote, that the end result would be the "dispossession of the savage and the occupation of his lands by civilized man" whatever policy was pursued. This was inevitable, but it should be accomplished as humanely as possible. Rather than paying the Indians for their land, allowing them to be robbed of the money by unscrupulous whites, and then fighting endless wars with them, the government should treat the Indians as wards, with the wild tribes under military control and the semi-civilized tribes removed from the disruptive frontier environment.[16]

Pope also had ideas about eliminating the abuses surrounding the Indian trade. He repeatedly called attention to the machinations of traders and the impossibility of enforcing the Intercourse Acts. Federal regulation of Indian trade had failed; the Indian country was flooded with liquor, and the Indian was robbed of all he had. The situation was disgraceful and dangerous, and Pope drew up a new set of trade regulations and requested authority to put them into effect in his department.

Under the existing laws the traders were "wholly uncontrolled and irresponsible" and were a common cause of hostilities. Concerned only with profits, they plied the Indians with liquor, cheated them of their furs, and provided them with arms and ammunition. Pope could see no reason why traders should not be compelled to follow the same rules of trade and fair prices in their dealings with the Indians as were required in dealing with white citizens. He was confident that his trade regulations would eliminate many of the abuses, especially with military enforcement.[17]

Intended to be an integral part of the new Indian policy, Pope's trade regulations are summarized as follows:

Trade Regulations

1. All previous permits to trade with Indians are revoked, and written authority from the War Department is now required to engage in Indian trade.
2. A copy of this authority must be given to the commander of

the military district in which the trading is done, with a bond as security that the regulations will be complied with.

3. The district commander will designate the points at which trading posts shall be established. Each trading post will be in the vicinity of a military post, and no trade is to be carried on except at that location.

4. District and post commanders are to be furnished with an invoice of the goods with the original prices attached.

5. A council of administration at the military post will fix a tariff on goods, and the prices will be publicly exhibited.

6. The council of administration will fix fair prices for furs and other goods offered by the Indian.

7. Each member of the council of administration shall be sworn to have no interest, either direct or indirect, in the Indian trade.

8. No money will be paid to the Indians under any circumstances, and the sale and possession of liquor are prohibited.

9. With the exception of Indian traders and their authorized employees, no whites will be permitted in Indian country except emigrants on their way West; and these emigrants are prohibited from trading with the Indians.

10. The schedule of prices and other regulations are to be explained to the Indians by the post commander.

11. Any Indian trader who violates these regulations shall be arrested and confined by the military commander; his store shall be closed, and his case acted upon by the War Department. All other whites found trading with the Indians shall be arrested, their goods confiscated, and they shall be escorted out of the Indian country.

12. Sutlers at all military posts shall be permitted to trade with the Indians.

13. In the event of hostilities, all trading posts in the area shall be closed.

14. These regulations are necessary to make clear to the Indians that they will be dealt with fairly and to encourage them to locate their permanent homes in the vicinity and under the supervision of military posts.

15. Post commanders are directed to furnish every possible assis-

tance to missionaries and other religious instructors who desire to work with the Indians for humane purposes.

16. Commanders of the military posts are charged with the enforcement of these regulations and shall make frequent inspections.[18]

This new policy, in which Pope placed so much hope, met with mixed reactions in Washington. Having served on the frontier, General Halleck gave his approval and support. Making sure that the proposals were not distorted, Halleck arranged for their publication in the *Army and Navy Journal.* At the same time, he warned Pope that they would be "strongly opposed by nearly everybody connected with the Department of the Interior." Speculators —especially those connected with Indian affairs—operated through Congress and the civil departments of the government, and they exerted a powerful influence on governmental policies. Those with a vested interest at stake were sure to oppose any attempt at revision and reform. Halleck slyly sent his cousin, Bishop Henry Whipple, to the Interior Department to call attention to the "Pope paper," and the Episcopal clergyman promised his support.[19]

Officials of the Indian Bureau, however, opposed the wholesale revision of Federal Indian policy which the Pope paper entailed. Dr. Walter Burleigh, agent for the Yankton Sioux, claimed that demoralization among Indians surrounded by white settlement, did not exist as Pope claimed. At least it was not true of his Yankton, he asserted. Launching an attack on Pope, the agent said that the general's "ten years' experience on the frontiers had failed to afford him that degree of knowledge which a person should possess before sweeping into oblivion with one stroke of his pen a system that has worked so well for nearly a quarter of a century."[20] Burleigh, one of the more effective agents at enriching himself at the expense of the Indians, had no desire to see the old system swept into oblivion.

The Commissioner of Indian Affairs, William Dole, received Pope's plan in silence and even pretended that it had been mislaid when Bishop Whipple visited him at the Interior Department. But Whipple's interest in the plan and its publication in the *Army and Navy Journal* forced Dole to reply. In defending the existing Indian policy, Dole completely distorted Pope's proposals and criticized statements that had never been made.

Dole admitted that "grave and serious mistakes may have occurred" in the management of Indian affairs and that the Indians had often been subjected to "cruel wrongs and indignities" which had caused them to go to war, but he found no reason to revise the government's policy or to attribute these failures to that policy. It would be difficult, he argued, to demonstrate that any other policy would have led to better results.[21]

Having thus disposed of the need for change, Dole discussed Pope's suggestions by distorting what Pope had said and attributing statements to him that he had not made. The proposals themselves were carefully avoided. Dole exhibited a remarkable ignorance of Indian policy, past and present. Forgetting that Thomas Jefferson had suggested the removal of eastern tribes to the plains region and ignoring the fact that the removal had been carried out, Dole wrote that no one would have considered such a policy sixty to eighty years ago and that if it had been suggested, no attempt would have been made to implement it. "To me," he said, "the proposition seems even now unwise and extremely impracticable."[22] John Pope had no desire whatever to move all the Indians to the plains. It was the very thing he wished to avoid.

Completely misrepresenting Pope's proposals, Dole charged that Pope wished to disarm some 300,000 Indians and send them into the barren high plains region where they would be unable to subsist. Dole was guilty of either deliberate distortion or careless handling of the facts. Pope had suggested that the reservation tribes be moved eastward away from the plains and that the Army control the wild tribes on the western plains. He had no desire to move all the Indians westward where they would remain a barrier to travel. He would not let them starve. He was genuinely concerned that they were a disappearing race, and he feared that if changes were not made, their extinction would be rapid. He complained that the Indians had been so often uprooted and moved from one location to another that some of the tribes had ceased to exist. Commissioner Dole apparently saw nothing wrong in this, for he had been the one who had approved the removal of the peaceful Winnebago from Minnesota in 1863, and then in 1864 proposed that they be moved again. [23]

Commissioner Dole had rejected Pope's "broad and sweeping" criticisms and suggestions by avoiding or distorting them. Confident that they would never be seriously considered, he predicted a general war with all the Indians in the country if they were implemented. With the Civil War in progress, he knew that Congress would never risk the outbreak of war with some 300,000 Indians.

Pope had become involved in a debate over Indian policy because of the Sioux war, but he was not alone in his criticisms or demand that changes be made. Others agreed that the policies were obsolete. In 1854, Commissioner of Indian Affairs, George W. Manypenny, had requested new trade regulations to replace the obsolete Intercourse Act of 1834, and he had insisted that repeated removals of Indians must stop. In 1858, Commissioner Charles Mix had voiced the necessity of locating the Indians on a permanent reservation where they could be prepared for assimilation. Mix also questioned the use of annuity payments because they made the Indians "the victims of the lawless and inhuman sharper and speculator."[24]

Other aspects of Federal Indian policy were questioned and criticized as well. In 1862, Secretary of the Interior Caleb Smith discussed the treaty system. "It may well be questioned whether the government has not adopted a mistaken policy in regarding the Indian tribes as quasi-independent nations, and making treaties with them for the purchase of lands they claim to own," he wrote. "They have none of the elements of nationality; they are within the limits of the recognized authority of the United States and must be subject to its control." The rapid progress of civilization meant that the Indians would lose their land. The nation could not permit large sections of land to remain in the hands of "savage tribes" as hunting grounds when it was needed for agricultural expansion. "Indeed," Smith wrote, "whatever may be the theory, the government has always demanded the removal of the Indians when their lands were required for agricultural purposes by advancing settlements." Title was acquired by treaty, he said, but "it is well known that they [the Indians] have yielded to a necessity which they could not resist." Smith announced in 1862 that a "radical change" in policy was needed. The Indians should be treated as wards of the government, he asserted. But no changes were made.[25]

Commissioner Dole himself had commented in 1862 on the disruptive influence of evil white men who surrounded the reservations when he claimed that the "pernicious effects" of contact with "vicious whites" damaged relations with the Indians and hindered their progress toward civilization. Bishop Whipple was more caustic in his criticisms.

"The history of our relations to the Indians," he wrote, "is one to make every American blush for shame. It may be doubted whether a sadder history of blunders, frauds, and crimes can be found in any civilized country." The treaty system with its theory of independent nations was based on "falsehood" and was a "shameful lie." Treaties, he said, were "often conceived in fraud, and made solely to put money into some white man's pocket." [26]

What was to be done with the Indians? How could they be civilized? How could war with them be prevented? These were problems with which Pope and other reformers wrestled. Bishop Whipple used his influence in Washington to bring changes, but in the early 1860s he found much opposition. Accompanied by General Halleck, Whipple called on President Lincoln and his cabinet during one visit to the capital. When Secretary of War Edwin Stanton saw the bishop, he remarked to Halleck, "What does Bishop Whipple want? If he has come here to tell us of the corruption of our Indian system and dishonesty of Indian agents, tell him that we know it. But the Government never reforms an evil until the people demand it. Tell him that when he reaches the heart of the American people, the Indians will be saved." [27]

Bishop Whipple publicized his demands and button-holed cabinet members and congressmen—influential contacts that were closed to military men. As an army officer, Pope had to transmit his reports and proposals through channels, but by 1864 he had made his views public, which was the most he could do. The War Department was too busy with the Confederacy to devote any attention to Indian policy, and the Interior Department refused to consider radical reforms that threatened vested interests.

In the search for a realistic and workable policy that would maintain peace on the frontier, Pope raised issues and made proposals that were to become the subject of much discussion in the post-Civil War period. Treaties, annuities, graft, removal, and other problems—all were within the scope of his interest. During the 1870s many of his ideas would be put into effect, although not always for the reasons that he first proposed them.

"Hell with
the fires
put out"

Early in 1864 Pope began to plan a summer campaign
against the Teton Sioux in the region west of the Missouri
River. During the winter and spring, some of the Sisseton
and Yanktonai Sioux began to surrender, and while others
also indicated a willingness to surrender, most of them,
especially the Teton bands, were still hostile. The subtribes
of the Teton Sioux—the Sans Arc, Blackfeet, Two Kettle,
Miniconjou, and others—were, like the Yanktonai, split
into hostile and peaceful factions, but the hostiles were in
the ascendancy, and they sought to prevent their tribesmen from making peace.

Support for Pope's new campaign came from several
sources: Commissioner of Indian Affairs William Dole
urged the establishment of more military posts along the
Upper Missouri. General Sully had established Fort Sully
at Farm Island about six miles below the trading post of
Fort Pierre, but the new fort and Fort Randall, located
some thirty miles above the mouth of the Niobrara River,
were the only military installations along the upper
stretches of this water route to the Montana gold mines.
John Hutchinson, acting governor of Dakota Territory,
also requested renewed military efforts and announced
that the hostiles must be hunted down and punished until

they were made to respect and fear the power of the government. [1]

With men like Hutchinson insisting on new efforts and with the Interior Department demanding that routes to the Idaho and Montana mines be opened and protected, Pope was authorized to begin his campaign to protect the frontier settlements and to open and maintain important routes of travel. Above all, he must encourage the Sioux to make peace and punish those who remained defiant. Pope had always believed in offensive movements, and the limited successes of the previous year had not caused him to change his mind. He knew that peace would never be maintained by simply stationing troops among the settlements. War must be taken to the heart of the Indians' homeland, for not until they learned the power of the government would there be peace.

The basic outline for the 1864 campaign included establishment of four new military posts in the heart of the Sioux country. Pope believed that more posts should be located in the Indian country to control the surrounding regions and protect the lines of travel. Fort Sully had been a start, but more were needed. New forts at Devil's Lake and on the James River would dominate Yanktonai country and screen the settlements of Minnesota and Iowa, while others would be located on the Upper Missoui and Yellowstone rivers. A military expedition was also planned. While troops from Sibley's district scoured the region east of the Missouri River to clear it of Indians, General Sully was to invade the Teton country west of the Missouri River and establish the post on the Yellowstone River. [2]

Plans were approved by the War Department in February, and Pope called Sibley and Sully to his headquarters in Milwaukee to work out the details. Reports from the

Upper Missouri indicated that the hostile Teton and Yanktonai along the river were making minor attacks and had
announced that they would allow no travel up the Missouri
or across their country. [3]

The Indians were trouble enough by themselves, but the
proximity of the Canadian border and the activities of the
half-breed traders made the situation even more difficult.
If the hostiles could flee to Canada and trade for arms,
ammunition, and food, the effect of the summer campaigns and the destruction of Indian supplies would be
negated. Sibley, like Pope in 1863, remonstrated about
this "refuge for these Ishmaelites of the Prairies."

In January 1864 Pope informed the War Department
that from 800 to 1,000 Santee Sioux had taken refuge in
British settlements along the Red River and were being
subsisted there. Since no British forces were in the region
to control them and to prevent raids into the United
States, he insisted that the British government was obli-
gated either to prevent their movement into United States
territory or to allow American troops on Canadian soil.
Secretary of State William Seward discussed the matter
with Lord Lyon, the British minister, but no agreement
was reached, and the military continued to be plagued by
the existence of the Canadian sanctuary.[4]

With the outbreak of the Sioux war half-breed traders
from the Red River settlements in Canada had begun to
trade with the hostiles and encouraged them to continue
the conflict. The Commissioner of Indian Affairs and
others believed that Confederate agents were working
through these traders to encourage hostilities and thus tie
up troops which were needed in the South. When reports
on the extent of the arms trade reached Pope at headquarters, he authorized Sibley to regulate the activity of
British half-breeds on United States soil.[5]

Migration to the Rocky Mountain gold fields added to the military problems in the Department of the Northwest. Montana gold was the topic of the day, often overshadowing the Indian war, and occasional bearded, weather-beaten prospectors coming down the Missouri with pokes of yellow dust caused great excitement along the Missouri and Mississippi rivers. Reports from the gold fields were front-page news in the Missouri Valley press, and demands were made for new roads to Virginia City.

Minnesotans had long been interested in the western gold fields. They thought of them in terms of the profits to be made from outfitting emigrant miners and the troops that would follow to protect the roads. They envisioned new western markets, and they saw Minnesota as an important link in the lines of communication across the continent. Promoters such as James W. Taylor, a close friend of Secretary of the Treasury Salmon P. Chase, and the Minnesota congressional delegation aroused interest and were influential in winning Federal support for the construction of new roads and the protection of travelers. The government provided support because western gold was needed to help finance the Civil War. In 1862, 1863, and 1864 James L. Fisk, a captain in the Quartermaster Corps, led government-sponsored emigrant trains to the Montana mines. And in 1864, Congress appropriated $40,000 for protection of gold seekers using the new roads across the Nebraska and Dakota territories.[6]

Pope was willing to provide assistance, and his decision to build new posts in Dakota was prompted in part by the desire to protect travel, but he was also aware that the emigrants would complicate the problem. Not only had the hostiles made it plain they would allow no travel through their country, which in itself promised bloodshed, but emigrants also demonstrated a special talent for

55

causing trouble. Wandering westward in small groups by whatever route seemed best and taking few precautions for their own safety, they presented an irresistible temptation to even peaceful Indians. Few warriors could forego the prospect of acquiring horses or a new trophy to hang from the lodgepole. "Such people are proverbially careless and imprudent," Pope said, but they invariably held the government responsible for all resultant suffering. [7]

To protect the careless and the foolish, Pope authorized General Sully to prevent civilian boats from passing up the Missouri beyond Fort Pierre until he believed it safe, and he issued a travel circular on March 14, 1864 which listed suggestions for all travelers. The circular of 1864 was in the form of advice and was intended to reduce demands on the troops in the department. But when the Indian problem continued, Pope issued travel orders in 1865 and 1866, establishing regulations for travel across the plains. [8]

In preparing for the military campaign, Pope was further hindered by demands for troops in the South and by the activities of his ever-present critics. Need for troops presented a special problem. While the military situation in the South was no longer critical, General Grant was searching everywhere for troops to strengthen his armies in Virginia and Tennessee. To him an Indian war was of secondary importance. When disasters occurred, as they did in the Red River campaign in Texas in the spring of 1864, troops that would have been used in the prosecution of the Sioux war were pulled from the Department of the Northwest. Pope accepted this situation philosophically. Although it cramped his operations, he told General Sully, "We must do the best we can." [9] In August, calls for troops became incessant. Grant, desperate for men to strengthen Sherman's advance on Atlanta, called for every man that could be spared and even ordered inspectors and surgeons sent to western hospitals to clear them out and forward the convalescents to the front.[10]

To make matters worse, and in an attempt to embarrass and discredit Pope, several members of Congress began to insist that he had more troops than were required, implying that he was not concerned enough with the success of the war in the South. At the same time the frontier settlements were clamoring for more protection. The exasperated Pope complained to the War Department that while he was being urged to furnish protection to travelers across the plains, "a set of people, ignorant of all the facts and perfectly unacquainted with the necessities of the department are besieging the authorities at Washington to deprive me of the very means necessary to do precisely what they seek with constant persistence."[11]

Pope defended himself in a caustic letter to Halleck. Lashing out at his critics, he specifically blamed "persons connected with our unfortunate Indian system, agents, Indian traders, whiskey sellers, contractors, &cs.," who wished to prolong hostilities and who wanted annuity treaties involving large sums of money and fat contracts. He explained that when hostilities ended and the Indians were driven beyond the reach of the Minnesota frontier, these groups would lose a lucrative business. For these reasons the traders, agents, and their friends were believed to have used their influence in Washington to reduce the strength of Pope's command, and there was something sinister involved as well. Applications for removing troops were made, he said, by political opponents of the government, "who seek means to make war upon the Administration," and the continuation of hostilities would furnish them with material for their attacks.[12]

To Pope's dismay and disgust the incessant criticisms finally bore fruit. In June, Lieutenant Colonel W. L. Duff

57

of the Inspector General's office was sent to investigate. Acting on verbal orders from General Grant himself and reporting directly to John Rawlins, Grant's Chief of Staff, Duff discovered that it was a common opinion among influential citizens in the Northwest that the Sioux war was not as serious as Pope and Sibley believed. Some critics went so far as to say that "the whole thing was a humbug." These individuals preferred a line of military posts garrisoned by a regiment of cavalry. Occasional emigrant trains could then be easily and safely escorted by a company of cavalry. But Duff also saw hidden motives behind the attacks on the military commanders, for he reported that many of the accusers were interested in keeping troops in the country.[13]

Pope protested bitterly that such irresponsible statements were taken seriously by superiors.[14] He was worried that Grant considered the charges serious enough to order an investigation and that the accuracy of troop returns was suspect.

General Halleck, aware of the events, wrote to General Grant on behalf of his friend, "It is a very great mistake to suppose that General Pope has retained an unnecessarily large force in his department." On the contrary, he said, "I have found him the most ready of all the department commanders to give assistance to others when asked, certainly quite a contrast to some of the present and former commanders of the Department of Kansas, Missouri, and Ohio."[15]

Angered by the constant harassment, Pope was in no mood to listen when Governor Stephen Miller of Minnesota requested more troops for the frontier. In the future, he said, the governor should send these requests to the Secretary of War. They would no longer be forwarded through Pope's headquarters. Pope also vented his anger on

General Sibley who, as usual, wanted more troops for his district.

When Pope discovered in mid-September that his department was again subject to an inspection, he was unable to control his temper. A second inspection within the space of a few months was too much, and he demanded written evidence of the charges against him and the opportunity to know his accusers. He did not believe "that the War Department will take action implying so insulting a charge against an officer as are these inspections, based upon statements of persons unknown to the officer in question, without furnishing him copies of the statements and the names of his maligners." [16]

During the time that Pope was defending himself, he had continued preparations for the summer campaign. By mid-March the details of the new expedition had been worked out. General Sully was to concentrate about 1,300 cavalrymen at Fort Pierre and move them up the Missouri River. At Bordache Creek on the Upper Missouri his force would be complemented by an additional 1,600 troopers from Sibley's command in Minnesota. Pope stressed, as he had previously, that no treaties with the Indians were to be made which provided for gifts or annuities. The Indians were to be told that they would be under military supervision and that as long as they remained at peace and did not molest the whites, they would be treated kindly and protected. Depredations, however, would bring immediate punishment.

Although the government had taken no action on Pope's policy proposals, Pope was determined to implement them if possible. He warned Sully that no communication was to be permitted with the Indians except on his authority. No Indian agents or others were to be allowed to negotiate with the Sioux. When the Indians surrendered, they were to be located near military posts under military control, and the semi-civilized Sioux were to be given seeds and tools to begin supporting themselves. [17]

To strengthen the Sully expedition, Pope requested that the distribution of annuity payments, supplies, and arms and ammunition be delayed until after the campaign. And for once the Commissioner of Indian Affairs was in agreement. In fact, he had already issued orders prohibiting the distribution of guns and ammunition to the Sioux of the Upper Missouri and instructed Agent Samuel Latta to confer with Sully before distributing clothing and supplies. The experience of the previous year had demonstrated the wisdom of withholding annuities. In July 1863, Latta had distributed goods to the apparently friendly Sioux bands at Fort Pierre and had then continued up river. A few days later the steamboat on which he traveled was attacked by the same Indians. [18]

Because the Indian Bureau was anxious to bring the Sioux war to a speedy conclusion Commissioner Dole decided that a peace mission was in order. In March he designated Father Pierre De Smet, the great Jesuit missionary, to confer with the Sioux along the Missouri and to make peace, but soon after De Smet left they engaged in hostilities. This was, he informed Dole, "a proof of the little reliance to be placed on their words and promises. . . . "[19] Since the peace effort had failed, Sully was determined to punish them.

On June 26, Sully sat quietly on his horse as the long blue column marched out of Fort Sully. The Indian expedition of 1864 had begun. Twenty days earlier Colonel Minor T. Thomas, after receiving last-minute instructions from Sibley, had led the Minnesota column from Fort Ridgely as the band played "The Girl I Left Behind Me." While Colonel Thomas marched westward from Minnesota,

Sully moved up the east bank of the Missouri River, pausing long enough to track down and capture the three warriors who had killed Captain John Feilner, his topographical engineer. Sully beheaded the captives and mounted the gory trophies on posts as a warning to others.

In early July the two columns joined on the east bank of the Missouri River opposite the mouth of the Cannonball River and crossed the Missouri to the site of Fort Rice, which Sully's men were building. They then moved westward up the Cannonball River with sixty days' rations and an emigrant train in tow. When the scouts brought reports of a large Indian encampment on the Knife River, Sully placed the emigrant wagons under a strong guard and turned northward looking for Indians.

On July 28 the command came upon the hostile village at the base of Killdeer Mountain. The Indians were waiting, eager for a fight. They had come upon Sully's scouts the day before, and so confident were they of victory that the village was still standing and the women and children were assembled to watch the massacre. The battle, however, did not go as expected. Sully used his artillery to full effect and quickly swept the warriors from the field. Scrambling women attempted to strike camp but were forced to flee. "Their haste to escape," wrote one participant, "was expedited by shells dropped into the village, which caused great consternation."[20]

Unable to pursue the Indians because of the nature of the land—he was on the edge of the Badlands—Sully destroyed their camp and returned to the emigrant train. He then decided to cross the Badlands to the Yellowstone River. But passage through this terrain was an ordeal. At first sight of the rough and broken country with its weird rock formations, Sully described it as "hell with the fires put out." At times the men had to cut a road to get the wagons through, and Indians resisted them every foot of the way. Artillery fire usually kept the warriors at bay, but one participant noted, "The red whelps harassed us all day."[21]

The command finally left both fighting Indians and rugged terrain behind and marched northward toward the Yellowstone River and the desperately needed supplies. Struggling through blistering heat and swarming grasshoppers, they passed the site of an abandoned Indian village whose size astounded Sully. "I should judge all the Indians in the country had assembled there," he wrote. "The space they occupied was over one mile long and half a mile wide, besides which we discovered camps all over the country close to this spot."[22] On August 12 the weary command reached the Yellowstone River and found two of the four expected supply boats, the *Chippewa Falls* and the *Alone,* waiting for them.

The condition of the troops and the loss of two shallow-draft steamboats with supplies forced Sully to abandon the plan of constructing a military post on the Yellowstone. He began his return to Fort Rice, and the emigrant train turned westward toward the Montana mines. Some troops were left at two trading posts—Fort Union at the junction of the Yellowstone and Missouri rivers, and Fort Berthold in the Mandan country—to increase the safety of river travel, for the Sioux were still hostile. Determined to resist any encroachment on their territory, they had attacked two steamboats, the *General Grant* and the *Chippewa Falls,* below Fort Union. Little damage was done, however, because the big gun of the *General Grant* hurled canister at the Indians and kept them at a distance.[23]

Sully had defeated the hostile bands of the Teton and Yanktonai and destroyed some of their confidence, but he realized that they had fought only because they had been confident of victory. He had learned much about fighting Indians in the broken country west and south of the Missouri River and had come to the conclusion that more extensive efforts were needed if the hostiles were to be routed. The reception that the Indians gave the Fisk train verified this.

James Fisk and an emigrant train had left Fort Ridgely on July 23, and after demanding an escort at Fort Rice, Fisk had moved due west toward the Badlands and gold fields of the newly created Territory of Montana that lay beyond. Fisk followed essentially the same route as Sully, but near the Little Missouri River he ran into a band of Hunkpapa and was forced to establish an entrenched camp until a relief force arrived to escort the emigrants back to Fort Rice. [24]

Despite continuing hostilities, Sully, like Pope, hoped that the Indians had been punished enough to make peace. He was aware that a major effort would be required to defeat them decisively. "If a war of extermination is called for," Sully wrote, "it will be necessary to shoot everything that wears a blanket; but it would be very expensive and I know such is not the wish of the Government." If extermination was the aim, other and less expensive methods were available. "The cheapest and easiest way to exterminate the wild Indian," he commented, "is to bring him into a civilized country in contact with the whites (the women would soon become prostitutes and the men drunkards)."[25]

During his return trip down the Missouri, General Sully had stopped at several trading posts, and he had observed the annuity system in operation, as well as the effects white traders had on the wild Indians. What he saw appalled him. "This system of issuing annuity goods is one grand humbug," he told Pope. The amount of goods was so small that it was impossible for every member of the tribe to receive a share unless they were issued "at the rate of spoonsfull of sugar and strips of cloth one inch wide per man." It was, he reported, "a matter that beats anything I have heard in rascality. . . ."[26]

Pope was not surprised at these discoveries; they simply supported his criticisms of the Indian system. Nor was he astonished at Sully's remarks about the traders. Sully, however, was aghast at what he saw. The extent of the whiskey trade was beyond anything he had expected. "Why can't the Government send all the traders out of the country," he complained.[27]

As Sully passed down the Missouri to Fort Rice, he was in contact with some of the hostiles. Many of them desired peace, but the problem was to get them to the military posts and protect them. The war faction among the Teton and Yanktonai kept watch over the encampments to ensure that none escaped to conclude peace with the soldiers. Sully, however, attempted to bring them in. He believed that, by rounding up those tribesmen in the vicinity of the military posts, by protecting them, and by giving them some food and clothing, a nucleus would be formed that would attract others, and missionaries could then begin the process of civilization and Christianization.

General Sully had definite ideas regarding the role that missionaries could play in preparing the Indians for their entry into white society, and he explained in detail the suggestions that Pope had made in more general terms. Sully believed that teaching must precede preaching; that the Indians must be civilized before being Christianized, and that if the religious groups understood the significance of such labors they would be more willing to support their home missionaries than those in distant lands. "They would have the satisfaction," he explained, "of feeling that while they were reclaiming the savage they were at the same time doing a great benefit to the welfare of their country."[28]

Pope and Sully were both emphasizing the need for missionary activity among the Indians at the very time that similar ideas were taking form in the mind of Bishop Whipple. It is probable that the three men influenced the decision to inaugurate President Grant's "Quaker Policy" which allowed religious groups to select Indian agents, since General Grant was familiar with Pope's papers on Indian policy.

The Indian campaign of 1864, like that of 1863, was but a partial success. Fort Rice on the Missouri and Fort Wadsworth on the Coteau des Prairies had been established, and small garrisons had been left at Fort Union and Fort Berthold. Soldiers had invaded the homeland of the Teton Sioux and had demonstrated that they and their terrible field artillery were more than a match for the poorly armed hostiles. And for the second consecutive year the Sioux had been attacked and lost most of their camp equipage and supplies. The prospect that they would suffer from this again forced many to ask for peace. In late November, General Sully reported that the Indians were anxious for peace. He believed that peace could be maintained "provided the proper course is adopted, and that is to treat the Indians in future with justice. Let them understand that the Government intends to see that they will no longer be the prey of dishonest agents and traders."[29]

Although the 1864 expedition had not lived up to expectations, Pope was well enough pleased with the results to recommend General Sully for a promotion and more than pleased when he suddenly received orders to report to Washington. On November 24, 1864 he boarded a train for the capital and then proceeded to General Grant's headquarters in Virginia. Pope did not know what was in the offing but assumed his summons could only be recognition for his accomplishments in the Northwest. Although serious charges had been levied against him by his critics, the inspections had cleared him. What, then, did Grant have in mind?

General Grant was looking ahead, since it was evident that the Confederacy was on the verge of collapse. William Tecumseh Sherman's tough western army had taken Atlanta, and Lee was fighting desperately to defend Richmond. Army commands would soon have to be reorganized, and Grant offered Pope the Department of the South. Pope, however, refused. Indian fighting was preferable to commanding occupation forces, and he realized that his statements in 1862 had not made him popular in the South. Frontier duty was more attractive and offered more opportunities for advancement. When Grant then proposed that the Departments of the Northwest, Missouri, and Kansas be combined into the Division of the Missouri, with Pope in command of the new military division, Pope eagerly accepted. All military operations on the plains would be coordinated under his control. Pope had, in fact, suggested such a unit of command in 1863.

Although unexpected, this development signified that Pope's achievements had been recognized, and that the tarnished record had been refurbished. But more important, the coordination and unity which Grant believed were essential, would be brought to military operations on the plains. "The importance of this change," he wrote, "is much increased because of the inefficiency of two of the commanders of the departments named, one of who [sic] I suppose cannot well be removed. I do, however, think it of very great importance that General Rosecrans should be removed." [30]

General Grant ordered Halleck to lay the matter before the Secretary of War and request an immediate change, for "with Pope in command we secure at least two advantages we have not heretofore had, namely, subordination and intelligence of administration." The change was forthcoming, but Pope did not assume command of the Division of the Missouri until the beginning of 1865.[31]

CHAPTER FOUR

"We must settle
with the Indians
this summer"

On assuming command of the Division of the Missouri, Pope was presented with an excellent opportunity to implement his Indian policy, and he was confident that he could do so. The new division, encompassing the entire plains region with the exception of the Confederate state of Texas, placed all the great tribes of the plains—Sioux, Cheyenne, Kiowa, and Comanche—within his power. He began to enforce his policy, believing that it would at least reduce the frequency of Indian wars and be of benefit to both the Indians and the government.

During 1864, Pope had already begun to put some of his ideas into effect. He had instructed Generals Sully and Sibley that only simple peace treaties be made, that all Indians who surrendered were to be placed under the exclusive control of the military, and that no civilians—not even agents of the Indian Bureau—were to have any contact with them. Since the War Department was aware of these orders and had not countermanded them, it had given tacit approval of what had been done.[1] And now, with the entire plains region under his command and with the great conflict with the Confederacy almost over, troops would be available to force the tribes into submission.

A peace that could be maintained under the new policy toward the Indians appeared to be within reach. The opportunity was there, but it was fleeting, for Pope found himself thwarted at every turn. Although there were a few military successes, 1865 proved a frustrating and largely unsuccessful year. Pope was hindered by public sympathy for the poor red man which had been stirred up by the Sand Creek massacre; he was also harassed by the conduct of the Union troops sent to the plains at the close of the Civil War. These men who had volunteered to fight to save the Union had no desire to fight Indians. Opposed by Governor Newton Edmunds of Dakota Territory, by Indian Agent Jesse Leavenworth, and by a Congressional Committee, Pope had to be content with meager results and watched his dreams fade away.

While the change in command in the West was taking place, the military outlook had also changed. Minor difficulties in the central plains region and along the Platte and Arkansas River roads during the 1860s had blossomed into a full-scale Indian war. While Pope was conferring with General Grant in Virginia, hostilities broke out along the Arkansas River. On November 29, 1864, Colonel John M. Chivington of the Colorado Volunteers launched a surprise attack on a Southern Cheyenne village at Sand Creek in eastern Colorado. The massacre and mutilation of the peaceful faction of the tribe, which believed itself to be under military protection, threw the entire West into a turmoil. Chivington, who had wanted an Indian war, succeeded far better than he knew.[2]

The hostile elements of the Southern Cheyenne lashed out with vengeance. Runners were sent to the southern Oglala and Brulé Sioux and to the Arapaho, and tribesmen gathered on the Republican River. The Cheyenne and their allies spread havoc across the plains. Striking along the

Arkansas and Platte roads, they burned and ravaged isolated ranches and settlements and destroyed the telegraph.
Twice they raided Julesburg, Colorado, one of the key
stations along the Overland Route, driving the residents
into the protective works of nearby Fort Rankin and pil-
laging the town. When on January 7, 1865 Julesburg was
first attacked, Colonel Robert R. Livingston of the First
Nebraska Cavalry at Fort Kearny telegraphed to General
R. W. Mitchell. "The Indians are masters of the Overland
road, and immediate action is imperative." Panic swept the
plains, and Colonel Thomas Moonlight of the Eleventh
Kansas Cavalry reported that Denver was completely isolated and expressed fear that the Colorado mining regions
would soon have to be abandoned.[3]

Reports of the devastation and desperate pleas for aid
reached the East, and demands for action flowed in from
the Missouri River to Utah Territory. Mail contractors
threatened to stop the stage service unless they were given
protection. The governments of Kansas and of Nebraska,
Colorado, and Utah territories demanded more troops on
the plains. Officials in Utah requested creation of a Department of the Plains to keep communications open. Not the
least of these requests came from Secretary of the Interior
Jacob P. Usher, who pointed to the necessity of removing
all Indians from the Platte and Republican valleys. Congress had granted charters to the Union Pacific Railroad
for the construction of the eastern segment of the transcontinental road, and the area had to be cleared of Indians
for the protection of the survey and construction crews.[4]

As reports and demands for aid and protection flowed
in to Washington, Federal officials became aware of the
seriousness of the Indian outbreak. While the Sand Creek
massacre was largely responsible, the activities of other
volunteer troops on the plains and their harsh treatment of

70

peaceful Indians also had created trouble. Military authorities ordered General Samuel Curtis of the Department of Kansas to investigate what had really happened at Sand Creek, but Curtis was reluctant to do so. He defended Chivington and urged Governor John Evans, who was in Washington, to quash the investigation. He wrote to Evans that the attack on Julesburg revealed a larger war party than usual and seemed "to be a daring thing at this season of winter," and he indicated that he was concerned about the attitude of government officials toward the Sand Creek massacre. General Halleck, in ordering the inquiry, had described Chivington's conduct "as being calculated to bring down all the Indians upon us," but Curtis disagreed. He wrote to Evans that harsh treatment would frighten the hostiles rather than increase their strength. "Terrible and shocking blows are necessary to quell the rascals," he said.[5]

To General Halleck, Curtis wrote that Chivington may have gone further than ordered but "still it is not true, as Indian agents and traders are representing, that such extra severity is increasing the Indian war." On the contrary, Curtis argued, it would bring them to terms. Yet in spite of all his arguments, Curtis discovered that more troops were needed to protect the Overland Route, and he requested Governor Evans to use all his influence to have additional men sent to his command.[6]

By February 1865, Curtis' connection with the Sand Creek investigation was over, and all he had to fear was that he might in some way be implicated in the massacre. Reorganization of the western military commands had meantime been carried out, and when Pope assumed command of the new Division of the Missouri, Curtis' Department of Kansas was abolished. Kansas was added to the Department of the Missouri, then under the command of

Major General Grenville Dodge, and Curtis was sent to Pope's old command in the Department of the Northwest.

While these changes were taking place, there were new reports of Indian activities along the Upper Platte. Colonel Robert R. Livingston reported that Indians had destroyed the Overland Road for one hundred miles from Julesburg to Junction Station and that no stages were running west of Camp Cottonwood, which was about halfway between Fort Kearny and Julesburg. He informed Dodge, "Feel assured, General, that this is no trifling Indian war." Livingston estimated that 2,000 warriors had participated in the attack of Fort Rankin and the sacking of Julesburg.[7]

While the military commanders assumed their new commands, the hostiles left the Platte Route and moved northward, scattering from the Black Hills to the Powder and Tongue rivers. General Dodge, unfamiliar with the Department of the Missouri, had to ask where the Powder River was. Pope, too, was unaware of the location of the hostiles, but his primary concern was to keep the roads open, and on February 9 he sent Dodge a terse message to reopen the Platte Route.[8] Although Dodge did not have enough men concentrated in the area to deal with this great gathering of hostile warriors, he did the best he could. One measure he took with Pope's approval was to regulate travel on both the northern and southern routes. Special Order No. 41 of February 10, 1865 applied Pope's 1864 circular to the Department of the Missouri, but it was no longer merely a suggestion. All travelers going westward were required to halt at Fort Kearny in Nebraska and Fort Riley in Kansas to organize for their own protection, and no wagon trains with fewer than one hundred men would be allowed to pass these posts.[9]

Entrusted with protection of the frontier, Pope was forced to deal with all the powerful plains tribes. The

Sioux had been hostile before, but now the Cheyenne and the Arapaho had joined them, and the Kiowa, Comanche and Kiowa-Apache were causing trouble along the Santa Fe Trail as well. Not having enough men, Pope had to keep the lines of travel open somehow, and he proposed a reorganization of districts and departments. He requested the creation of a Department of the Plains that would include the two overland roads and would free General Dodge to deal exclusively with Rebel troops and bushwackers in the Missouri region. On February 17, Secretary of War Edwin Stanton brought more effective control and unity to the overland routes by adding the Territory of Utah and most of Nebraska to the Department of the Missouri. By March the wisdom of Pope's suggestion became evident, and a District of the Plains was created under the command of Brigadier General Patrick Connor, a favorite of westerners. Consisting of the territories of Nebraska, Colorado, and Utah, the new District included the Platte Road.[10]

There were many duties to attend to, but most important was the necessity of getting troops onto the plains to protect the lines of travel. In May, Indian activity along the road west of Fort Laramie made this evident as the telegraph line was destroyed and stage stations were attacked. Later in the month Schuyler Colfax, Speaker of the House of Representatives, personally discovered that western travel was dangerous and telegraphed Stanton from Fort Kearny that the Indians were attacking the entire stage line west of the Missouri River and that he believed a state of emergency existed on the plains.[11]

Some soldiers came from an unusual source. Enlistment of former Confederate soldiers who preferred Indian fighting to languishing in Yankee prison camps had begun early in 1864. Pope had been skeptical at first, but he soon welcomed the United States Volunteers or Galvanized Yankees as they were designated. He needed troops, and they were good fighting men. In February 1865 Pope informed General Dodge that he would receive two regiments of Southern troops from the Rock Island Prison. It would take time to organize them and provide officers, but in the meantime the Overland Road had to be opened. It was "the all important matter with us now," he said, as he ordered Dodge to strip Kansas of troops to get the job done.[12] Pope was so pleased with the performance of the Southern troops that he requested additional regiments. "They answer well for such service, and relieve regiments which can be sent elsewhere," he reported. "They are in excellent discipline and well drilled, and they have passed through Iowa and Kansas, better behaved than any troops on hand."[13]

Pope based his plans for the summer campaign of 1865 on the fact that Civil War veterans would be available for duty in the West, and preparations were made for three major expeditions. General Connor would march northward from Fort Laramie into the Powder River country to deal with the Sioux and Cheyenne who had wintered there, while General Sully would move westward through the Black Hills to the same region from his base on the Missouri River. Once again Pope would resort to a giant pincer movement designed to engage the various subtribes of the Teton Sioux. It was expected that Sully would deal with the eastern subtribes and drive them before him while Connor would attack the Oglala and their Cheyenne allies, and the Teton Sioux would be trapped between the two forces.

According to the original plans, the Powder River expedition was to be in the field by early summer, but by mid-June preparations were still being made, and plans had been changed. Political pressure from Minnesota caused Pope to withdraw Sully from the campaign west of the Missouri River and divert him toward Devil's Lake in the northeastern portion of Dakota Territory. That left it up to Connor to deal with the hostiles in the Black Hills region and to establish a new post on Powder River. One of the three columns would move through the Black Hills from a base at Omaha, Nebraska Territory, while the two others would operate out of Fort Laramie.

Pope's aim was to clear the major land and water routes —the Platte Road and the Missouri River—and to open the Powder River Road or Bozeman Trail between Fort Laramie and the Montana mines, as well as to defeat the hostiles and convince them to accept peace under a new Indian policy. His goal in the southern portion of the division was the same, and an expedition against the Kiowa, Comanche, and hostile elements of the Southern Cheyenne was planned. The objective was to clear the Arkansas River Road and to push the Indians north of the Platte Road and south of the Santa Fe Trail, and to leave Kansas and much of Nebraska Territory free of Indians.

By the time Brigadier General Patrick Connor assumed command of the newly created District of the Plains in March of 1865 and began preparations for the Powder River campaign, the hostiles had already moved north of the Platte River. During the spring, army officers committed serious blunders that increased the hostility of the western Sioux. Two Oglala chiefs, seeking peace, approached Fort Laramie to return a captive white woman. Denounced by the hysterical woman, the chiefs were immediately hanged in artillery trace chains. [14]

General Dodge added to the difficulties by ordering friendly Sioux camped near Fort Laramie to be sent eastward to Fort Kearny. The encampment was composed mainly of the Laramie Loafers—a collection of Oglala and Brulé who had abandoned the nomadic hunting life and settled in the vicinity of Fort Laramie. They had always been friendly, but General Dodge ordered them sent to Fort Kearny, which was in the homeland of their mortal enemies, the Pawnee. The Indians were collected and began the march down the Platte River under a military escort, but after several days on the road they decided they would go no farther. Their women had been mistreated by soldiers of the escort party, and they refused to enter Pawnee country. When the soldiers attempted to make them move, there was bloodshed. Because the Indians had not been disarmed and one of the officers refused to issue ammunition to part of the escort, the Indians drove the soldiers back and then crossed the Platte River to freedom.[15]

Colonel Moonlight left Fort Laramie in pursuit, only to demonstrate his incompetence. He went into camp one night on Dead Man's Fork about 120 miles northeast of the fort, and, despite the protests of experienced Indian fighters, turned his horses out to graze. The Sioux immediately relieved him of his mounts and left him to walk back to Fort Laramie and an immediate discharge. But a greater damage had been done; through the folly of General Dodge, the friendlies had been driven away.

Connor, a bombastic and overconfident Irishman who hungered for glory and was determined to crush the haughty Sioux and Cheyenne, was also beset with difficulties. He talked of chasing the hostiles clear to the Heart River if necessary and planned to "carry the war into Egypt." Connor, an exterminationist, instructed his officers, "You will not receive overtures of peace or submission from Indians, but will attack and kill every male Indian over twelve years of age." The Indians, he told

Dodge, "must be hunted like wolves." The words might easily have come from Chivington who operated under the principle that "nits make lice." Westerners might applaud such sentiments, and General Dodge gave his approbation, but Pope neither applauded nor approved. When he learned of the orders, he immediately countermanded them. He told Dodge, "These instructions are atrocious, and are in direct violation of my repeated orders." There would be no extermination in his command, and Connor had better learn this quickly or "it will cost him his commission, if not worse."[17]

The Powder River campaign was grand in scope, but success depended on volunteer troops. As the men in these regiments marched westward, their attitude became evident, and it did not promise success. Having enlisted to fight "Johnny Reb," they were not at all eager to tangle with painted Sioux and Cheyenne warriors. Governors and state legislators were demanding that the troops be sent home, and the soldiers themselves wholeheartedly approved of these demands. Mutinies were common, and desertions decimated the ranks. Even the Galvanized Yankees were affected. Sully reported that the battalion of the Fourth United States Volunteers on the Upper Missouri was "fast mustering itself out by desertion." Throughout the Division of the Missouri troops were sullen and unwilling to serve, and Pope commented that one-fifth the number of willing troops could do the same job and do it better. He protested to General Sherman that the applications of governors to have the troops mustered out could be met only if the whole country west of the Missouri River were abandoned to the Indians. General Dodge complained that about one-fourth of the troops sent West had deserted.[18]

Conner, especially, endured the dissatisfaction of the

Volunteers. When part of the First Nebraska Cavalry demanded their discharge because the war was over, the mutiny was suppressed "with grape and canister." The Sixth Michigan Cavalry arrived at Fort Laramie half-armed and very dissatisfied. The Sixteenth Kansas Cavalry, which was to form the center column of the Powder River expedition, had left Fort Leavenworth on the Missouri River on February 14, but by mid-March nothing had been heard from them, and no one knew where they were. Brigadier General Robert Mitchell, looking for the Sixteenth Kansas and unable to find them, wrote to General Dodge, "the most miraculous event of the war is the loss of the Sixteenth Kansas. I cannot hear of them by scout or otherwise." Dodge did not know where they were either, but when they were still "missing" in early April, he remarked that there had been time enough for them to walk to Fort Kearny and return twice.[19]

The Sixteenth Kansas finally arrived at Fort Laramie, but the sullen troopers continued to cause trouble. With the Sixth Michigan, the Eleventh Kansas, and the First Nebraska Cavalry in various stages of mutiny, the Sixteenth Kansas decided to mutiny as well. Having no desire to hunt "scalp lifters," the men claimed their terms of service would be up before the expedition terminated and said that they "had not lost any red devils and were not disposed to hunt for any." They changed their minds, however, when they found themselves looking down the barrels of two "double shotted" howitzers.[20]

There were other problems as well. Rations and ammunition were in short supply, and there was not a horse at Laramie fit for service. The supply problem was serious. In early July, Connor wrote to Dodge, "I fear that rascally contractor will starve us out," and when conditions did not improve, he wrote again, "I wish they [the Indians] had Contractor Buckly under their scalping knives."[21]

While the preparations were underway and the Volunteers were marching westward, General Pope became increasingly aware that he must settle the Indian problem that summer. Governor Newton Edmunds of Dakota Territory was preparing to make treaties with the Sioux along the Upper Missouri, and a congressional committee was pursuing the same end on the southern plains. Pope realized that he must hurry if he were to defeat the hostiles before the peace groups and humanitarians had their way, but the primary reason for urgency was the military situation. Pope had ample troops for the summer campaign, but he would not have them long. The Volunteers were being mustered out; Congress was determined to reduce expenditures, and already he was receiving complaints about expenses.

A policy of retrenchment had begun, and Pope wanted to terminate the Indian war while he still had the men. "The pressure upon me about expenses on the plains is tremendous," he wrote to Dodge. "Whether reasonable or not, the demands of the Government must be complied with." He warned Dodge to cut expenses and to be prepared, when the campaign had ended, to protect the overland routes and nothing more. He also told Dodge, "If you cannot accomplish results with what you have they must be left undone."[22]

Though the need for speed was imperative, extreme confusion delayed the expedition. Troops already in the Indian country were being mustered out while others were being sent West. Supply problems were enormous. And the commander of the eastern column, Colonel Nelson Cole of the Second Missouri Light Artillery, was still in Omaha in June. He was delayed by lack of supplies and the discovery that most of the mules had never been broken. When he was finally ready to leave, two companies of his own regiment, whose members had not been paid for eight months, refused to march.

On the first of July, Cole managed to get the eastern column underway. With guides who did not know the country he marched up the Loup Fork and across the barren and desolate country of Nebraska and Dakota territories. His troops suffered from thirst and scurvy and, eventually, from cold and Indians. One soldier wrote that he "would sooner face death in battle in Dixie then suffer so intensely from thirst in this inhospitable country."[23]

In August, Cole and his men were joined by the center column under Lieutenant Colonel Samuel Walker of the now fabled Sixteenth Kansas Cavalry. Walker had marched out of Fort Laramie on the fifth of August and, having crossed the Black Hills, joined Cole on the Belle Fourche River. The two columns, marching separately but close together, moved in a northwesterly direction to the Little Missouri River and then to the Powder River. Here they found the Indians, or at least the Indians found them. Short of supplies and surrounded by hostiles, the dispirited troops did little more than halfheartedly defend themselves. Reduced to eating horse and mule meat, the frightened half-starved soldiers suffered from the weather as well. A Wyoming sleet storm and plunging temperatures had left over eight hundred animals dead or unfit for service.[24]

Walker and Cole had accomplished nothing. They were constantly harassed by the hostiles; their men were starving, and they could not find General Connor and his supply train. On September 13, Connor's scouts finally discovered the disgruntled soldiers and directed them to the recently established Fort Connor on Powder River, the location of which was unknown to both Cole and Walker.

Connor also accomplished little; he had left Fort Laramie on July 30 with 675 men, guided by Mountain Man Jim Bridger and with Captain Frank North's Pawnee scouts providing a protective screen. As soon as Fort Connor was constructed and garrisoned, Connor marched northward to the Tongue River. Attacking an Arapaho village under Chief Black Bear, he managed to capture a number of horses and take several prisoners. Though little else was accomplished, Connor wanted to continue the war and informed Dodge, "We should fight them like the fiends they are until they come begging on their hands and knees for mercy."[25]

The hostiles, however, did not "come begging." On July 26 some 3,000 warriors attacked the troops at Platte Bridge, and in August they dealt with Connor's columns. The Powder River campaign, aimed at crushing the Sioux and Cheyenne and opening the Powder River Road to eager gold seekers, was a disastrous military failure. The only results of the campaign were the establishment of Fort Connor and the fact that the presence of troops north of the Platte River had caused the Indians to retreat from the lines of travel. It was the Indians—not the troops—who had attacked and at a time and place of their own choosing. Events of the summer had increased the confidence of the hostiles and strengthened their determination to drive all white men from the Powder River country. General Pope, forced to take further action to open the Bozeman Trail, made plans to build additional posts along the road.[26]

Events on the south central plains were no better and would have been ludicrous if human lives had not been involved. Peace movements and military expeditions were organizing simultaneously while government officials vacillated. It was not until the Joint Congressional Com-

81

mittee under Senator James Doolittle of Wisconsin took up the matter that affairs were straightened out and a treaty was made with the tribes of the south central plains.

Following the Sand Creek massacre the Cheyenne had decided on war, while south of the Arkansas River the Kiowa and Comanche were troublesome. Colonel Kit Carson had led an expedition against the Comanche in 1864. Operating from New Mexico Territory, Carson had marched down the Canadian River and met a superior concentration of warriors near the remains of the old trading post of Adobe Walls in the Panhandle of Texas. He had extricated his command with skillful use of artillery, but the Indians continued to raid the Arkansas Route.

In the summer of 1865 the Kiowa and Comanche were still active along the road, and this pleased General Dodge. While disappointed with his assignment as Commander of the Department of the Missouri, he was determined to use it, as well as his important political connections, to make a name for himself. He wanted action and though he preferred to kill rebels in gray, killing redskins in breechclouts would do. He was certainly not averse to an Indian war, and he was prepared to punish all raiding parties who ventured near the Santa Fe Trail. While he wanted no "Sand Creeks," he believed that the hostiles must be punished. One of his officers, Colonel James Ford of the Colorado Volunteers, promised to do the job. He informed Dodge, "I will guarantee to make it so hot for the Indians before fall that they will hunt a cooler district or throw up their hands and retire from the game."[2 7]

Though Pope had authorized the summer campaign, his purpose was to clear the Arkansas Route and force the tribes of the south central plains to remain south of the Arkansas River, and he considered this expedition of secondary importance to the Sioux and Cheyenne war to the north. General Dodge, however, persisted in wanting war even after he discovered opposition to his plans.

A former army officer, Jesse Leavenworth of the Upper Arkansas Agency, informed the military that he had been in contact with the Indians and that they wanted peace. He was confident that with army cooperation he could bring peace to the whole Santa Fe Trail. Not about to be thwarted by an upstart agent, Dodge appealed to the War Department and was informed that "the military have no authority to treat with the Indians. Their duty is to make them keep the peace by punishing them for hostilities." Satisfied with this support, Dodge prepared to deal out punishment, and Colonel Ford stood by to give the Indians "one good thrashing" so that a peace could be made "that will last forever."

Undeterred, Agent Leavenworth hurried to Washington and conferred with General Halleck and Senator Doolittle of the Committee on Indian Affairs. Dodge demanded authority to attack. Pope, unsure of the situation, refused to unleash the impatient general until he heard from Washington. If, as Leavenworth reported, the Indians would make peace and agree to stay south of the Arkansas River, Pope was willing to accept it. On April 29, Secretary of War Edwin Stanton telegraphed that the Secretary of the Interior had said that Leavenworth had no authority to make any treaties with the Indians and, "there is no reason why Dodge should not proceed vigorously with his campaign at once."[28] Unsupported by his own department, Agent Leavenworth could do little more. But Colonel Ford, for all his bombastic statements, was not ready to move. And before he was, Senator Doolittle's congressional committee intervened.

The committee, authorized to treat with the hostiles, was convinced that peace could be made. The southern tribes, wrote Doolittle, were "the greatest horsemen in the world" and a war to conquer them would require about 10,000 troops and cost approximately $40 million or more. Opposed to the military and to Indian wars in general, the committee claimed that to date there had been little bloodshed except for the "treacherous, brutal, and cowardly butchery of the Cheyennes on Sand Creek" and concluded, "It is time the authorities at Washington realized the magnitude of these wars which some general gets up on his own hook, which may cost hundreds and thousands of lives and millions upon millions of dollars."[29]

This generalization was hardly fair to the harassed military men in view of the fact that they were constantly pressured by frontiersmen who wanted the Indian exterminated or at leased moved aside. On the other hand the influence of the humanitarians and their colleagues in the Indian Bureau who were opposed to any punishment for the poor Indian was equally important. Commissioner of Indian Affairs William Dole, commenting on the report of the congressional committee, represented the humanitarian attitude when he wrote that it was better to supply the simple wants of the Indians than fight them. Dole blamed the army for constantly thwarting all peace efforts.[30]

From his headquarters in St. Louis, Pope studied the course of events along the Arkansas River and listened to Indian agents, army officers, and the congressional committee. Concentrating on the Sioux war and struggling to prevent Governor Edmunds of Dakota Territory from purchasing peace, Pope did not press for war with the tribes of the south central plains. He had no sympathy with demands that the Indian be exterminated, and he realized that the Cheyenne had been wronged at Sand Creek. But, above all, he lacked the men and supplies to fight another major Indian war, and the congressional committee had secured presidential approval to make peace along the Arkansas River.

Commissioner Dole and Senator Doolittle were correct in their belief that peace should be made. Hostilities were in part due to the massacre at Sand Creek, and in a pointed reference to this affair, the Indians told Agent Leavenworth that "they would not do as the white soldiers had done to the Cheyenne." But the general attitude of Dole and the humanitarians was neither realistic nor logical. It presumed that peace could be maintained by supplying "the simple wants of the Indians" and disregarded the fact that the entire social and political structure of the plains tribes was based on warfare. It also ignored the fact that the Kiowa and the Comanche were a proud and bold people who were determined to do as they pleased until otherwise forced. Unlike Pope, the humanitarians failed to understand the situation on the plains and did not recognize that a crisis was developing as the pressure of white settlements pushed the Indians on all sides. More and more settlers were moving westward; new roads were being opened, and the Indian's homeland and hunting grounds were being seized and destroyed.

While Jesse Leavenworth and the congressional committee worked for peace, they were both somewhat embarrassed by the activities of the Indians. Leavenworth was relieved of his horses and supplies and almost lost his hair while trying to bring the Indians together. War parties struck all along the Santa Fe Trail and boldly raided the horse herd at Fort Dodge, causing Inspector General of the Army Delos B. Sacket, who was at Fort Larned, to call for an immediate campaign to open the road. Further west, the agents sent to the Kiowa and Comanche by General James H. Carleton of New Mexico were sent back with the information that the Indians intended to raid as they pleased.[31]

Despite these events, there were indications that the Indians wanted to make peace. Kit Carson and William Bent were confident that they could conclude a peace with these tribes, and Bent was willing to "guarantee it with his head." Major General John B. Sanborn, who had replaced Colonel Ford, was ready to march all the way to the mountains of southern Texas to punish the Indians, but he went no farther than the Little Arkansas River because he realized that the Indians wanted peace. On August 15 he met the chiefs of the Kiowa, Comanche, and Kiowa-Apache at the mouth of the Little Arkansas River. A truce was made and arrangements were set for treaty negotiations in October.[32]

Along the Upper Missouri, however, the situation was entirely different. Though peace moves were underway there as well, Pope attempted to block them because they threatened his plans to defeat the Sioux before making peace under his Indian policy.

CHAPTER FIVE

"Want of vigilance
and such inefficiency"

While the plains tribes were frustrating military efforts farther west, preparations were made for new military operations along the Upper Missouri. During the early months of 1865 Pope perfected his plans to increase the pressure on the hostile Teton bands west of the Missouri. Sully had dealt the Sioux a hard blow at Killdeer Mountain in July 1864, but they had not been conquered. During the winter, however, many Indians, starving as a result of loss of supplies, indicated that they were ready to surrender. Reports from the Upper Missouri indicated that many of the Indians along the river also desired peace. And groups of friendlies collected near Fort Rice were using their influence to bring the bands in.

Certain elements, however, favored a continuance of the war, and Canadian traders were apparently working for this end. Though army officers throughout the upper country—including Sully who had protested bitterly—continued to report the activities of these half-breed traders and claimed that they were supplying the hostiles with arms and ammunition, little had been done to correct the evil. The Canadian traders not only supplied arms and ammunition, but also encouraged the Indians to remain hostile. The Yanktonai chief, Two Bears, and other members of the friendly camp at Fort Rice provided detailed information on the activity of the traders. They reported in late January that the Canadians had visited the hostile camp below Fort Berthold with ten sleigh loads of goods. They had ridden into the camp, flying the English flag, and announced: "This flag will not be put down for anybody, only for God Almighty. Those who join us will not get hurt. Those who join the Americans will get hurt." They presented the hostiles with powder and bullets, traded more, and promised to return with a fresh supply and to help clean out Forts Berthold and Rice.[1]

Despite the advice, encouragement, and aid of the Canadian traders, large numbers of Indians were making peaceful overtures, and Pope was presented with the problem of what to do with them. On February 1, 1865 he restated his policy and ordered it into effect, instructing Sully and the post commanders to confer with the surrendering Indians and inform them that "the United States will maintain peace with them simply on the basis of their good behavior and assist them in protecting themselves against hostile Indians." All traders were to be located at military posts under the supervision of the post commanders, and it was hoped that the Indians would camp in the vicinity of the posts where they too could be watched and protected by the military. Pope stressed that the Indians must be warned to remain north and west of a line from Forts Abercrombie and Wadsworth to Fort Pierre and the Missouri River. No other treaties would be made.[2]

Pope's orders were explicit, for he was determined to implement his Indian policy. The War Department had allowed his earlier orders to stand and had apparently given its approval of what he had done. The Indian war had suspended the treaties and the payment of annuities, and Pope was resolved that they would not be renewed. He would not pay the Indians to be good; he would not bribe them to make peace, for that, in his opinion, only encouraged them to renew hostilities when they wanted more goods.

When Pope called Dodge and Sully to his headquarters in St. Louis in March 1865 to confer on the strategy for the coming season, he planned to use troops from both the Department of the Northwest and the Department of the Missouri against the hostiles west of the Missouri River. Sully would march westward from Fort Pierre on the Missouri River in mid-May with 1,200 cavalrymen and a detachment of artillery to drive the hostiles from the Black Hills and establish a post on the Powder River. The other units from Fort Laramie would also operate in the same region.

Soon after the plans for this coordinated Sioux campaign had been formulated, Minnesotans—including military commanders, government officials, newspaper editors, and ordinary citizens—called so loudly and so insistently for increased military aid and protection from what proved to be imagined bodies of hostile Indians, that Pope had to acquiesce and so changed his plans that the effectiveness of the Sioux campaign was destroyed.

General Sibley, always something of an alarmist, which had irritated Pope before, was very responsive to the pressures and fears of the citizens of his state. In March 1865 he reported serious danger of an outbreak by the Chippewa tribe and suggested that Canadian half-breeds and traders and possibly Rebel agents were behind the discontent. At first General Samuel Curtis, commanding the Department of the Northwest, tended to discount Sibley's fears. Minnesotans had been making similar claims for years. The Chippewa were discontented because members of the tribe were being abducted and sold into the Union

Army as substitutes for men who had been drafted, but he thought there was little danger of an outbreak.[3]

Sibley, however, continued to spread alarm throughout the spring and summer, bombarding Curtis and Pope with cries of danger. Having raised the specter of a Chippewa war, he next turned his attention to the Sioux and painted a dark picture of the prospects on the Minnesota frontier when hordes of red savages descended on the unsuspecting and unprotected settlements. Large camps of hostile Sioux were reported at Devil's Lake and Turtle Mountain in the northeastern portion of Dakota Territory, and Sibley feared that there were several parties of hostiles near the settlements waiting for the opportune moment to strike. There was, he said, great alarm on the border, but it is doubtful that it could match his own fears. To protect the frontier, Sibley planned to establish a line of posts and to "destroy utterly" all raiding parties.[4]

Though the Minnesota settlements had adequate protection, Sibley's alarms began to influence General Curtis, who soon communicated similar demands to General Pope. In May he wrote that he must have a line of posts from the Niobrara River in Nebraska Territory to Spirit Lake on the Minnesota-Iowa border. He also began to question the wisdom of sending Sully westward, urging instead that the Minnesota and Iowa frontiers must receive effective protection first.[5]

Early in May, Sibley excitedly informed Pope that formidable raids had been made near Mankato in southern Minnesota. General Curtis believed that the raiders were from "the great hive of hostile Sioux" near Devil's Lake, and he expected continued attacks along the frontier. There was much excitement among the settlements; the militia was being organized, and plans were formulated for using bloodhounds to hunt down Indians. Resulting criticisms in the Minnesota press strengthened demands for additional troops. The fact that the Mankato affair turned out to be the murder of one family by a few Indians, with a half-breed deserter from the Union Army as their leader, did not deter Sibley and Curtis although it clearly irritated Pope.[6]

Throughout May alarming reports continued to flow in as Sibley reacted to any unconfirmed report of danger. He feared that the Chippewa, Assiniboin, and other tribes were plotting war despite the fact that they were ancient enemies of the Sioux. He wrote Curtis that he needed more troops. He had barely enough to protect the settlements, he said, and an attack on the hostiles was imperative. "At the risk of being considered somewhat of an alarmist," he wrote, "I am frank to express my conviction that the Indian difficulties in this part of the country will continue to increase in their proportions unless the most vigorous measures are taken to suppress them."[7]

Despite the steady stream of alarms from Sibley and then Curtis, Pope was unmoved. He had listened to Sibley's fears before and put little faith in them. His strategy had always been that the best defense is a good offense, and events of the past two years had proved him right. Pope informed Curtis that a campaign to Devil's Lake would not be considered because the sanctuary of Canada so near at hand would make it ineffective, that there was a stampede in Minnesota every spring, and that stories from the frontier were always greatly exaggerated. Sully would proceed to the Powder River as planned.[8]

Soon after the entreaties of Sibley and Curtis were rejected, Pope began to vacillate. On May 22 he asked General Grant to seek permission to pursue hostiles into Canada, for he wished to send a cavalry force to Devil's Lake. He was considering such a move only if authorized to cross the border in hot pursuit. At the same time he sent Brigadier General Alfred Pleasonton to investigate the situation, informing him that only one small Indian raid had been made near Mankano. "The whole affair," Pope wrote, "shows such utter want of vigilance and such inefficiency (to call it worse) . . . that I am wholly at a loss to understand it."[9]

Despite his irritation, Pope had begun to meet the demands from Minnesota, and on May 23 he surrendered completely. Orders went out that Sully would suspend the move to the Black Hills and march instead to Devil's Lake. It was now General Sully's turn to be upset, and he protested vehemently; the change of orders was unwise and unnecessary, he thought. The main concentration of hostiles was west of the Missouri River, and it was evident that all the subtribes of the Teton Sioux had taken up arms against the government. Sully wrote to Pope that Cheyenne, Arapaho, and portions of the Brulé and Blackfeet Sioux were gathered at Bear Butte on the Big Cheyenne River waiting to fight. The Cheyenne were loudly boasting of their successes along the Platte Road and promised similar victories on the Missouri River.[10]

Despite indications that the Sioux bands, which normally made their home along the Missouri River, favored peace; the remainder, and especially the wild Hunkpapa, were determined to fight. The hostiles had moved north of the Platte River in February and scattered in small encampments from the Missouri to the Tongue River, but with the arrival of spring they were gathering to "take the war out of the bag." The western Sioux and Cheyenne were also making their presence known along the Missouri River. Logging parties and horse and cattle herds were attacked near Fort Rice, and on April 26 some 300 Indians attacked the heavily guarded horse herd within a mile of the post. Other raids followed, and on May 26 and June 2 hostiles struck within several hundred yards of the fort itself.[11]

It was evident to Sully that the real danger lay to the west and that little could be accomplished in the Devil's Lake region. If any hostiles were there, they would simply move across the Canadian boundary when the troops approached, but more important such a movement would leave hostiles in control of the Missouri Valley, giving the appearance that the troops were afraid of the western tribes. The hostiles had thrown out the challenge and if it were not met, Sully feared that the friendly Indians would join their hostile brethren.

Sully was not the only one to protest Pope's change of orders. Congressman Asahel W. Hubbard of Iowa, who was interested in opening new roads to the Montana gold fields, urged Pope to carry out his original plan. The safety of emigrant routes and especially the Sawyer Road depended on troop protection. Congress had appropriated funds for the survey of a wagon road from the mouth of the Big Cheyenne River to the Bozeman Trail which ran northward to Montana through the Powder River country, and James Sawyer of Sioux City, Iowa was in charge of the expedition. Pope had made up his mind, however, and was not about to change it again. Orders were sent that Connor would now have to cover the Black Hills region and establish a post on the Powder River.[12]

The issue remained so controversial, however, that Pope continued to doubt his decision. His letters demonstrate that he had no faith in the reports from Minnesota and that he expected few if any results from the Devil's Lake expedition. On June 2 he forwarded one of Sibley's alarming reports to General Grant with the comment, "It seems difficult to know what reply to make to such communications. They exhibit a panic which I hardly know how to deal with, except by asking you to send me an officer to command in Minnesota who is not subject to such uneasiness." With about 2,500 soldiers in Minnesota, Pope could not understand how anyone could fear Indian attacks, especially when 700 men had provided adequate protection during the previous summer. "Such a force as this in Minnesota," he wrote, "is unheard of in all previous time. I cannot believe that it is not abundantly sufficient if properly posted and handled."[13]

The demands for additional protection were met, and Pope assumed that Minnesotans would be satisfied. Such was not the case, however, and Governor Stephen Miller requested that an additional force of a "regiment or two from Minnesota" be sent to Devil's Lake as well.[14]

Once Sully had been ordered to Devil's Lake, dispatches from the Department of the Northwest indicated that the move was unnecessary. On June 3, General Curtis informed Pope that there was little danger from the Chippewa, yet at the same time he requested additional cavalry for his department. Curtis supported the demands for an additional movement to Devil's Lake from Minnesota, while admitting that the Sioux were far from the frontier. Only small bands had come down into Minnesota, but they created "great trepidation" and Curtis wished to prevent a stampede by the settlers.[15]

Sully continued to protest the new orders, repeatedly warning Pope that nothing would be accomplished and begged him to reconsider. Sully was also dissatisfied with Curtis, his superior, and made no attempt to hide this from Pope. That Sully was justified in his warnings can be seen in the reports of Lieutenant Colonel C. Powell Adams from Fort Abercrombie, indicating that the Sioux had moved West of Turtle Mountain on the Canadian line and that the few who remained were without mounts and arms and were starving. Adams believed that a quick strike by 200 to 300 men would destroy them.[16]

Pope's decision for a thrust to the Northeast was made in spite of all these facts. Sully warned Pope that the hostile Teton and the Cheyenne were active along the Missouri and were encouraging all the bands to continue the war. They boasted that they had destroyed the whites along the Platte Route and promised they would drive them from the Missouri as well. Throughout June and July Sully begged for permission to march against these braggarts, but his requests were denied. On July 23, the thoroughly disheartened general led a column of about 1,000 men from his camp opposite Fort Rice to Devil's Lake, which they reached on July 29. Scouring the region eastward to the James River and finding nothing, Sully moved northward to the Mouse or Souris River near the Canadian line and then returned to Fort Berthold on the Missouri River.

Additional troops were also sent to Devil's Lake from Minnesota. Colonel R. H. Carnahan of the Third Illinois Cavalry searched the region with his regiment and a detachment of artillery, but he was unable to find either Indians or Sully's command. These military expeditions were wasted effort which occupied troops that were needed west of the Missouri River. Pope had expected few results, and he was not disappointed. He had acquiesced to political demands and committed a large force to a fruitless search for nonexistent hostiles. It was unwise from a military point of view, although how unwise he did not fully realize until the disastrous results of the Powder River campaign were known. In insisting on the Devil's Lake expedition, Pope had demonstrated excessive sensitivity to the pressures from Minnesota while ignoring the reports from the Upper Missouri. He undoubtedly believed there were enough troops in the Powder River country to crush the hostiles, but whatever the reasons. the Devil's Lake campaign was a serious military blunder.[17]

Pope had made his decision with a good understanding of the situation in Minnesota, for he was familiar with the traditional frontier demands for protection. And while the fears of the settlers were real, especially among recent immigrants, Pope undoubtedly realized that politicians and contractors were exploiting these fears. This acquiescence placed him in an awkward position because he realized that the western tribes must be dealt with.

In retrospect it is evident that Pope had not reckoned with the quality of officers and men in his command, and undoubtedly he believed that many of the Sioux were ready to surrender. Confident that he had strength enough to deal with the hostiles on the Powder River, Pope was amenable to political pressure. This was not pressure from old critics like Rice. It came instead from former associates and subordinates, such as Sibley, Alexander Ramsey, and Governor Stephen Miller, men who had defended him and supported him under attack. This was undoubtedly one of the many considerations running through his mind as he dealt with the complex problems in the Division of the Missouri.

Also on his mind at this time was his struggle to reform Federal Indian policy. He bombarded General Grant with suggestions, and repeatedly called attention to his earlier letters and requested approval to implement his ideas in the Division of the Missouri.

Pope hoped that General Grant would approve the measures which had already been taken and that he would urge the government to accept Pope's policy recommendations in their entirety, but he had not expected the interference of Governor Edmunds of Dakota Territory. Edmunds and other territorial leaders were concerned with the effect of the Indian war on the territory. With the outbreak of 1862 there had been an alarming recession on the frontier line, and whole towns had been abandoned. Emigration in suceeding years had slowed to a trickle. With their thinking centered on territorial development as well as on their pocketbooks, at least some Dakotans clamored for the end of the Sioux war.

In 1863 the Dakota territorial press complained that "these savages block the way to the whole system of Northwestern development," but continuation of the Sioux war diverted emigration to more peaceful regions and Dakotans were concerned.[18] The territory must grow; population must be attracted, and the Indian war must be ended. One citizen commented that unless something were done to attract settlers, Dakota would remain "a mere political lemon, to be squeezed more or less by politicians of either of the dominant parties who happen to get it into their fingers."[19] Dakotans were thinking of emigration, railroads, new routes to Montana, opening the Black Hills, and permanent military markets. Some, like Walter Burleigh, were interested in the money to be made from exploiting the Indians.

With the outbreak of the Sioux war in 1862 Dakotans had begged for military assistance, and in 1863 they had welcomed the appointment of the old Indian fighter, General Alfred Sully, to the command of military forces along the Missouri River. The *Yankton Dakotian* had commented, "We have a real live General in command," but when the war continued, this attitude changed.[20] By 1865 the demand was for peace, and during the winter of 1864-65 Governor Edmunds journeyed to Washington to win support for the demands of the territory. Formerly chief clerk in the surveyor general's office, Edmunds had strong connections in Washington where his brother held the important position of Commissioner of Public Lands.

Soon after his appointment as territorial governor in 1863, Edmunds had begun to criticize military strategy in the Department of the Northwest. In the autumn of 1863 and again in 1864 he had disparaged the military expeditions. They had not brought peace and had not protected the frontier, he said. Edmunds preferred having cavalry units stationed in new military posts throughout the territory, and many Dakotans agreed because the economic benefits of this plan would be great and long lasting, assuring a dependable market for many years.[21]

Governor Edmunds' first visit to Washington was successful. He convinced President Lincoln that peace could be made with the Sioux, thus ending the needless expense of large-scale military operations on the northern plains, and he also received the support of Senator James R. Doolittle of Wisconsin and other congressmen who were becoming interested in he Indian problem. On March 3, 1865, Edmunds was awarded an appropriation of $20,000 to negotiate a peace with the Sioux, and a few days later President Lincoln appointed General Samuel Curtis, General Henry H. Sibley, Orrin Guernsey, and Henry Reed of Iowa to join Edmunds on the peace commission.

Despite the willingness of the Federal government to have a negotiated peace with the Sioux, Edmunds was not to have his way so easily. General Pope had, by operations of the previous years, forced large numbers of the Sioux to suffer and he did not intend to sit back and allow Edmunds to take advantage of his work and negotiate an annuity treaty with these Indians. When Sully learned that Edmunds wished to accompany his expedition, he wrote to Pope, "I'll try to euchre him, for I don't want him to get the credit for our work."[22]

Pope was determined that there would be no more old-style annuity treaties in the Northwest. He had given orders that no whites other than military officers were to negotiate with the Sioux and that all treaties were to be simply peace treaties. Since the War Department had not countermanded his orders, Pope intended to enforce them. Thus Edmunds met resistance when he requested military aid for his peace movement. Pope tersely informed the governor on May 8 that "there were no Sioux Indians in Dakota Territory with whom it is judicious to make such treaties of peace as you propose." The hostile Sioux were "public enemies" in a state of war and were therefore under jurisdiction of the military authorities. No assistance would be given to the peace commission, nor would such negotiations be permitted.[23]

With his treaty plans blocked by the obstinate general, Edmunds complained to Secretary of the Interior James Harlan and Commissioner of Indian Affairs William Dole. Harlan discussed the matter with the War Department, but Stanton refused to countermand Pope's orders.

The Yankton press, unhappy with these events, turned on the military. The *Union and Dakotaian* charged that Sully desired an Indian war to retain his rank as general, for with the Civil War over he would revert to his former rank of major. "It is whispered that he has a personal grudge towards portions of the Territory and some incidents of the past six months would seem to confirm this," the editor concluded.[24] When it was learned that Pope had prohibited negotiations with the Sioux, the editors called him a "military butterfly," among other calumnies, and announced to their readers, "The military ornament at St. Louis who commands this 'department' has issued orders prohibiting treaties of peace with the Indians."[25] Serving as the mouth piece of the Edmunds coterie, the *Union and*

Dakotaian attacked the military authorities and all others who opposed their policy. Referring to the "imbecile administration of affairs" by Pope and his officers, the editors charged, "As well might we rely upon the Army of the Potomac—as upon the Army of the Yellowstone." Still not satisfied, they questioned the integrity of Sully and his officers, proclaiming that there were "stupendous swindles connected with our Indian Expeditions."[26]

What upset Dakotans more than anything else was the fact that military contracts were filled largely in Sioux City, Iowa rather than in Yankton. Although the Dakota economy benefited from military contracts, the *Union and Dakotaian* asked, "We would like to know in what manner our people have benefited either last year or the present. General Sully for a petty personal reason cut us a year ago, and [Quartermaster] Bagg has been our enemy ever since our people found fault with him for giving his patronage to traitorous copper-heads."[27] In September the editors admitted, "We never could see any particular use for these expensive luxuries except to put money in the pockets of the favored few, principally located in and about Sioux City."[28]

The abuse heaped on the military authorities by the Dakota press outraged Pope, and he reacted immediately. Aware of the source of these diatribes, he instructed Sully that if any publication which abused army officers included "the contents of any official communications which can be directly traced to any officer of the Indian Department," he wished to be informed. Pope also protested to General Grant and the Secretary of the Interior. Official communications were not for public consumption as far as Pope was concerned, especially when they were "paraded in the newspapers in the unfairest possible manner." The protest brought an apology from Secretary

Harlan and resulted in a circular from the Indian Bureau prohibiting agents and superintendents from using the public press to vilify their opponents. This effectively stopped Governor Edmunds' further use of the territorial press to attack the military commanders.[29]

Working to strengthen his position with the authorities in Washington, Pope attempted to clarify his position and again sent out orders to his subordinates that no treaties were to be made by civilians unless authorized by the War Department. In a series of letters to General Grant, Pope explained what he had done and defended his position. If the government would accept his Indian policy, the Indian problem could be settled. By going to war, the Sioux forfeited their treaties, and it was now within the power of the military to manage them so that there would be little danger of future massacres. He had, he informed Grant, located the surrendering Sioux at military posts away from the frontier and had supplied them with seed and equipment to put in crops. No white men except religious instructors and military officers were allowed among them, and authorized traders were required to locate at the posts where they were under army supervision. Pope expected officials of the Indian Bureau to object to military control and the prohibition on presents and annuity treaties, but it was certain, he said, that the hostiles should not be given presents and new annuities, for "this practice seems to be to reward hostile Indians but not peaceful Indians."[30]

In an obvious attempt to block the Edmunds peace plan, Pope also protested against any activity that might restrict the expeditions then getting underway. "I think," he wrote to Grant, "the Government will find it true economy to finish this Indian war this season so that it will stay finished." He had the troops on the plains to do this, and believed that if the government would do away with the old Indian policy "everything would go right."[31]

Pope, having been in the West for several years, had observed the rapidly changing conditions on the plains. The movement to the mining regions of the Rocky Mountain West had increased greatly, even during the Civil War, but now such travel far surpassed anything that had gone before. During the month of May 1865, over 4,500 wagons were reported to have passed Fort Kearny, and more were expected during the summer. The ever-mobile emigrants were pulling up stakes and moving West, and the Indian country was being "penetrated everywhere." New roads were being opened; game was being killed, and the proud tribes of the plains were being crowded out and would soon face the threat of starvation. "Of course they are becoming exasperated and desperate and avail themselves of every opportunity to rid the country of the whites. We can, by sending troops enough, beat these Indians wherever they appear, but what is to become of them?" Pope asked. "Every day is reducing them more and more to actual suffering for food."[32]

The government must make a decision as to the future of these great tribes. "Wisdom and humanity alike seem to demand some policy which shall save the Indian from complete and violent extinction," wrote Pope. The Indians could either be exterminated by force or disarmed and located at fixed points where "they can be subsisted and protected and subjected, under the most favorable circumstances, to all the influences of education and Christianity." Grant commented that undoubtedly Indians required as much protection from whites, such as the whiskey sellers and the dishonest Indian agents and traders, as whites did from Indians. "My own experience has been that but little trouble would have ever been had from them but for the encroachment and influence of bad whites,"[33] he wrote.

Pope was aware that criticism would be extreme and that his name would be subjected to abuse and misrepresentation by those who had a vested interest in the continuation of the old policy, but he continued to fight for reform. On June 14 Pope wrote Grant sharply attacking the Edmunds proposals and requested that this letter be laid before Secretary Harlan. Surveying past events, he pointed out that the Sioux had been attacking everyone in their country, had raided in Minnesota and Iowa, and just recently had attacked Fort Rice on the upper Missouri. "If these things show any desire for peace," he wrote, "I confess I am not able to perceive it." The Edmunds treaty was presumed to be a typical Indian Bureau treaty with offers of presents and annuities. "In other words, the Indians are bribed not to molest the whites," Pope said. "Past experience shows very conclusively what the Indians think of such a transaction. No country ever yet preserved peace, either with foreign or domestic enemies by paying them for keeping it. It is a common saying with the Sioux," he continued, "that whenever they are poor, and need powder and lead, they have only to go down to the overland routes and murder a few white men, and they will have a treaty to supply their wants." If this is the kind of treaty the government desired, he said, he was confident that Edmunds could make it with the Sioux or any other tribe. [34]

Pope also pointed out that the Sioux had signed such treaties before and then had broken them, and there was no reason to suppose they would change their ways. Simple treaties of peace were the only solution, but they were objectionable to the Indian service because there was little opportunity for profit. It was clear from his experience that Indians would keep the peace only when they had reason to fear the consequence of breaking it and "not because they are paid (and badly paid too) for keeping it."

It was evident, Pope declared, that divided jurisdiction over the Indians had proved a failure, and he again suggested that the military should have sole control of Indian affairs. Joint jurisdiction brought only controversy and conflict. "The Indian officials are anxious, in season and out of season, to make treaties, for reasons best known to themselves." Military commanders opposed "these bribing treaties" knowing full well that they would be held responsible for the hostilities which inevitably would result. There were, he said, two methods to end the evils of joint jurisdiction: (1) the transfer of Indian affairs to the War Department, and (2) the making of treaties in which neither money nor goods were involved. Extermination of the Indians was also possible, but surely, he wrote, "such cruelty cannot be contemplated by the government." Pope, having no desire to exterminate the Indians now requested formal approval of his policy, for the tacit consent inherent in the silence of the War Department was no longer enough since Edmunds was searching for Indians with whom to negotiate.[35]

On June 15 Grant finally authorized Pope to carry out his recommendations and confided his belief that there would be no deviation from them. The victory, though sweet, was shortlived. Secretary Harlan, although he had claimed to agree with many of Pope's recommendations, pointed out that the implementation of Pope's policy required congressional action, and he gave no indication of pressing for such action. To clear up these difficulties, Pope journeyed to Washington in early July, but his conferences with Harlan and Stanton were disappointing. Victory, within his grasp, had again eluded him, and he was forced to give his reluctant support to the Edmunds peace effort. He did this with outward cheerfulness, but the defeat rankled.[36]

When Pope assumed command of the Division of the Missouri early in 1865 he believed that he could punish the hostile tribes of the Great Plains and conclude a lasting peace under a new Indian policy, but the year which began with such promise ended in defeat. Although he had opened and protected the Platte and Arkansas roads—the two great routes to the Rocky Mountain West—and kept the central region between the rivers clear of hostile Indians, his efforts to conquer them and terminate the Sioux problem had failed.

Acquiescing to political pressure, trying to defeat Edmunds, and campaigning against the western Sioux, Pope had attempted too much. Although he understood the Indian problem far better than his critics and opponents, he lost control of the situation, and the peace efforts, on the Arkansas and Missouri rivers, went on without him.

"A cracker-and-molasses peace"

While Pope was battling Indians and the Indian Bureau during 1865, major changes had occurred in western army commands. The shifting of departmental and divisional boundaries began that spring with the addition of the Department of Arkansas and Indian Territory to the already unwieldy Division of the Missouri. Pope was required to devote more attention to the Confederate forces under the command of Generals Sterling Price and Kirby Smith during the dying days of the Confederacy, and for a time he directed negotiations with Smith, who ultimately surrendered to General E. R. S. Canby in New Orleans.

Changes came quickly once the war ended, and while they did not please Pope, there was little he could do about them. In June 1865 a change of command was again in the offing, and flint-eyed William Tecumseh Sherman was on his way West to command the newly created Division of the Mississippi, which included all of Pope's division and more, stretching from Ohio to the Rocky Mountains and from the Canadian boundary to the Rio Grande. Sherman, the hero of Atlanta, and second only to Ulysses S. Grant in the military hierarchy, requested a western command, and it was Pope's position which he received. The Division of the Missouri was eliminated, and

Pope was reduced to a less important departmental command—the Department of the Missouri—within Sherman's new division. Being commanding officer of a department was no insignificant position, but the change in status must have distressed the sensitive Pope.[1]

The Department of the Missouri retained essentially the same boundaries as the former division. Arkansas and Indian Territory were no longer included, but it contained the northern and central plains region. Extending from Wisconsin on the Great Lakes to the Montana gold regions, and from the Canadian border to Indian Territory, it was a large and important command; and as the summer passed amid bullets, arrows, and harsh words, it was enlarged to include the territories of Colorado, Utah, and New Mexico.

The change of commands promised no less work and did not alter the nature of Pope's duties. As the heat of summer changed to Indian summer and to autumn, the heat of battle passed away as well. The Indian Bureau stepped back into prominence through the activities of Newton Edmunds, Jesse Leavenworth, and the Congressional Committee, and treaty negotiations began with the still powerful plains tribes. The Union Army was being mustered out; the blue-clad veterans, men who had opened the Mississippi River, taken Atlanta and finally Richmond itself would not settle the Indian problem. Treaties would be made to bring peace. Then travel could move unhindered, and the West could be opened for the construction of the western railroads.

Because of pressure from governors, local politicians, and the soldiers themselves, the volunteer army was on its way home. With an ear to demands from the local communities and from the expanding class of powerful businessmen who insisted on economy in government as long as land grants and other benefits were not discontinued,

Congress was returning the army to its prewar size. During the autumn of 1865, long lines of dusty and tired veterans marched eastward from Wyoming, Dakota, Kansas, and Nebraska to be replaced by the small regular army.

Regular regiments arrived undermanned. For example, when the Tenth Infantry reported to the Department of the Missouri, it numbered only 250 men. And the Third Infantry, which arrived in late October, totaled ninety men, eighty of whom were due to be mustered out during the winter. Pope protested to General Sherman, "I cannot exactly understand what is the use of ordering this regiment here without men." Sherman also complained to General Grant that the regular regiments were "mere squads."[2]

While the veterans marched homeward, government officials hurried to the appointed Indian treaty grounds. Although the traditional treaty system was an anathema to Pope, he was determined that the new agreements should be as effective as possible. For this reason he recommended that two experienced frontiersmen, Kit Carson and William Bent, be members of the peace commission for the southern tribes. Their knowledge of Indians and their influence among these tribes made their presence indispensible. Because Secretary of the Interior Harlan recognized the wisdom of this advice, Bent and Carson joined General John Sanborn, Major General William Harney, Kiowa-Comanche Agent Jesse Leavenworth Thomas Murphy of the Central Superintendency, and James Steele of the Indian Bureau on the treaty commission.[3]

Meeting at the mouth of the Little Arkansas River in early October, the commissioners commenced their work, and the results were all that Pope had feared. Kiowa, Comanche, Arapaho, and Apache warriors and chieftains were there, but the Southern Cheyenne were represented by only eighty lodges under the peace Chief, Black Kettle. This chief, who had seen his people slaughtered at Sand Creek, represented only a fraction of the tribe, and he questioned the wisdom of the negotiations. The remainder of the tribe, including the influential warrior societies, was still in the Powder River country where they had experienced a summer of successful warfare.

The commissioners were determined to have a treaty, however, and on October 14 the Cheyenne signed the agreement, accepting annuities and a reservation south of the Arkansas River. A few days later the Kiowa-Apache, Comanche, and Kiowa signed a similar agreement. Peace was made, but it could be only partial and tenuous, bringing little more than a lull in the conflict. The Kiowa and Comanche would remain quiet only as long as it suited them, while the majority of the Cheyenne—and the most hostile element of the tribe—had not yet signed.[4]

William Bent had said he could make a treaty with the Southern Cheyenne and would guarantee it with his head, but he had planned to locate the tribe on a reservation between the Platte and the Arkansas rivers. But by October this was impossible, for the Smoky Hill Trail had been opened in Kansas, and Indians were no longer permitted in the region. With this change in circumstances it is doubtful that Bent would now be willing to make any guarantees or that the warrior societies would ever give up this rich hunting ground although the commissioners hoped that they would.

General Pope, disappointed with the treaty and the payment of money annuities, was determined to make the best of it. He hoped it would be a lasting peace and did his best to ensure this. It would be impossible to convince the Cheyenne Dog Soldier bands to accept the treaty if Washington sent some petty eastern politician as their agent. Only an agent who knew the Indians and held their confidence would accomplish this. Major Edward Wynkoop of Colorado, an outspoken critic of Chivington and former post commander at Fort Lyon on the Arkansas River, was known and respected by the Indians, and Pope begged Secretary Harlan and President Andrew Johnson to appoint him. Unless this was done, Pope warned, the treaty was not worth the paper it was written on.[5]

Wynkoop was appointed special agent to the Southern Cheyenne, and Pope was pleased. He instructed his officers to give the new agent every possible assistance, and arrangements were made for William Bent to winter with the Cheyenne and Arapaho to help keep them at peace. Pope ordered his subordinates to listen to Bent's advice before they took any action regarding the two tribes. If they did not, he warned, they would answer to him.[6]

Wynkoop had a job that nobody would want. He had to maintain peace with the treaty Indians and convince the influential Dog Soldiers of the tribe that they should accept the treaty. The Dog Soldiers were angry when they discovered the new Smoky Hill Road running through their favorite hunting grounds and were not at all inclined to approve of the cession of this region to the White man. The activities of local whites were of no assistance either. A Mr. Boggs provided a good example. Boggs went to the Indian camp "without any authority whatever" and traded eleven $1 bills to an unsuspecting warrior for eleven $10 bills. When the Indian discovered that he had been robbed, he went looking for the thief. Failing to find Boggs, he discovered Boggs' son, and Cheyenne justice was satisfied when the scalping was completed. An officer investigated the affair but reported, "I think this case needs no further comment."[7]

Nor did Agent I. C. Taylor of the Upper Arkansas or Cheyenne-Arapaho Agency provide any assistance. Taylor, who was in a perpetual state of intoxication, refused to leave Fort Zarah or to deliver any goods to the Indians. From the safety of the fort, he suggested that the only way to gain permanent peace was to have the army exterminate the Dog Soldiers. He informed the Indian office that he had talked with the warrior societies and bluntly told them that "the Smoky Hill must go through if it has to be done at the point of a bayonet," and promised extermination to all those who resisted it. That Taylor said anything to the Cheyenne at all is doubtful, and he was soon replaced by the competent Wynkoop,[8] who managed to preserve the fragile peace. Wynkoop convinced the Dog Soldier bands to accept the treaty when they moved down from the Powder River country, but there was little hope that the treaty would be permanent. Even Wynkoop could not do the impossible.

Far to the north on the banks of the Upper Missouri, treaty talks were also underway. In October 1865 the Edmunds peace commission had traveled up the river to terminate the Indian war in Dakota Territory. Treaties were made with the representatives of nine separate bands or subtribes, but they were of little value. The season was late, the river was low, and little effort was made to contact the hostiles. The Indians who did sign the agreements were what the hostiles derisively termed the "stay around the fort" people. There was nothing wrong with making treaties with friendly Indians, but the commissioners announced that they had made peace with an estimated 16,000 Sioux.[9] Governor Edmunds and General Curtis knew which bands were hostile and that they had not treated with these bands, but still they lied, announcing that they had brought the Sioux war to an end.

At the very moment when commissioners were negotiating with the hastily collected friendlies along the Missouri, Sitting Bull was camped west of the river taunting the army to come out and fight, and Red Cloud was proud of his successes against Connor's soldiers on the Powder River. George Hyde, one of the outstanding historians of the Sioux, estimates that these two groups numbered from 3,500 to 4,000 lodges. The peace commissioners, aware of these facts, still announced that the Sioux were at peace.[10]

It soon became evident that the treaties failed when raiding activity continued along the Platte Road, and in the spring of 1866 the peace commission, in an open admission that the war was not over, again set out for the Indian country. The hostiles on the Powder River under the Oglala war chief, Red Cloud, had taken no part in the negotiations of the previous year and did not learn until afterward that they had even been held. To meet this failing, the peace commission divided into two groups, with Edmunds returning to the Upper Missouri, and E. B. Taylor of the Northern Superintendency traveling to Fort Laramie.

Before Taylor arrived at Fort Laramie, efforts had been made by Colonel Henry E. Maynadier, the commander of the post, to bring the hostiles in for talks. The army had taken the initiative in attempting to bring the Oglala and their allies to terms. Acting under orders, Colonel Maynadier attempted to contact the hostiles, but despite proclamations that the Sioux were at peace none of the whites or mixed-bloods at the Fort were willing to risk their lives to test the validity of this declaration. Maynadier eventually persuaded Big Ribs of the peaceful Laramie Loafers to undertake the mission. Big Ribs rode northward in October and was not heard from for months. Maynadier feared that he had met his fate at the hands of the hostiles, but in January 1866 he emerged from the frozen Powder River country with the news that Red Cloud would listen to the words from Washington. [11]

Negotiations began in June. The Laramie Loafers and Spotted Tail's Brulé Sioux were present, as were Red Cloud and Man-Afraid-of-His-Horse, two great war leaders, with their warriors. The Powder River hostiles had come to Fort Laramie to listen, but what they heard and saw did not please them. Superintendent Taylor was not candid with them and did not explain that the government was determined to open and protect the Bozeman Trail through the Powder River country. The Indians quickly discovered this, however, because Colonel Henry Carrington and the Twenty-Seventh Infantry arrived at Fort Laramie during the negotiations. Carrington was en route to the Powder River to construct forts to defend the short cut to the Montana mines, and his arrival disrupted the peace talks. Red Cloud and Man-Afraid-of-His Horse stalked out of the council and led their people northward with the announcement that they would fight all who came into their country. [12]

Taylor, who had been heard to say that he would make a treaty even if it were made with just two Indians, ignored the dramatic exit of the hostiles, rounded up the friendlies, and negotiated a treaty. The only important name on the agreement was that of Spotted Tail of the Brulé, who was friendly with the whites and who, like the other signatories, had no interest in the Powder River country. With a treaty in hand, Taylor was less than candid with the Indian Bureau, giving the impression that Red Cloud was the leader of a small and unimportant band of Sioux. [13]

And so the Indian Bureau and the peace groups had their day, and treaties were made on the Platte, Missouri, and Arkansas rivers. The Sioux, at least the peaceful Sioux, had conceded the right of travel through their land in return for increased annuity payments, and the Indian Bureau announced that the Sioux war was at an end.

Pope expected little from the treaties, and he was soon vindicated. Aware that the hostiles along the Missouri River remained defiant, he expected the war to be renewed along the Platte Road and had instructed his western commanders to be prepared; he also recognized that the treaty of the Little Arkansas was extremely fragile although he did his best to preserve it.[14] Understanding the rapidly changing conditions on the plains, he warned that a crisis was developing and predicted that continual warfare would be the normal state of affairs. But Pope was ignored.

Westerners were outraged by the events at Fort Laramie. They predicted failure and hurled invectives at the Indian Bureau when ammunition was distributed to the Indians during the negotiations. The Denver *Rocky Mountain News* trumpeted the question many frontiersmen were asking, "When will the Government wake up, and abandon the worse than useless peace policy it has been pursuing with these savages?" In spite of the treaty that had been made and the peace that had been declared, raids continued. Although the army was reduced in size and the troops drawn away, the Indian Bureau gave "these inhuman fiends" arms and ammunition "to be used in their hellish work."[15]

During the spring of 1866 while Congress was ratifying the Edmunds treaties and preparations were being made to send the peace commissioners back to the Indian country, Pope's connection with the Sioux came to an end. General Sherman, under whose command Pope's department fell, concluded that the Department of the Missouri was too large and unwieldy, and in March it was divided. The Department of the Platte was created, embracing Minnesota, Iowa, Nebraska, Montana Territory, and portions of Dakota Territory. The Sioux fell within the new department, leaving Pope to deal with the Cheyenne, Comanche, Kiowa, and the mountain and desert tribes of New Mexico and Colorado territories. There were duties enough as Sherman predicted, although Pope grumbled at the reduction of his command.

When General Sherman arrived in the western country in June 1865, Pope sensed a kindred spirit and looked forward to having an influential colleague in his struggles with the Indian Bureau. With Sherman eager to learn of conditions in the new Division of the Mississippi, Pope found a willing ear. The two men, both headquartered in St. Louis, held numerous discussions on military and Indian affairs, and Pope provided his commander with a storehouse of information on past events and future prospects. Sherman nodded in agreement when Pope related tales of the stupidity of Indian officials and insisted that the needed reforms could best begin with the transfer of Indian affairs to the War Department where they rightly belonged and where some semblance of honesty and fair dealing could be achieved.

Sherman agreed wholeheartedly about the matter of transfer, but there were more pressing things to be done such as the long stretches of roads to be protected from Indian attack. There was time enough in the future to engage the Indian Bureau in verbal duels as Pope had done, but these had been barren of results except to provide interesting entertainment for the reading public. There was no reason to believe that the Indian Bureau could change its policies at the suggestion of a military man, and there was no prospect that the wholesale changes Pope envisioned would be realized without the action of Congress.

Treaties already ratified could only be changed by Congress as Secretary Harlan had clearly told the disappointed Pope in 1865. It would be better to wait until Congress turned its attention to Indian affairs and the transfer issue; then would be the time to speak up, for people would be willing to listen.

Sherman preferred to wait before becoming embroiled in debate over Indian policy although he sniped verbally at some of the more outrageous actions of the Indian Bureau. Pope, however, could not wait, although the constant flow of policy papers which he directed to Washington during previous years had produced no results except perhaps to weary Washington officials.

Pope not only unburdened himself to his superiors in Washington but took delight in collecting corroborating testimony from other experts on the Indian question as well. Sully and Sibley had always provided reliable support, and General Grenville Dodge made his contributions as well. But the participation of Kit Carson and William Bent in the treaty of the Little Arkansas provided Pope with a rare opportunity to gather more information and support, and Pope called them to St. Louis.

Old-timers on the plains, Bent and Carson were indeed experts on the Plains Indians. Both had been intimately connected with Indians for years and were well informed on many aspects of Indian affairs. Certainly, Pope believed, their view would have an impact on Washington bureaucrats. Bent, long the great trader on the plains and founder of Bent's Fort on the Arkansas River, was respected by white and Indian alike. His intimate and friendly relationship with the Cheyenne was of long standing, and his influence with them was probably greater than that of any other white man. He had married a Cheyenne woman, and two of his sons were with the hostile Dog

116

John Pope
during the
Civil War.

John Pope
later in
his career.

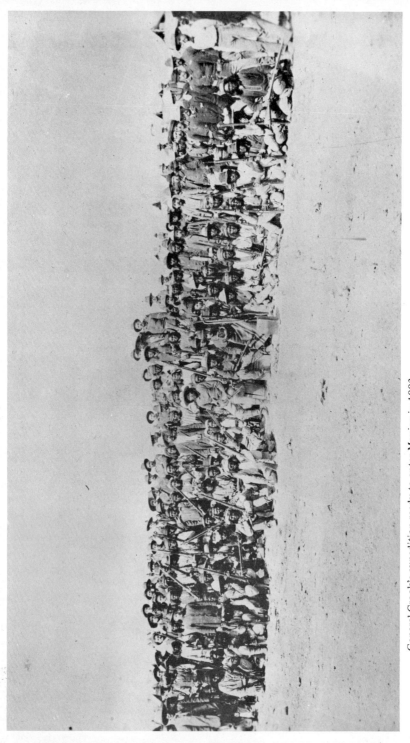

General Crook's expedition ready to enter Mexico in 1883.

General Crook and two Apache Scouts.

Edward Hatch,
of the Ninth Cavalry.

Ranald S. Mackenzie
as a young officer.

Patrick Connor, who directed
the Powder River campaign.

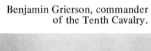

Benjamin Grierson, commander
of the Tenth Cavalry.

Nelson Miles as a young officer.

Victorio, Warm Springs Apache.

Vincent Colyer, secretary of the Board
of Indian Commissioners, disliked by
Westerners.

Alfred Sully, who led expeditions against
the Sioux in 1863, '64, and '65.

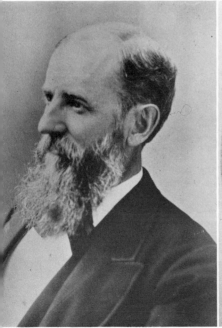

Satanta, Kiowa "Orator of the Plains."

Old Nana, Warm Springs Apache.

Big Tree, Kiowa warrior.

Soldier bands on the Powder River. Carson's stature was if anything greater than Bent's. The mountain man, soldier, and Indian agent was recognized as an outstanding authority on Indians. For these reasons and because the two were in general agreement with some of the major tenets of Pope's Indian policy, Pope had suggested their participation on the treaty commission of 1865.

At Pope's request Bent and Carson submitted a written report regarding Indian policy which pleased him and drew warm praise from Sherman as well. The Indian trader and the former Indian agent, familiar as they were with the workings of the Indian system, were "satisfied that it offers no security, either to the Indian or Government, against the rapacity and cupidity of the Agents." They had seen too many agents retire as wealthy men, and they recounted the Indians' lament at the treaty council that the Great Father in Washington was good and was honest but his agents were not. The Great Father, said the Indians, made big bales of goods for his Indian children and entrusted them to the agents in whose hands they became smaller and smaller "so that when they get to us they are hardly worth receiving." And when the Indians, in protest, threatened to cause trouble, the agent—to conceal his thefts—would call in the military.[16]

To Bent and Carson military control of Indian affairs was the only solution to the Indian problem. It would not only reduce graft and remove the control of the Indians from irresponsible civilians but would also enable the reservation system to become workable. Bent and Carson also believed that placing Indians on reservations under military control was the only way to save them from extermination. Bent and Carson also emphasized that volunteer soldiers and officers of the Chivington stripe would not suffice; regular troops and experienced officers were

needed, for it would be a difficult and trying task to protect the Indians and keep them on the reservation. Furthermore, the army could, by strict enforcement of the
trade laws, prevent exploitation of the Indians by unscrupulous traders. Bent and Carson confirmed Pope's assessment of the Indian problem, and he fully expected that
their views would have some influence.[17]

Pope sent the Carson-Bent report to General Sherman
and provided him with a number of other detailed reports
on conditions in his department. He was also careful to
supply the general with copies of his former letters on
Indian affairs. Sherman read them all with care and found
himself in basic agreement with Pope. So impressed was he
with his departmental commander's views and judgments
that he sent the reports on to Grant with a comment on
the continued conflicts between army officers and members of the Indian Bureau. "If the whole management of
the Indians, their treaties, annuities, and traders could be
transferred back to the War Department," he wrote, "it
would much simplify our work."[18]

In the spring of 1866, Pope provided Sherman with a
comprehensive report on the Department of the Missouri.
It was as Grant said, a "very admirable report." Pope's
long experience as a military explorer in the West and his
participation in the railroad surveys of the 1850s had made
him familiar with the geographical area within his command. The arid Great Plains, the home of the blanket Indians, was the trouble spot. Pope, like Sherman, believed
that it would always remain an uninhabitable desert unsuitable for agriculture. It was, however, bounded by a
farm belt on the east and the Rocky Mountains mining
regions on the west and was crossed by the great roads
along the banks of the Platte and the Arkansas rivers.

Travel by these and other routes was increasing and the

Department of the Missouri had as its foremost task the protection of travelers and lines of communication. Pope realized that wagon transportation, inefficient and expensive as it was, would be of importance for some time to come. How soon it would be inadequate to supply the needs of the booming population of the West, Pope could not guess. But the answer to these needs, the transcontinental railroads, were already edging toward the Great Plains. The prospects for the development of the nation were tremendous, and the man who had surveyed the southern route for the railroad in the 1850s was quick to grasp the significance of the transcontinental railroad for the nation. He also understood its importance to the military which would benefit more than any other department of the government.

Considering the geographic size of his department, Pope thought long and hard on the problems he faced. It was without a doubt a huge and unwieldy command although he would not admit this. Stretching from Indian Territory to Canada with New Mexico Territory jutting down in the southwestern corner, it included all the important tribes of the high plains and all the great roads. Controlling the area was a thankless job with the tiny force available, but Pope accepted it eagerly. There were already too many roads to properly protect, yet westerners were demanding more; and the travelers made their own trails, wandering everywhere across the Indian country, often becoming one more trail statistic and one more trophy for some eager young brave.

There was in Pope's mind only one way to provide adequate protection for the long, thin lines of travel: the Indians must be collected and placed on reservations on the navigable rivers east of their homeland where they could be cheaply fed, civilized and taught to support themselves. There were other possibilities, of course, but they held little promise of success. To restrict travel to several selected routes was out of the question, because "the American emigrant cannot and will not be restricted in either the direction or extent of his movements."

The old system of Indian management could be continued and was indeed "the only course which can be legally pursued" under existing laws. But it was difficult to see how Indians could be expected to keep a treaty when the government itself was encouraging the western movement, causing settlers and miners to invade the Indians' land and slaughter the game. Because the white man ignored the treaties, the military was forced "to wink at direct violations of our treaty obligations." The white man was determined to go where he pleased, and it was foolish to ignore this situation or pretend it did not exist. Such a system could only result in a state of almost continuous war—regardless of how many treaties were made, and the Indians, gradually forced into an ever-diminishing section of territory, their means of subsistence already almost destroyed, could only fight for survival.[19]

Pope's report was a long and detailed assessment of conditions in the Department of the Missouri. Although he approached the problem as a military man attempting to carry out difficult if not impossible duties, he showed an understanding that members of Congress and officials of the Indian Bureau did not. His thinking was national in scope, and he envisioned the rapid development of the American West. While he was mistaken in his belief that the Great Plains would never be settled, he understood that American travelers and settlers would go where they pleased and settle where they wished, and the government and Indians be damned. There was little hope for peace.

Sherman forwarded a copy of Pope's report to Grant as

"the best, most clear and satisfactorily condensed description" of the department and its problems and urged his friend to read and study it at his leisure. "My own opinion," Sherman told Pope, "is that unless we have absolute control of Indian affairs, we cannot be responsible for harmony of action and the safety of the Frontiers or emigrants in transition." Sherman also instructed General Philip St. George Cooke to give close attention to Pope's description and suggestions when Cooke assumed command of the Department of the Platte.

General Grant, like Sherman, was impressed with Pope's "very admirable report" and wrote to Sherman of the questions that it had raised. Like most military men with experience in the Indian country, Grant was convinced that "the matter of first importance. . . for the economical and safe control of Indian affairs depends upon getting the Indian Bureau transferred from the Interior to the War Department."[20]

In addition to reports and suggestions, Pope had many immediate duties to attend to: treaties to be made and maintained, demands of westerners to be heard, and the all-important lines of travel to be protected—a task that had been difficult enough with thousands of troops and was now almost impossible for the tiny peacetime army. With just one regiment of regular cavalry at his disposal in March 1866, Pope defended the roads as best he could and hoped that the Indians would not be too active. More troops were marching westward, but even they would not be sufficient. The undermanned Army had to make do with what was available.

There were roads to protect, but there were roads to open as well. There was above all the Powder River Road or Bozeman Trail as it was called. Cutting 500 miles from the journey to the Montana mines, it was important and valuable. The Powder River campaign had made a very weak start toward opening the road with the establishment of Fort Connor, renamed Fort Reno, but the hostiles under Red Cloud still controlled the Powder River country. Pope had ordered Colonel Henry B. Carrington of the Twenty-Seventh Infantry to construct two additional posts along the road to provide the necessary protection. The Sioux were bound to object to the invasion of their last great hunting ground, and their attacks on the Connor expedition and their angry departure from the treaty talks at Fort Laramie in June served as fair warning. But the road was important and "must be opened and made secure" as Sherman said. By the time Carrington undertook this task, however, the Bozeman Trail and the Sioux became the responsibility of the new Department of the Platte.

Before the Department of the Missouri was divided, however, Pope had planned for additional posts in Dakota Territory. A post on the north side of the Black Hills would permit travel by way of a new road from the Missouri River to the Bozeman Trail. It was a project which was dear to the hearts of the people of Minnesota, Iowa, and Dakota Territory, but they were to be disappointed because the reorganization of departments and the lack of troops thwarted the project.[21]

More significant than posts that were never built was the publication of Pope's General Order No. 27 in February. Designed to ease the duties of the small body of troops in the department and to increase the safety of the western roads, the new order attempted to regulate travel. All wagon trains were required to rendezvous at designated points and organize for defense, and travel was restricted to trains with a minimum of twenty wagons and thirty armed men. The order was not well enforced and was often ignored as travelers straggled westward alone or in small groups regardless of the dangers. Order No. 27, however, did bring some regularity and safety to the westward movement, and Sherman approved of it and applied it again in 1867.[22]

Although the travel order was often disregarded, there was remarkably little bloodshed, and 1866 was a quiet year on the south central plains. It would not be so in the future when others inherited the task of dealing with the Cheyenne, Comanche, and Kiowa. While Pope was touring his department in August, new orders arrived. He was appointed to the Third Military District in the defeated South, and Major General Winfield Scott Hancock was ordered to assume command of the Department of the Missouri.

He had served four difficult years on the frontier. During this time he sharply questioned the wisdom of the old Indian policy and waged a major battle for reform. He realized that a crisis was rapidly developing on the Great Plains. He understood that the government was working against itself and that, while treaties were made with the Indians on the one hand the government was encouraging emigration to the West, on the other hand, thus ensuring that the treaties could not be enforced. The great tribes of blanket Indians were being encircled, and pressure on them was mounting from every side. The Sioux problem, which began during Pope's tour of duty in the West, was not settled, and the haphazard policy which the government followed in succeeding years was barren of results. Cavalry charges and Indian ambushes continued and it was not until after George Armstrong Custer and his troops fell on the slopes above the Little Big Horn that the Sioux were forced onto the reservation.

General Pope, Bishop Whipple, and many others pleaded

for a realistic Indian policy, but they were solitary voices lost in political inactivity. Pope left the West in 1866, but the wisdom of his assessment of the Indian problem and the bankruptcy of the old system were apparent. Peace had not been made with the hostiles on the Powder River although the Indian Bureau had declared that that war had ended, and while a treaty had been made with the Cheyenne, Comanche, and Kiowa, it proved meaningless.

Soon after Pope departed for his new command in the South, warfare again swept the West. First the Teton Sioux and then the Cheyenne, Kiowa, and Comanche took up carbine and lance. The hatchet did not remain buried, and scalping knives were once again red with blood. The treaties of 1865 and 1866 did not last. The Interior Department declared the Sioux war to be ended in 1865, and E. B. Taylor announced that the Indians who had refused to sign the treaty at Fort Laramie in June 1866 were a small and insignificant band under the leadership of Red Cloud. It was these "peaceful" Indians, an "insignificant band," who harassed the troops along the Bozeman Trail and placed Colonel Carrington's new posts under what amounted to a state of siege. On December 21, they lured Captain William J. Fetterman and eighty men into a trap and exterminated them. Fetterman boasted that with eighty men he could ride through the whole Sioux nation, but he only rode several miles before being massacred by determined Sioux warriors.[23]

Events on the south central plains were little different. The Treaty of the Little Arkansas lasted for slightly over a year. In 1867 the Kiowa and Comanche returned to their traditional pattern of raiding into Texas, while the Southern Cheyenne renewed their depredations along the roads and among the settlements north of the Arkansas River. General Hancock and Lieutenant Colonel George Armstrong Custer campaigned against the hostiles in Kansas, but the government decided that treaties would bring peace at a lower cost. In October 1867, the Medicine Lodge Treaty was made with the tribes of the south central plains by members of the Peace Commission, created by an act of Congress on July 21, 1867, because of the war on the Powder River.

The Peace Commission was an unusual collection of dignitaries, some of whom were opposed to military action against the Indians. Senator John B. Henderson, author of the bill creating the commission, was the chairman of the Senate Committee on Indian affairs and an outspoken peace advocate. N. G. Taylor, the Commissioner of Indian Affairs and a former Methodist minister; John B. Sanborn, a former military officer; and Samuel F. Tappan, a New England Congregationalist who had lived in Kansas and Colorado but had lost none of his humanitarian zeal, were among those selected by Congress and were peace advocates with a strong religious bent, with the possible exception of John Sanborn. The three men chosen by President Andrew Johnson were military men: William Tecumseh Sherman, clearly the best known figure on the commission; General Alfred Terry, commander of the Department of the Platte; and William S. Harney, though in retirement, a well-known Indian fighter.

Vilified by the western press, the commissioners met in St. Louis in August 1867 and began to tour the West to pacify the hostile tribes. They traveled up the Missouri, and then went to Fort Laramie where they encountered some difficulty; Red Cloud and his Oglala were too busy in the Powder River country to talk to peace commissioners. Peace was not made with the determined Oglala chieftain until 1868, when the government conceded the Bozeman Trail, but in the meantime the commission journeyed southward without General Sherman to meet the southern tribes at Medicine Lodge Creek in southern Kansas.[24] The gathering was inauspicious from the beginning. Five hundred troopers from the Seventh Cavalry and a battery of Gatling guns rode escort for the dignitaries and thirty wagonloads of presents for the Indians. Treaties were made with the Kiowa and Comanche, and Arapaho, but the Southern Cheyenne were outspokenly opposed to a treaty. Few of them attended the councils, and it was only with great reluctance that they eventually signed the new agreement.[25]

Once again treaties were made; the traditional pattern of warfare and treaty that Pope criticized so strongly continued. Again the Indians were being bribed to be good. Pope had expected the Treaty of the Little Arkansas to fail, and he had been proved right. He had warned the government that annuity treaties would not succeed, and the treaty of Medicine Lodge Creek proved him right again, for it did not even last as long as its predecessor.

In 1868, warfare again swept the south central plains, but this time with Major General Philip H. Sheridan commanding the Department of the Missouri. A tough little cavalryman with a brilliant Civil War record, Sheridan had ruled with an iron hand in the defeated South. Now he took the field against some of the finest light cavalry in the world. In October, after General Grant had informed the Peace Commission that the settlers must be protected even if it meant the extermination of the Indian race, Sheridan rode at the head of his troops to accomplish one or the other.

Preparations for a winter campaign were soon under way, and during the autumn several columns scoured Indian Territory. On November 27, Custer launched a dawn attack on Black Kettle's Southern Cheyenne village on the banks of the Washita River. His Seventh Cavalry troopers struck hard and retreated quickly as large numbers of warriors gathered from other villages strung out along the river, but the lesson had been learned. The Cheyenne, Kiowa, and Comanche knew that they were no longer safe even during the winter months; they could no longer "put the war back in the bag" when the raiding season was over and expect to be undisturbed until the grass grew again.

As Sheridan continued to apply pressure, the Kiowa, Comanche, and Kiowa-Apache surrendered. Part of the Cheyenne tribe quickly followed suit, but it was not until General Eugene Carr of the Fifth Cavalry surprised the hostiles near Summit Springs in eastern Colorado in July 1869 that the remainder decided to leave the war trail. The severe mauling that the Dog Soldiers received, coupled with the death of their leading chief, Tall Bull, ended the war on the south central plains, at least for a time. [26]

The events of the late 1860s confirmed Pope's criticism of Federal Indian policy. The bankruptcy of the old system was evident to most men who were interested in the Indian problem. The treaty system failed time and again, and it was apparent that the plains tribes could not be bribed to remain at peace. Pope recommended that the trade laws be strengthened and enforced and attempted to do this within the limits of his command in 1864 and 1865. The congressional committee investigating the condition of the Indians acknowledged the need for more effective regulation of the Indian trade, and the Peace Commission of 1867 agreed. Pope also argued that the Indians were on the road to extermination, and again the congressional committee made similar findings. Reform,

Pope insisted, was necessary to prevent the extermination of the race and to terminate the state of continuous warfare with the blanket Indians, and every study of the Indian supported his contention. It remained to be seen if reform would come and what form it would take.

CHAPTER SEVEN

"Surely it isn't
an unreasonable request"

Early in May 1870 a familiar figure stepped off the train in St. Louis. John Pope was returning to the Department of the Missouri, replacing Major General John Schofield. During the intervening years Pope had dealt with problems of reconstruction and reunion in the Third Military District in the South. Negroes, carpetbaggers, scalawags, and recalcitrant Southerners had held his attention, and then after a brief stint in the Department of the Lakes, he returned to his old command.

Pope was pleased to be back in the West and set to work immediately. At first appearance things had changed, for a new Federal Indian policy promised great things. It was not long, however, before Pope realized that the only real change was in the character of the agents of the Indian Bureau. All the old conflicts, in somewhat different form, were still unresolved, and Pope soon found himself again struggling with the Indian Bureau.

When Pope had begun his earlier struggle for reform, few others evinced similar concern. Bishop Henry Whipple, however, was a leading exception. Whipple's efforts bore little in the way of immediate results, but he did interest President Lincoln. Following the Sioux outbreak of 1862, Whipple discussed the Indian problem with the President, and in reply to the Bishop's criticisms Lincoln said, "Bishop, a man thought that monkeys would pick cotton better than negroes could because they were quicker and their fingers smaller. He turned a lot of them into his cotton field, but he found that it took two overseers to watch one monkey. It needs more than one honest man to watch one Indian Agent." Lincoln acknowledged the corruption in the Indian service and promised, "If we get through this war, and I live, *this Indian system shall be reformed.*"[1]

Lincoln did urge Congress to reorganize the Indian system, but during the Civil War Congress had little interest in Indian affairs.[2] The atrocities at Sand Creek finally aroused some concern in Congress, and on March 3, 1865 Senator James Doolittle's joint resolution was passed creating a joint committee to investigate the condition of the Indian tribes. Congressional interest soon waned although Doolittle, Senator John Henderson from Missouri, and Representative George W. Julian of Indiana led a small "peace party" in Congress. The struggle with President Andrew Johnson over Reconstruction occupied much of the energies of Congress, but politicians had little interest in Indian affairs. Only when well-publicized massacres occurred did the legislators arouse themselves to action.

The Fetterman massacre of 1866 had this effect, and Congress responded by sending an investigating commission to Fort Laramie. When the war on Powder River continued, Congress created the Peace Commission to settle the Indian troubles and bring peace to the plains region. Congress saw little need for further action, but the report of the Peace Commission, which was published in 1868, caught the eye of other Americans. Humanitarians who had fought long and hard for the liberation of the slave now began to turn their attention to the "noble red man." Abolitionists Lydia Maria Childs, Peter Cooper, the founder of Cooper's Union in New York City, and Henry Ward Beecher, the noted New York minister, began to agitate on the Indian question. All were well known and had been connected with the abolition movement. Wendell Phillips, one of the best known abolitionists, began to indicate interest in the cause of the Indian, and anti-war groups such as the Universal Peace Society joined the movement.[3]

Religious denominations, too, began to demonstrate increased concern for the Indian. Pope, Whipple, and Sully had long encouraged churchmen to recognize the opportunities for missionary activities within the bounds of the United States, but it was the publication of a similar request in the report of the Peace Commission which aroused interest. Whipple won support from fellow bishops and began to work closely with interested leaders from the Society of Friends.

The Quakers had long been interested in the American Indian, and their missionaries and teachers had been active since the colonial period. Soon after the election of Ulysses S. Grant to the presidency, representatives of the Orthodox and Hicksite Friends visited the President-elect and petitioned him to reform the Indian service. Grant's aide-de-camp, Ely S. Parker, replying for the general, asked the two Quaker groups to submit a list of suitable men for agents. Grant was willing to experiment. He preferred having Indian affairs transferred to the control of the War Department, but congressional efforts in this direction had been defeated. He had said that the settlements must be protected, and to solve the Indian problem he was willing to experiment.

After the inauguration Grant gave the Quakers control of two superintendencies. The Quaker Policy had begun:

131

the Hicksite Friends were given control of the Northern Superintendency and the Orthodox Friends were placed in charge of the Central Superintendency, which included the Southern Cheyenne, Arapaho, Kiowa, Comanche, and other smaller tribes. It was an administrative policy and was strictly on a trial basis. Grant followed his natural propensity for military control of Indian affairs by placing army officers in control of the other superintendencies, although he was partly motivated by the need to find positions for the surplus officers on hand.[4]

In 1870 the Quaker Policy was expanded. Congress, interested in patronage and unconcerned with corruption, ruled that army officers could no longer hold civilian posts in the government. Grant could easily have acquiesced, but he was determined that the corruption in the Indian service must cease, and the experiment with Quaker agents was apparently working well. Rather than return the Indian service to the control of politicians, Grant expanded the Quaker Policy by bringing other denominations into it. The superintendencies were divided among the various religious denominations as equitably as possible.[5]

Congress, too, reacted to the mounting pressure from humanitarians and religious groups and on April 10, 1869 authorized the President to appoint a board of ten philanthropists as a commission to watch over the disbursement of Indian funds. The members of the Board of Indian Commissioners, who served without pay, also functioned as advisers on Indian policy.

The Indian Service needed reform, for it had long been a haven for party faithfuls and was rent with corruption and inefficiency. Reformers had leveled criticisms at the government and begged for honesty in the Indian Bureau. Those familiar with the problem charged that corruption was one of the main causes of Indian wars. Pope, Sully, Bent, Carson, Whipple, and the Indians themselves had made similar charges. "It is a common saying in the West," said Pope, "that next to, if not indeed before, the consulship to Liverpool, an Indian agency is the most desirable office in the gift of the Government."[6] Wendell Phillips and other humanitarians, although they lacked firsthand knowledge, agreed with these charges, as had the earlier Congressional Committee of 1865 and the Peace Commission of 1867. While government officials acknowledged the existence of wholesale corruption, changes were made only because of the influence of the humanitarians and religious groups. Pope and Whipple had laid the groundwork for reform with their protests and suggestions in the 1860s, but they had been without influence. Reform came in 1869, and it is interesting that it came under Ulysses S. Grant whose administration is noted for scandals rather than for reform.

At the same time that the Quaker Policy began, the Peace Policy went into operation. The Peace Policy envisioned the assimilation of the Indian into white culture, and its basic tenet was to make the reservation system workable. The Indian would be made comfortable on the reservation and uncomfortable off it. Once they were settled on their reservations, education and preparation for citizenship would begin. The Peace Policy did not preclude the use of force, for the army was expected to enforce the policy by driving recalcitrant Indians to the reservation and keeping them there.[7]

Grant and his Commissioner of Indian Affairs, the full-blooded Seneca, Ely S. Parker, were military men, and they lacked the moralism and idealism of the humanitarian and church groups. Their desire was a policy which would be of benefit to the Indian, but, like Pope, they realized

133

that the Indian could not stand in the way of national development. Unlike the settlement of the Canadian frontier, the American settlers were unregulated; they went where they wished, and all that the government could do was to protect them. The motive behind the Peace Policy, therefore, was to clear the land for white expansion, for once the Indians were placed on reservations, huge areas of their land would be opened to settlers.

The Quaker Policy and Peace Policy were two innovations of the Grant Administration.[8] The Quaker Policy was administrative, with the purpose of bringing some degree of honesty to the Indian service, while the Peace Policy sought to regulate relationships between the two races. Since they originated simultaneously, the two policies were often lumped together and considered by many to be one. Westerners complained bitterly and vilified the changes brought about by the two policies, referring to them interchangeably, but what westerners really opposed was the manner in which the Peace Policy was carried out. The churchmen in charge believed that moral suasion rather than force would bring the Indians to the reservations and keep them there. But the Peace Policy did not function as intended; the Indians were neither persuaded nor forced to the reservations, and those who went were not kept there. As a result the westerners protested and had only scorn for the humanitarians who did not "know the difference between a war dance around a scalped victim suspended over a slow fire, and a religious ceremony."[9] The *Boulder County News* of Colorado was typical in its belief that "these gentle 'wards of the nation' must be exterminated."[10]

Much to the joy of the frontiersmen, the New York *Herald* agreed with western sentiments. Under the headline "A CHORUS OF INDIAN SHRIEKERS" the *Herald* reported, "Just as we used to be deafened by the freedom-shriekers when the nigger was the great topic—as all the unoccupied old ladies who do the humanitarian gabble gave their attention to that man and brother—so now it is all Indian and philanthropy, and the barbarism of our conduct nationally. Exactly the same class of people take up all the isms and grind the monotonous tune of agitation." [11]

But despite the outraged protests of westerners and their desire to have some of the humanitarians fall victim to a Kiowa or Apache religious ceremony, the sentimentalists were in charge, and the Peace Policy was enforced according to their interpretation, which meant that it was rarely effective. Because humanitarian agents believed that honesty and kind treatment would eventually convince the Indian to give up his old life and adopt the white man's culture and religion, they often refused to apply force when needed and allowed their Indians to run wild. Humanitarians seemed to show more concern for the Indian than for white settlers, and Indian raiding parties often fled to the protective arms of their agents. The Denver *Tribune* aptly summed up western attitudes toward the humanitarians and their painted wards under the headline, "TWO MORE INDIAN ATTACKS."—"Go in Red Skins! Peel the Bark, Clean out the Frontier; Help yourselves to Blood. We are the Reigning Mogul at Washington. Those d———d White-Livered long haired, Humanitarian, New England whelps, will help us on the 'Peel.' " [12]

At the time of Pope's return to the Department of the Missouri, the Central Superintendency, which roughly corresponded to the Department of the Missouri, was staffed by Quakers. Enoch Hoag was superintendent; Brinton Darlington was agent for the Southern Cheyenne and Arapaho, and Lawrie Tatum, an Iowa farmer, was agent for the

Kiowa and Comanche. At first Pope was delighted, for he had recommended that the missionary societies interest themselves in the American Indian, and the Peace Policy was certainly an improvement over former policies. Now the military was simply entrusted with keeping the Indians on the reservations where they could be prepared for assimilation into white culture.

Pope soon realized that his struggles with officials of the Interior Department were not over and that there was a wide gap between his interpretation of the Peace Policy and that of Quaker officials in the Central Superintendency. Pope therefore renewed his struggle with the Indian Bureau and began to send criticisms and suggestions to Washington. As before, he was concerned with the condition of the Indians as well as with the protection of western settlements. He did not abandon his desire for major reform, but realizing that his goals were unattainable, he sought a more workable solution to specific problems as they arose. He did his best to prevent hostilities and, by speeding the process of assimilation, to save the Indians from extermination.

Studying conditions in his department, Pope was impressed with the changes that had occurred in the few short years of his absence. Most momentous was the work of the railroads. Like Sherman, Pope understood the value of the railroads to the nation and to the military. The Kansas Pacific Railroad, which had just begun to inch out onto the plains in 1866, was near completion and would provide an important new link between the Missouri Valley and the mining regions of Colorado and New Mexico. It was already the keystone of the Texas cattle industry, for Joseph G. McCoy had shown cattlemen the significance of the railroad when he made Abilene, Kansas the destination point for the long drive north in 1867. The railroad was important and had to be protected.

The Kansas Pacific had already passed Fort Harker in western Kansas, and, to provide protection for the crews, Lieutenant Colonel C. R. Woods of the Fifth Infantry was placed in charge of the whole line from Fort Wallace to Denver. Construction could not be allowed to stop because of lack of protection, and with the troops of Forts Halleck, Lyon, and Reynolds at his command, Woods had enough men to protect the crews.

Further to the east were the rapidly spreading Kansas settlements, and Pope ordered Lieutenant Colonel George A. Custer of the Seventh Cavalry to establish a summer camp near Fort Hays. Charged with the protection of settlements along the Saline, Solomon, and Republican rivers, Custer was instructed to keep his troops in motion, watching for hostiles and calming the fears of uneasy settlers. Lieutenant Colonel A. D. Nelson at Camp Supply on the North Fork of the Canadian River was instructed to keep a close watch on the Cheyenne and Arapaho near his post. The military, he was told, must keep informed as to the intentions and movements of the tribes on the reservations to prevent surprise attacks. [13]

Almost immediately after Pope's arrival trouble erupted along the western stretches of the Kansas Pacific Railroad in Colorado. On May 14 a party of raiders struck the line near Kit Carson killing ten men and driving off 300 head of stock. Additional troops were sent to Woods; Major Marcus Reno of the Seventh Cavalry went in pursuit of the raiders, and Custer's command moved to prevent the Indians from going eastward. Pope was confident that "they will make the Country north of the Rail-road too hot for the Indians," but the hostiles managed to escape detection. [14]

Reports of Indian depredations continued. Stock was

stolen, and employees were killed and wounded at the Kiowa-Comanche Agency. On June 12, some 200 to 300 Indians attacked the cavalry herd at Camp Supply but were driven off. A day later a Kiowa raiding party was more successful, stealing 73 mules from Fort Sill. Although the harried Negro troopers of the Tenth Cavalry at Fort Sill and Camp Supply were having continuous troubles with the Indians, it was the Texas frontier that suffered most. Kiowa and Comanche war parties raided at will, driving out many settlers, and Lawrie Tatum reported that raiders had pushed the frontier back 150 miles. The Peace Policy was not working well, especially with the Kiowa and Comanche. There was danger of a major outbreak, and demands for protection increased.[15]

The situation was threatening, but Pope was hampered by the division of authority over the Indians. Not at all pleased by the restrictions on his authority, Pope protested to his superiors. He asked that the relationship between the military and the Indian Bureau be clarified. How could he be responsible for protecting the roads and settlements, he asked, if he lacked the power to deal with hostiles on the reservations? All he wanted was the authority to prevent hostilities before they began. To prohibit military action on the reservations until requested by the agents was foolish and impractical. Pope fumed because his hands were tied. Even though the army might have information that raiding parties were making preparations to attack, he was forced to "remain passive and permit them to raid" before he could act.[16]

What upset Pope most was the fact that although he was powerless to take preventive action, settlers held him responsible for the consequences. He protested bitterly, "The Indians having the power to nurture their plans and make their preparations unmolested, and the choice of points to strike along an extensive frontier but scantily supplied with troops, must of course always be successful on their first move." All the army could do when news of a raid was received was to futilely chase the long-departed savages. This was bad enough, but the inability to punish hostile acts on the reservations was more distressing. The troops could protect themselves if attacked, but they could not search out and punish the Indians who had stolen mules from the quartermaster's corral at Fort Sill. Pope's protests had little effect. He instructed his officers in Indian Territory to watch the Indians closely and attack them the moment they left the reservation. But when soldiers were killed and army property stolen, the officers could only request the agents to deliver the guilty parties for punishment. "I am well aware," Pope told Lieutenant Colonel Nelson, "that this proceeding will be a mere form without satisfactory results, but it is the only course left the military. . . ."[17]

The wild Indians had been placed on the reservation and were required to remain there, although it would take years before they could be expected to abandon their nomadic life for that of settled agriculturists, and nothing yet had been accomplished in that direction. In Pope's mind, there were two methods of keeping the Indians on reservations and thus protecting lines of travel and exposed settlements. One was to place troops on the reservations with authority to watch the Indians and prevent raids by seizing the instigators and impounding their ponies until the danger subsided; the other was to disperse the troops among the settlements and along the roads. The first method was clearly the best and, in Pope's opinion, the only one which could be effective. Settlements could not be protected effectively when raiders were allowed to make their preparations and plans without interference. As things stood, Pope pointed out, the raiders could choose their objective, strike, and, by the time the army was notified and the troops were in motion, be back on the reservation where they could not be touched.

What galled Pope most was that the military was blamed for the raids. Pope compared the army to the police and argued that neither group should be held responsible for crimes if they "were restrained from intercepting the criminals until they had accomplished their purpose." Although the army was small, about half the troops in the department were located at posts on the reservations, but they were powerless to act. Pope suggested that the posts be broken up and the troops scattered among the settlements; in this way he could make full use of every available man.[18]

In the past Pope had been the leading exponent of complete military control over the Indians. He had not abandoned this goal even though it had been defeated in Congress and he had to work within the system. He did, however, request more authority for the military if troops were to remain on the reservations. If the agents would keep well informed about the activities of their Indians and call in troops when raids were being planned, bloodshed could be prevented. Whether this was done under military authority or at the request and under the direction of Indian agents was unimportant; the important thing was that force be applied in time.

No action was taken on Pope's requests, and Indian troubles continued both on the reservations and along the frontier. Supply trains between Fort Dodge and Camp Supply required large military escorts. Farther south, Lawrie Tatum, the Kiowa-Comanche agent, was warning his superiors that there would be extensive raids by the Kiowa and Comanche. The situation was so dangerous that the other Quaker agency employees fled to safety leaving only Tatum and a few brave school teachers to deal with the intractable Indians. In July, Tatum reported that all the Indians were off the reservation and that they were doing all they could to provoke an attack by General Benjamin Grierson at Fort Sill. This, they knew, would bring them more annuities as the government would bribe them to be good. The situation was ludicrous. The Indian Bureau refused to use the military, but when Superintendent Hoag shipped supplies to the Cheyenne-Arapaho Agency, he was forced to request an escort so that the Cheyenne and Arapaho would not steal the supplies before they ever reached the agency. Pope replied sarcastically that Hoag had not said what danger was feared and that this information was necessary before an escort could be assigned.[19]

In July, Pope inspected the posts and checked the disposition of troops along the Kansas Pacific Railroad, and his observations led him to discount reports of Indian trouble in Kansas and to turn down requests for more troops. Although Governor James Harvey of Kansas continued to report rumors of Indian uprisings, he was told that his state was adequately protected, that the Indians in the region were peaceful hunting parties from the Osage and Kaw reservations, and that if Kansans were upset about the Indians in the western part of the state, they could complain to the Indian Bureau because the Indians were off their reservations with the approval and authority of their agents.[20]

Throughout the summer of 1870, army officers and Indian officials continued to differ regarding the situation on the reservations. Lieutenant Colonel Nelson at Camp Supply and General Benjamin Grierson at Fort Sill reported depredations as they occurred and feared that the situation

141

would get worse rather than better. The Indian agents hoped for the best and attempted to protect their own Indians, often blaming other tribes for depredations which did occur. Agent Tatum was an exception. A brave and honest Quaker, he understood his charges and reported their crimes. He was learning that kindness, honesty, and good treatment would not turn the Kiowa and Comanche into peaceful farmers. The Kiowa were especially bad. Tatum believed that they were the worst Indians on the continent and that they could never be trusted. Pope, in complete agreement, described them as "the most faithless, cruel, and unreliable of all the Indians of the plains."[21]

Tatum worked closely with General Grierson in attempting to maintain some control of the Indians and securing the return of captives when possible. With the approval of mild-mannered Grierson, Tatum began to withhold rations to force the Indians to return captives, and in August the two men—the soldier and the Quaker—met with the Kiowa chiefs at the agency and urged them to follow the white man's road. Their words had little effect upon the Kiowa. Satanta, the "Orator of the Plains," announced that he preferred the breech-loading rifle and the scalping knife. Good Indians received nothing from the government, he stated, but the bad Indians were well treated and well fed. It paid to be bad.

While the talks were going on, the warriors were flexing their bows, snapping cartridges into their guns, and sharpening their scalping knives. The effect of these threats was lost, however, for when Lone Wolf went over and put his hand under Tatum's vest to see if the "scare" had worked, he found the heartbeat normal and sat down. The Kiowa promised to be good, but Tatum placed little value in their words, and raids into Texas continued.[22]

Throughout the autumn Grierson and Nelson continued

to report discontent among the tribes. Pope forwarded their reports to Washington and pleaded that the Indian Bureau do something to pacify the Indians and prevent general hostilities in the spring. He requested that the Interior Department be informed of the situation and that it confer with the Indians. There was no doubt in his mind that the Arapaho especially had good cause for complaint, "for they find that they really get less (and have more trouble to get it) from the Government by keeping the peace than by going to war," and they were constantly reminded of this by the treatment that Kiowa and Cheyenne raiders received. [23]

Pope pointed out the heart of the problem when he said that the reservation, if it were to succeed, must provide the Indians with the means of subsistence so that they would have no excuse to wander over the countryside. The Indians would never be civilized if they were forced to spend much of their time hunting and if they were allowed to indulge in the customary raiding activity. The Indians must be forced to remain on the reservations. If they were to be fed and clothed entirely by the government, he wrote, they would need no arms and could be brought into the neighborhood of the agency. This would prevent raids and allow the process of assimilation to begin. [24]

Throughout 1870, Pope became increasingly irritated with the actions and lack of action by the Indian Bureau. The blanket Indians were allowed to run wild and go unpunished. The Cheyenne and Arapaho were dissatisfied, but nothing was done to mollify them. The Ute of Colorado were discontented with a recent treaty and claimed they had been deceived. They refused to accept their reservation, and since they had always been peaceful, Pope suggested that talk rather than force be used to settle this difficulty.

There was also the problem of removing white intruders from the reservations of the peaceful tribes. It was common for white settlers to move onto the reservations and begin farming. Because reservation boundaries were not always well marked, some westerners invaded a reservation unknowingly, but many intentionally disregarded the boundaries and took the land they wanted in the belief that it was too good for the Indians. When the Indian agent called for troops to remove the white intruders, he became a target for abuse from the frontier press. Removing white settlers from a reservation was a distasteful and unrewarding task, and in an attempt to reduce the criticism heaped on the troops, Pope always insisted that the Indian agent direct the removal in person.

During the summer of 1870, Pope had approved the use of troops to remove intruders from the Kaw and Cherokee reservations. But when the Indian Bureau requested troops to clear the Miami reservation and Pope received orders to do so in late December, he protested. The Miami reservation, located in one of the most densely settled counties in Kansas, had a population of 4,000 white settlers who had been there for some time, but to uproot them in midwinter would be cruel. Yet this is what the Interior Department wished to do. Pope requested that the removal be delayed until spring, and he also suggested a governmental inquiry in the meantime. It was inconceivable that some 4,000 people could have moved onto the reservation, begun permanent settlements, and farmed "under the immediate eye, if not with the tacit sanction of the Indian Department." Pope wanted to know why this had been permitted. [25]

In only six months Pope had become well informed on the situation in his department. He had observed the operations of the Peace Policy and the Quaker Policy and was unimpressed. Nor was he pleased with the location of the reservations within his command. He could find no wisdom in locating a reservation in a tribal homeland where the Indians knew every trail, waterhole, and hiding place. He had few hopes that his criticism would be heeded, but he offered it anyway.[26] Neither Pope's criticism nor his recommendations for change was acted upon, and throughout the winter of 1870-71 danger signs were common in the Indian country south of the Arkansas River.

Colonel Nelson continued to report that the Cheyenne and Arapaho were dissatisfied and predicted raids in the spring. Grierson and Tatum also expected trouble, for Kicking Bird and other friendly Kiowa warned of raiding parties already headed for Texas and that as soon as the grass was good raids would increase. Pope, who trusted the reports of his officers, relayed these warnings to Washington and pleaded for action.

If only the Indian Bureau would confer with the Indians, Pope thought, perhaps the causes of discontent could be removed. When the Secretary of the Interior failed to take any action, Pope wrote directly to Commissioner of Indian Affairs Ely S. Parker. He was most concerned about the Southern Cheyenne who had shown signs of improvement but who were now talking of war. Pope instructed Lieutenant Colonel John Davidson, the new commander at Camp Supply, to keep a close watch on the Indians and sent him two Gatling guns and additional mountain howitzers to strengthen his position. He also sent patrols into the field much earlier than usual to prevent the Cheyenne from moving north into Kansas if they decided to go to war.[27]

In January Commissioner Parker sent Superintendent Hoag to the Cheyenne Agency to check the validity of the military reports. When Hoag discounted them, Pope was so disturbed that he finally turned to President Grant in hopes that something might be done. Pope's only wish was to avert hostilities, and he believed that if a "reliable person" were sent to confer with the Cheyenne, peace could be maintained. Hoag treated the whole affair as an attack on himself and on his agents and replied with a long defense of their work in civilizing the Indians. Pope explained that he was not attacking the Indian Bureau; he was simply attempting to maintain peace. He had, he said, the President's policy at heart, "but somehow there seems to be a constant feeling of suspicion that the military authorities are in opposition to the Indian Bureau and I fear my letters have been misinterpreted by that Bureau. . . ."[28]

Pope also wrote to Sherman, pointing out his lack of authority to act to prevent raids. "If any raids are made we are held responsible no matter what the Indian Department has said or done," he wrote. "Between these horns of a dilemma it is not easy to decide what is best to do." Hoag visited Fort Leavenworth, and Pope gave him all the material he had on the Cheyenne problem, but the Quaker superintendent discounted Pope's reports and claimed to have more reliable information. The angry Pope told Hoag that if he would promise there would be no hostilities, Pope would not move a trooper from his post. Hoag declined this offer and spoke of bad men among the Indians. It was, of course, Pope told Sherman, from these "bad Indians" that trouble was expected.[29]

Pope was disturbed that Sherman, by endorsing the Indian Bureau papers, appeared to believe the allegations against army officers. He immediately defended his officers. They were stationed in Indian country, and if they did not know of what they wrote, it would be "very strange" indeed. "That they intentionally misrepresent the state of facts," he wrote, "I am sure you do not intend to imply." [30]

When he returned the papers to the Adjutant General's office, he again defended his officers and the accuracy of their reports. He explained, as he had before, that his only interest was to avert hostilities. He reminded the Adjutant General that he had urged pacific measures in the treatment of the Indians for years and "that the present Indian policy is substantially what I have again and again recommended, the only real difference between my views and those now in operation being as to the *location* of Indian reservations." He did not want war, and he did not believe that any portion of the army favored war with the Indians. In such a war army officers and soldiers had everything to lose and nothing to gain, he said. If they succeeded in expeditions against hostile Indians, they were denounced in the East as murderers and assassins; if they failed, they were denounced in the West as inefficient and worthless. [31]

Pope could not understand why authorities in Washington continued to ignore his reports and refused to take any action. No one wanted an Indian war, and a war, or at least extensive raids, could be prevented by conferring with the Cheyenne and learning the causes of their discontent. If the Indian Bureau was correct that no trouble need be expected, such a conference could do no harm; if they were wrong, a conference could settle the difficulties. Why the Indian Bureau refused to confer with the Indians was beyond all understanding. "Surely it isn't an unreasonable request," he said.

It seemed like a reasonable request, but Superintendent Hoag did not agree. Pope protested sharply that Hoag merely contradicted the military reports and denounced the officers in language that was "insulting and unjust." This in itself brought Pope's temper to a boil, but more

147

serious was the fact that Hoag's report on the Cheyenne did not even show that an investigation had been made. This impression was confirmed when Hoag visited Fort Leavenworth, for Pope reported that he learned in conversations with Hoag that an investigation had not yet been conducted. [32]

When Hoag and Cheyenne-Arapaho Agent Darlington requested the withdrawal of troops stationed at the Cheyenne-Arapaho Agency, Pope was astounded. The two Quakers believed that the presence of troops at the agency embarrassed the Indian Bureau and said that army officers had no desire to help carry out the present Indian policy. This, replied Pope, was "destitute of truth." There might be some truth in the charge if it meant that army officers did not approve of all the agent did. "If every one in this region of the country who does not endorse the proceedings of Superintendent Hoag and his agents is to be withdrawn my belief is that this entire region would be almost, if not quite, depopulated," he commented. Pope himself did not agree with all the Indian Bureau did, and neither did Sherman or Sheridan, but he "emphatically rejected charges that his officers were opposed to and attempted to undermine the present policy." He withdrew the troops from the agency as requested, and angrily requested authority to withdraw them from Camp Supply as well. If the Indian Bureau were to blame the soldiers every time trouble occurred, he would be only too happy to place them where they would be of some value. [33]

In the spring of 1871 Pope must have felt that the Indian Bureau had singled him out as the object of all their dislike. He was all but ignored when he predicted raids by the Southern Cheyenne. With all his troops disposed to turn back raiding parties from the South, he did not need any trouble in the northern part of his department, but this is what the Indian Bureau provided. In March they gave Spotted Tail and his Brulé Sioux permission to hunt south of the Platte River.

Pope struggled by himself to avert a Cheyenne war, but now Sherman came to his aid. The General sharply protested giving these hunting permits to the Sioux. If peace were to be maintained, he wrote, it would be better to supply them "with buffalo meat collected by white hunters." Spotted Tail was a peace chief, but the presence of armed Sioux warriors was guaranteed to throw the frontier into a panic regardless of the fact that they were hunting buffalo and not scalps. An Indian was an Indian, and settlers did not wait to feel the razor edge of a scalping knife before they judged whether he was friendly or hostile. Trouble was bound to occur, and Sherman warned, "this hunting privilege will create alarm, misrepresentation and finally violence and I warn the Indian Bureau that it will surely result in collisions wherein their Indian friends will come out second best." Sherman was forced to accept the decision of the Indian Bureau, however, and although Pope also protested, he could only fume silently and warn the settlers in the hope that trouble would not ensue. [34]

Maintained in the winter by government rations and with their ponies beginning to regain their strength from the new spring grass, the Kiowa, Comanche, and Cheyenne were about to begin the raiding season. Faced with the prospect of extensive raids, the Indian Bureau finally decided that there might be some validity in Pope's reports, especially as Tatum was warning his superiors that the Kiowa were determined to provoke war and had already sent raiding parties against the Texas frontier. The decision was made to bring the principal chiefs of the four great southern tribes to Washington.

Pope was elated, for he was confident that hostilities

could be averted, at least with the Cheyenne. His only fear was that action had come too late and that raids were already in progress. Now that something was being done, Pope could chuckle at Hoag's predicament, for Hoag did not know where the Cheyenne and Arapaho were and was forced to turn to the army to have them brought in. This was done, and in June, Little Robe and Stone Calf of the Cheyenne joined the Arapaho and Wichita chiefs for a visit to Washington. After conferences with government officials, the Indian chieftans visited other eastern cities where they spoke before enthusiastic gatherings of humanitarians and listened to the moral platitudes of reformers like Wendell Phillips. The visit was a grand success. During the absence of their chiefs, Little Robe and Stone Calf, the Cheyenne tribe remained quiet, and the chiefs, impressed with what they had seen and heard, kept the tribe at peace after their return.

The visit of the chiefs was not a complete success despite its effect on the Southern Cheyenne. Kiowa and Comanche delegates were noticeably absent. They had rejected the invitation to meet with the Great Father just as they had refused to attend a peace meeting sponsored by the Okmulgee council of the civilized tribes in May. Kiowa and Comanche warriors had more important things to do. Good talks, government rations, kindness, and honesty were fine when snow covered the south-central plains, but with spring the raiding season returned, and the Kiowa had no inclination even to talk of peace. There were too many horses and trophies to bring back from Texas, and the Kiowa and Comanche insolently rejected all invitations to talk. Pope and Tatum warned there would be increased raiding, Texans were crying for mercy, and the state legislature was demanding protection. William Tecumseh Sherman listened and decided to see for himself. [35]

Accompanied by Inspector General Randolph B. Marcy, who had explored parts of north Texas in 1849 and again in the 1850s, Sherman inspected Forts McKavett and Concho and then moved north towards Forts Griffin and Richardson. Texas appeared quiet and peaceful as Sherman's party, with an escort of seventeen troopers of the Tenth Cavalry, crossed the open prairie near Salt Creek between Forts Griffin and Richardson, a large Kiowa war party peered down from a nearby hill and watched them pass. The medicine man promised success if they let the first party pass without striking, and the warriors waited somewhat impatiently for the second party. When Henry Warren's wagon train came into view, Satanta, Satank, Big Tree, and their warriors struck hard. [36]

Sherman, at Fort Richardson, meanwhile was listening to the citizens of Jacksboro, Texas complain of visitations by the reservation Indians. He admitted that it was "a great outrage if Indians who received annuities from the United States made their reservation a refuge for stolen stock," but he believed that the stories of depredations were exaggerated. During the evening, however, while he was being feted by the officers of Fort Richardson, survivors of the Warren train massacre staggered into the post, and Sherman learned how near his close-cropped red hair had come to hanging from a Kiowa lodgepole. [37]

When he learned of the massacre, Sherman immediately sent Colonel Ranald S. Mackenzie, the brilliant young commander of the Fourth Cavalry, in pursuit with 150 cavalrymen, and ordered troops from Fort Griffin into action as well. As Sherman thoughtfully rubbed his hair, he ordered "that this case be followed up with extreme vigor" and that the raiders be pursued onto the reservation if necessary. Sherman then hurried on to Fort Sill to await results. [38]

Conferring with Grierson and Tatum, Sherman found that the progress of these reservation Indians was "a farce," but he was surprised to find himself in agreement with Tatum, the Quaker agent, whom he found "a good honest man." Tatum was disturbed that the raids increased in frequency and magnitude in spite of the fact that the Indians were being fed and clothed by the government and had already urged his superiors to allow him to arrest the raiders and send them to Texas for trial. Tatum had at last concluded that hostiles must be punished and wrote to Enoch Hoag, "I see no reason why they should not receive the same punishment as whites for similar offences." With these sentiments Sherman heartily agreed.[39]

Tatum believed that the recent raid had been led by Satanta. He heard reports that Satanta had been in Texas, and later Satanta himself verified it. On May 27, Satanta, Satank, Eagle Heart, and other chiefs and warriors came into Tatum's office for a talk, and Satanta proudly boasted of leading the attack. He described the massacre in detail and then asked for rations.

Tatum immediately sent a note to Sherman requesting the arrest of the chiefs and then sent Satanta to talk to the "Big Chief from Washington." When Satanta arrived, Sherman was ready. The Negro troopers of the Tenth Cavalry were mounted and armed in the new stone corral where they were out of sight, while others were stationed inside Grierson's quarters. On the porch, Satanta again boasted to Sherman and Grierson of the raid, but when he learned that he was to be sent to Texas for trial, he quickly disclaimed any participation in the massacre. It was a tense scene. The Kiowa were armed, and their weapons were cocked, but they found themselves surrounded by a contingent of the "Buffalo Soldiers" with leveled carbines.

Sherman, his eyes blazing, made it clear that the chiefs were going to Texas, and the Kiowa, with Satanta saying, "No! No! Don't shoot," decided not to test the determination of the General from Washington. [40]

Clapped in irons, Satanta, Big Tree, and Satank were turned over to Colonel Mackenzie for delivery to the Texas courts. As the column left Fort Sill, Satank began to chant the death song of the Koitsenko warrior society. Freeing himself from his chains, he attacked the guard and attempted to escape, but a volley of quick shots cut him down, and he was left dying in the dirt as the column proceeded on its way.

Westerners were delighted with the arrest of the chiefs, and military men on the frontier shared this feeling. Major J. K. Mizner of the Fourth Cavalry wrote Sherman that he was overjoyed and felt assured "that on Texas soil they will find an early grave." He urged that justice be swift and the execution immediate, for he feared that sentimentalists would rouse themselves to prevent it. Pope, too, was delighted and felt that the arrest was a "most righteous act," but he feared that the Interior Department might criticize it as a violation of the Peace Policy. Pope's fears were soon realized. [41]

Tatum, eager to have justice done but also concerned with the attitude of his charges, suggested that the two remaining chiefs, Big Tree and Satanta, be tried and sentenced to life imprisonment. They should never be allowed to regain their freedom, he believed, but they should not be executed, for they could serve as hostages for the good behavior of the tribe. The Texas courts, however, thought differently, and on July 8, 1871 Big Tree and Satanta, that "arch fiend of treachery and blood" as the prosecutor called him, were sentenced to be executed. [42]

The Kiowa were shocked by the sudden turn of events. Never before had they received such treatment from the government. The arrest of raiders was something new, and Sherman believed that they were debating peace or war. Sherman for his part was ready for war. He had ordered Pope to send Grierson the absent companies of the Tenth Cavalry and authorized Mackenzie to pursue all raiding parties onto the reservation until "they realize that if they persist in crossing [the] Red River they will be followed back."[43]

The Quaker interpretation of the Peace Policy had been tried and found lacking. The Kiowa and Comanche listened to the kind words of the Quakers, ate government rations, and did as they pleased. Following the Warren train massacre and the General's close brush with death, Kiowa style, the military interpretation of the Peace Policy was put into effect, and all future raiders were to be punished. The Secretary of the Interior agreed that raiding parties should be pursued onto the reservation, and he agreed with Tatum's and Sherman's request that only those Indians who remained on the reservation would receive government rations.[44]

Military operations began as soon as Mackenzie and Grierson took the field. Although the summer campaign produced little in the way of punishing Indians, the presence of the weary, long-suffering troopers of the Fourth and Tenth Cavalry on the plains of Texas, coupled with the arrest of the chiefs, had a great effect on the Kiowa. Tatum found them more subdued than ever before. They were very anxious to know whether raiding parties would always be followed onto the reservation, and they were now quite willing to return some of the stolen stock.[45]

This was the military way, a way that Pope had long

suggested. Raiders must be punished. This was what the Peace Policy had intended. The effect of the new policy was immediate and positive, but not for long. The humanitarians were soon to regain control of the enforcement of the Peace Policy.

"The Kiowas
and . . . Comanches
are uncontrollable
by me"

During the summer of 1871 military control of Indian affairs on the southern plains increased, but it was not long before the humanitarians regained their former influence, and the effect of the military policy of holding Indians accountable for their actions was soon lost. The Quaker-style Peace Policy was again in effect, and the failure of this policy helped prepare the way for the outbreak of full-scale war in 1874.

The Kiowa and the reservation Comanche remained quieter than normal throughout the autumn of 1871, but there was some raiding activity by the younger Indians, and Lawrie Tatum doubted that the chiefs could control them. He continued his forceful policy, however, and reduced rations when parties were off the reservation. Tatum's problems were great, but he bore them like a good Quaker. He was encouraged when he learned that a large band of about 1,000 plains Apache, who had never been attached to any agency, had elected to leave the Llano Estacado or Staked Plains of west Texas and come to his reservation. This caused a flurry of excitement, for the Indian Bureau apparently knew little or nothing about this band. If only the Kwahadi Comanche would do the same, Tatum would be much happier. The Kwahadi, like the

Apache, had never been attached to a reservation, and, refusing all overtures of peace, they raided at will from their homeland on the Llano Estacado.[1]

During the late fall and winter of 1871-72 the tribes were quiet. Even the Kiowa remained near the agency. But with the return of spring, young Kiowa warriors began to prepare for the summer raiding season. In April, Big Bow and White Horse destroyed a freight train in Texas. Other parties were also out, and in June, White Horse massacred Abel Lee and his family near Fort Griffin.[2]

The Kiowa also struck to the north as well and managed to drive off the mules belonging to a Sixth Infantry baggage train near Fort Dodge. When Pope first learned of this loss, he was incensed. It was a disgrace not only to the command but also to the entire army. He wrote to Sheridan that no explanation for this inexcusable carelessness would satisfy him. It was "inconceivable that a party of Indians could drive away more than a hundred wagon mules from a command of four companies of troops, without the loss of men on either side, unless there was the greatest carelessness on the part of the troops." At first Pope was not at all sure that the theft was the work of Indians, but he ordered Lieutenant Colonel John Davidson to investigate and ascertain whether any Indians on the reservation had the stolen stock.

When Pope learned what had actually happened, his anger mounted, and he fired a verbal blast at Captain Orlando Moore, who commanded the troops, announcing that he held the captain fully responsible for the affair. Four companies and their baggage train had been moving north to the railroad and camped for the night near Fort Dodge. Without examining the country and without setting guards, the command let the mules graze loose and settled down for the night. When seven astonished Kiowa happened by and recovered from the surprise of finding such a tempting scene, they could not resist and made off with 121 mules. The sleeping soldiers, taken by surprise, made no attempt to pursue.[3]

Pope called upon Superintendent Hoag to recover the mules and warned him that the raiders should be punished. If they were allowed to go unpunished, they would be encouraged to raid again, but Pope had little hope that anything would be done. Since the reservation was under the jurisdiction of the Indian Bureau and the army could not punish the Indians there or use force to recover the mules, there was nothing else that the angry general could do.[4]

The situation on the southern plains, at least as far as the Kiowa were concerned, was tense, and Pope feared that there would be war. Military couriers from Camp Supply were fired on, and raids continued on the ravaged Texas frontier. Pope did not want war, but he believed it was inevitable if robberies and murders went unpunished. The presence of large parties of Cheyenne and Arapaho in the area north of the Arkansas River added to the danger. Although they were apparently peaceful, their very presence could cause an incident that would lead to trouble with those tribes as well. Pope requested that Hoag bring the Cheyenne and Arapaho back to the reservation and also ordered his commanders in the area to warn the Indians that they must return to the reservation. At the same time he attempted to calm the fears of Kansas authorities and to answer petitions from the Kansas settlements by explaining that these off-reservation Indians were peaceful.[5]

While the wandering Cheyenne and Arapaho were troublesome, the Kiowa were running wild and striking savagely at the Texas frontier. Agent Tatum warned his superiors that he could not control the Kiowa; they did as they pleased and were proud of it. He requested authority to stop the issue of all rations and annuity goods until the raiding stopped. He wrote, "My own view is that they should receive nothing more from the Government at present, unless they return the stolen animals and then the leaders of the parties who commit murders." Since this was the only punishment that he could inflict, it should be done, for "the Kiowa are uncontrollable [sic] by me. . . . " Tatum grew increasingly concerned about the attitude and activities of his charges. During June they killed Frank Lee, a cowboy, near the agency, and the Kwahadi stole 51 animals from the corral at Fort Sill. The Kiowa killed a number of people in Texas and openly boasted of prisoners. Again Tatum informed Hoag, "The Kiowas and Quahadas are unmanagable by me."[6]

It was obvious that something had to be done with the Kiowa, but apparently Hoag did not know what to do. Tatum, Pope, and other military men, however, did know. They wanted guilty Indians punished, but this was something Hoag would not allow. When the civilized tribes of Indian Territory came forward with a proposal that avoided punishment of the Kiowa, he was quick to accept it. In June the representatives of the civilized tribes meeting in the general council at Okmulgee decided to send a delegation to confer with the wild tribes and encourage them to keep the peace. Led by Daniel Ross of the Cherokee, Chilly McIntosh of the Creek, and other members of the civilized tribes, the delegation assembled on June 22, 1872 near the old Fort Cobb on the Washita River. The Kiowa were noticeably absent, and as they were the primary reason for the conference, every attempt was made to bring them in. Finally on July 31 the Kiowa began to arrive. White Horse, who had murdered Abel Lee and taken several of his children captive, surveyed the scene and announced that if there was anyone there worth killing he would do it, but as there were no prominent men present, he would let the others go. He made it plain that while the old men might talk of peace, he would not.[7]

It was an inauspicious beginning for peace talks, and the defiant manner of the Kiowa did not change with time. Lone Wolf, speaking for the tribe, said that they did not want peace and would raid where they pleased. They might consider peace if Satanta and Big Tree were released, if their reservation stretched from the Rio Grande to the Missouri River, and if Fort Sill and the other military posts within those boundaries were removed, Lone Wolf announced.[8]

Little was accomplished other than the recovery of some captives and stolen stock, and even Tatum saw no prospect of stopping the raids by pacific means. The Interior Department still felt otherwise, however, and while the council at old Fort Cobb was in session, plans were being made for an official council with the wild Indians. On July 22, Captain Henry Alvord, who had served on the southern plains before retiring from the army, and Professor Edward Parrish of Philadelphia were chosen as commissioners to visit the tribes of the southern plains to warn them that the government had determined that they cease their depradations and remain on their reservations. If they refused, the Interior Department would authorize the military to punish raiders, and all Indians leaving the reservation for Texas would be treated as hostile. The reservation would no longer be inviolate to military activity, and all raiding parties would be followed to their camps and punished. [9]

In August, Commissioners Alvord and Parrish conferred with Superintendent Hoag and then with Generals Pope and Grierson, and on September 5 they met with representatives of the southern tribes near the Wichita Agency. Arapaho and Comanche delegates attended, but the Kiowa, the primary reason for the conference, were conspicuously absent. The attitude of the Kiowa toward peace was evident, for a few days before, they had solemnly promised to attend. The commissioners received an instant education in Kiowa honesty and promises.

The council dissolved on September 7, and Alvord began to tour the other agencies but with little hope for peace. He had learned that whatever promises the chiefs might make, the young men of the tribe could not be controlled. This had been openly admitted by all. Still hoping to meet with the Kiowa, Alvord visited the agency near Fort Sill. Some of the Kiowa came in to talk, but they were not inclined to have delegates from their tribe join the chiefs of other tribes who were going to Washington. Faced with a blunt refusal, Alvord finally promised that they would meet Satanta and Big Tree en route. Only then did the Kiowa agree to the Washington visit.

Alvord was authorized to promise the return of Satanta and Big Tree if the tribe remained on its good behavior for six months, but his experiences with Kiowa dishonesty and sullenness convinced him that this would be a disastrous move. A pledge of good behavior for six months would be just long enough to carry them through the winter months when they had no desire to be hostile and preferred to be fed by the government. When this conditional period ended their horses would have recuperated and would be in fine shape for the spring raiding season.

It was clear to Alvord and other well-informed officials that the pledge of a Kiowa warrior could not be relied on. Not only had they raided without cause and in violation of former promises, but they had also made overtures to other tribes for a general war. To promise the release of the prisoners would be regarded by all the plains tribes as an acknowledgment of weakness on the part of the government and would only encourage more atrocities. As a result, Alvord did not promise the release of the prisoners, although he did arrange for the prisoners to meet with the Kiowa delegation en route to Washington.[10]

In his report to the Commissioner of Indian Affairs, Alvord showed an understanding of the situation on the southern plains that many officials of the Indian Bureau lacked, and he made some cogent comments concerning the wild tribes and the policy the government should follow toward them. It was apparent that the Peace Policy was not working on the southern plains, for the Indians did not remain on the reservations. The Kiowa and large numbers of Comanche and Cheyenne were rarely on the reservations, and even the peaceful Arapaho were often absent. Alvord, like others before him, recommended that the warriors be ordered to the reservations, that the order for them to remain there be enforced, and that the issuance of their subsistence and annuities be dependent on obedience and good behavior.

Alvord devoted more of his attention to the Kiowa and wild Comanche than to the other tribes, for these two, he said, were the primary problem. His report and recommendations did not appeal to humanitarians and Quakers like Hoag who believed that peaceful persuasion and trust in the Indians would solve the problem. Alvord pointed out that the Kiowa were unrestrained; they raided at will and boasted of it. He estimated that at least one-half of their depredations had never been reported to the Interior Department, but their known depredations during the past two years had included about one hundred murders. They had stolen approximately a thousand horses and mules, including over two hundred taken within the last few months from the troops and agencies in their vicinity. He predicted that the Kiowa, as they had before, would profess friendship when the cold weather approached, but that they would resume their raids in the spring. Their promises of good conduct were, he concluded, "utterly worthless."

The Kiowa were proud and defiant and had no desire for peace. They had always raided into Texas and had every intention of continuing this tradition. They had told their agent that if the President did not want them to raid into Texas, he should move Texas far away where their young men could not find it.

Alvord, who understood these problems, agreed with Tatum that the Kiowa were uncontrollable. Tatum believed that "nothing less than military authority, with perhaps some punishment by troops, will bring them into such subjection as to again render the services of a civil agent of benefit to them," and Alvord concurred. Alvord strongly urged that the government dictate terms to the Kiowa. They should be ordered to move their camps to the vicinity of Fort Sill where they could be watched by the troops. All stolen stock should be returned, and the three most prominent raiders surrendered for trial. If the demands were not met by the stated time, he maintained, military reprisal should be immediate. The policy of appeasement had failed, and the time had come for the government to enforce the reservation system. It was inconceivable to Alvord that the reservation system could be declared effective when a large portion of the Comanche, the Kwahadi band, had never been on the reservation.[11]

It was apparent that the results of the special commission did not sit well with Superintendent Hoag and his Quaker friends although it verified and supported the reports and proposals of Tatum and Pope, who were in basic agreement that Indian raiders should be held responsible for their crimes. Tatum had gone as far as recommending military control and military action, if necessary, but in so doing he was certainly not supported by his superiors. Hoag, with his own ideas regarding Indians, criticized the special commission and urged that in the future such work be left to employees of the Indian Bureau. Hoag reiterated that the Kiowa "require full confidence and trust in their integrity. When once received, the same virtues are most invariably reciprocated."[12]

Tatum, who was in the field, found himself at odds with the ideas and beliefs of his superiors. He had begun the policy of withholding rations in an attempt to force good behavior and to recover captives and stolen animals from the Indians. He was adamant against the practice of accepting Kiowa professions of peace at the beginning of each winter so that they could be fed and clothed by the government during the winter when the weather and the conditions of their horses restricted their movements. He was opposed to paying the Indians to be good. "To purchase a peace of the Indians by giving them an increased amount of rations and annuity goods upon their promise to cease raiding and war has a very injurious effect, not only on the party who thus indirectly receives a bonus for their atrocities, but upon other Indians also. We had as well attempt to hire the murderers and desperadoes in our large cities to cease their depredations as to pay the Indians to do the same." He urged that they be held responsible for their actions, for "the leniency of the government in letting guilty ones go unpunished is accepted on their part as cowardice or imbecility on the part of the whites."[13] Pope had made similar statements many times in the past. Bribery of the Indians was a major reason for his long-standing opposition to the treaty system, and Tatum was learning from experience that Pope had been right. This fact was driven home when his peaceful Indians protested that the government gave the most rations and annuities to those who behaved the worst.

The murder of the Richard Jordan family and the abduction of Mrs. Jordan near Ellis, Kansas in 1872 further emphasized the necessity of keeping the Indians on the reservations. This crime, committed by some Cheyenne who were moving north, brought immediate protests from Kansas authorities, as well as petitions from settlers for protection. The incident demonstrated that the army could not possibly provide adequate protection when Indians could wander off reservations—with or without the permission of their agent.[14] Incidents like that led to Pope's outburst against the practice of allowing the Indian to wander at will throughout his department. It was a wrong to frontier settlers to permit reservation Indians to leave their reserves on any pretext. If whites were forbidden to intrude on Indian reservations, it was the right of whites, Pope argued, to prohibit Indians from intruding on settlers' land. If game was essential to the Indian diet, he said, it would be better and cheaper to hire white hunters to supply meat. [15]

In September, Alvord took a group of Indian chiefs to Washington. During October and November they conferred with officials of the Interior Department and toured the cities of the East. Impressed with the peaceful demeanor of the chiefs, Washington officials decided to demonstrate the goodwill of the government by releasing the imprisoned Kiowa chiefs, Satanta and Big Tree. The promise was made on the condition that the Kiowa remain good until March, which as Alvord pointed out was just in time for the raiding season to begin again. Apparently the officials of the Indian Bureau were so unimpressed with the logic of men like Alvord and Tatum that they ignored them.

Hoag was overjoyed with the decision and piously announced that with proper treatment Satanta would use his great influence for peace. Satanta, as Tatum had discovered, was as great a liar as he was an orator. Satanta, not at all happy in the Texas prison, was willing to do or say anything to secure his release. Claiming to be head chief of all the wild tribes on the southern plains, Satanta impressed the Quaker officials with this inflated position and sagely promised that if released, he would keep all these Indians from raiding. The humanitarians seized upon this promise and approved Satanta's release. Although they knew nothing about Indians, they thought they knew everything and refused to listen to those with greater knowledge.[16]

Tatum, a Quaker himself, knew Satanta and had listened to his promises and lies before. He knew that Satanta could not even control the young men of his own band much less the whole Kiowa tribe and other tribes as well. It would be impossible to stop the raids, even if Satanta wanted to, and Tatum doubted that he wanted to. Instead of releasing Satanta and Big Tree, Tatum wanted to jail more of the raiders. To the disillusioned Quaker, the promise of freedom to Satanta was "like a dark and rolling cloud on the western horizon," but the promise had been made. Convinced that he would now have absolutely no control over the tribe and realizing that he was opposed to the policies of his superiors, Tatum resigned[17] and sadly left the Kiowa-Comanche Agency.

Tatum's replacement, James Haworth, was much more amenable to the wishes of Hoag and the Quaker Executive Committee. The committee, believing that Tatum had been too harsh with his charges and disagreeing with his policy of "firm restraint" instructed Haworth to be more conciliatory. Haworth followed his instructions, and soon after assuming office, he wrote Hoag that all the Indians made very strong promises of peace and that his confidence was "strong that the Indians of this agency intend to follow the friendly and peaceable road this summer." Haworth believed that the release of Satanta and Big Tree would have a *"very good effect* upon the Indians and be a strong leverage in their control." A few days later he reported that the beef ration was not large enough, and "it pains my heart to see them hungry." If he could feed them better, he said, he "could do more with them in keeping them quiet than two military posts could do." He showed his distaste for the military by dismissing the guard at the agency, much to the joy of the Kiowa.[18]

Haworth and Hoag were in agreement that the captive chiefs must be released, and they recommended unconditional pardon. Hoag was encouraged by the peaceful appearance of the Kiowa and Comanche, and in a letter to Secretary of the Interior Delano stressed the necessity of releasing the chiefs and following a humane policy toward the tribe. He urged that the Secretary of the Interior "allow no apparent or real hostility of disaffected tribes, nor the consequent demands of an excited public press to influence the government to break faith with the Kiowas, who, were they disposed to renew hostilities, are rendered no more formidable by the release of the chiefs referred to." Texans who had suffered from raids led by Satanta could have attested differently, however, but then not many had survived to disagree.[19]

Not content with demanding the unconditional release of the chiefs and predicting war if it were not done as promised in March, Hoag also insisted that the agency should be moved away from Fort Sill. The Indians regarded the fort as a standing menace, he said, and this was wrong. "They know right well the reason for establishing forts on their reserves. They feel that confidence in their loyalty has no place in the heart of the people or government, and, as a natural result they reflect and reciprocate the same distrust," Hoag wrote. "They require full confidence and trust in their integrity. When once received, the same virtues are most invariably reciprocated."[20]

Hoag found a warm supporter in Haworth. The new agent distrusted the army and opposed Tatum's practice of allowing troops to pursue raiding parties onto the reservation as he did not believe it to be part of the Peace Policy. He complained that army patrols were sent out without consulting him, and he could see no need for them. The soldiers should remain in the fort, he maintained, because the Indians were peaceably disposed.[21]

The Kiowa agreed that the agency should be moved because they wanted to be free of the watchful eyes of the army. With few exceptions, they cared little about trust or distrust; they would do as they pleased regardless. They did not claim to have grievances, nor did they claim that they raided because of hunger. They raided because the Texans were there. They had always done so and did not intend to change their traditions. As they had said before, if the government did not want them to raid Texas, then let the government move Texas far away where the young men could not find it.

As March came and went, however, and Satanta and Big Tree were not released, the Kiowa became increasingly sullen. The Modoc War had broken out in northern California, and General E. R. S. Canby was murdered during negotiations with the Modoc chief. The Interior Department decided to delay the return of the Kiowa chiefs because the public was so outraged by the Modoc treachery. It did not matter that the Kiowa had never heard of the Modoc.

The Interior Department also failed to take into account the anti-Kiowa sentiment in Texas. The Kiowa chiefs had been tried by a Texas court and were in a Texas penitentiary, and Federal officials had no authority to release the chiefs. The promise of release was greeted as an outrage. The Texas legislature voted unanimously against a pardon, and Governor Edmund J. Davis was warned that if he pardoned "these brutes," he would be held accountable "for the wanton abuse of the pardoning power."[22]

The pressure of humanitarians and Federal officials was nevertheless great enough that Governor Davis finally agreed to pardon the chiefs if the Kiowa tribe accepted certain conditions. A council was arranged, and Davis and Commissioner of Indian Affairs E. P. Smith met with the tribe on October 6. The council came very near to ending in the death of Davis and Smith, but Davis was eventually prevailed upon to modify his conditions. Satanta and Big Tree regained their freedom.[23]

When Sherman learned of the event, he wrote in contempt, "If I ever come to Fort Sill, and any of those Indians come about bragging of killing people in Texas, I won't bother their courts, but will have the graves dug at once." To Sherman, the release of the chiefs was the work of "humanitarians who regarded murder on the part of Indians as a mere exhibition of moral insanity." He wrote to Davis that he had risked his life in touring the Texas frontier and promised that he would never again voluntarily take such a risk. He believed Satanta and Big Tree would have their revenge and expressed the hope that if they were to take scalps, "yours is the first that should be taken."

The harried governor protested vehemently. He wrote to

Sherman that he could appreciate the General's indignation that these scamps had the impudence to imperil "even your life," but every male in the tribe was just as bad. "Satanta and Big Tree and their party are specially condemnable *only* because their exploit happened to scare the General In Chief of the United States Army," he replied.[24]

Despite the promises made upon the release of Satanta and Big Tree, Comanche war parties continued to ravage the Texas frontier, proving that Sherman, Tatum, Pope, and others had been right. Young Kiowa warriors, eager to make a name for themselves, began to join the Comanche, as well as leading raiding parties of their own. In early December the army learned that a large war party was on the Lower Nueces River. Troops were sent, and on December 9, Lieutenant Charles Hudson of the Fourth Cavalry surprised the raiders near Kickapoo Springs. A short fire fight put the raiders into flight leaving nine dead on the field, one of whom was Tau-ankia, son of Lone Wolf, and the Kiowa chief was determined to have revenge.

Kiowa and Comanche raiding parties were soon on their way to Texas, and Cheyenne warriors joined them in increasing numbers. The Southern Cheyenne had been relatively peaceful for several years, but trouble was brewing during 1873. The Cheyenne had a number of grievances: the wanton slaughter of the great buffalo herds was beginning to be felt by the Indians, as was the booming whiskey trade. Although Indian agents and military men had complained about this for years, and steps had been taken to stop it, little could be done under the ineffective Intercourse Acts. In January 1873, John Miles, who had become the agent for the Cheyenne and Arapaho on the death of Brinton Darlington in 1872, complained that unless something were done the country would soon be flooded with whiskey. Miles knew what he was talking about, for he had seen 1,200 Cheyenne "drunk as loons." In February a number of Arapaho ran into some whiskey-trading buffalo hunters on the tributaries of Bluff Creek and traded most of their ponies for whiskey. When the orgy was over and they realized what they had done, they were quite upset. They found it very uncomfortable to be on foot.[25]

The military was more than willing to cooperate with the Indian Bureau to stop the whiskey trade because it was connected with the arms trade, and drunken Indians could easily start a major conflict unintentionally. When Miles discovered the location of one group of whiskey traders, troops were sent to arrest them, and 400 gallons of liquor were destroyed. Traders, buffalo hunters, and members of the peaceful tribes were important sources of whiskey, but the *Comancheros* were the most despicable. These traders from New Mexico—whites, Spanish-Americans, and Pueblo Indians—regularly crossed the Llano Estacado in carrying on their extensive trade with the blanket Indians of the southern plains. For arms, whiskey, and other goods, they received captives and stolen stock.

Pope did everything in his power to destroy this illicit trade, but with only minor results. Troops in the summer cavalry camp on the Canadian River near old Fort Bascom were given special instructions to destroy this flourishing trade. Some traders were captured with their supply trains and large herds of stolen Texas cattle, but when they were turned over to territorial authorities in New Mexico, courts there refused to convict them. Pope proposed that in the future such traders be turned over to Texas authorities for trial. Conviction would then be guaranteed, he believed, for the captives and stolen stock had been taken by the Comanche, Kiowa, and Cheyenne during their raids in

Texas, and it seemed just that they should be returned to Texas. Even though the War Department approved Pope's proposals, the trade continued. And Pope lacked the troops to take effective measures against the *Comancheros*.[26]

The liquor trade could and did result in trouble. During one orgy some Cheyenne warriors decided to form a war party to fight their ancient enemy, the Ute. Seventeen young men started west looking for the Ute and traveled into the mountains west of Fort Bascom. Finding no Ute, the youths started back toward the reservation but were surprised by troops and severely punished. As a result the Cheyenne, spoiling for revenge, not long afterward obtained a great supply of whiskey. About 1,500 Cheyenne went on a binge during which four government surveyors were killed southeast of Camp Supply. When the War Department learned of the murders, it requested information from Pope, but he explained that there was little he could do. The murders had been committed on the reservation where he had no jurisdiction, and furthermore he had not been advised that a survey party was in the region. This in his mind, was the kind of recklessness that invited trouble. Pope disagreed with the Indian Bureau reports that the attack was in retaliation for punishment dealt the Cheyenne near Fort Bascom. The troops had been enforcing the Peace Policy, for the Cheyenne, as well as all reservation Indians, had been repeatedly warned that they would be treated as hostile if found off the reservation.[27]

During the spring of 1873 Pope followed his usual practice of establishing cavalry camps where they could best cover the railroads and settlements. With camps near Wichita, Grinnell, River Bend, Fort Hays, and old Fort Bascom, he believed that he could restrict the movements of Indians from the reservation and that scouting would keep him informed of their movements. With almost the entire cavalry force of the department—1,558 men in the field—he was confident that the Indians would not be able to wander about unnoticed and could be peacefully forced back to the reservation when they left it.

Troops were fairly effective in controlling the southern tribes, but, as before, Pope was burdened with the presence of wandering Sioux from the Department of the Platte, who had moved to the upper reaches of the Republican River to hunt. He was deluged with protests and requests for protection, but since a clause in the Treaty of 1868 gave the Sioux the right to hunt on the Republican River "so long as the buffalo may range thereon, in such numbers as to justify the chase," there was little he could do.

Because of the protests of Pope and Sheridan and the demands of the Kansas settlers, Sherman decided to act. He had been a member of the commission that negotiated the Treaty of 1868 and had opposed this clause at that time. His fear then was that Indian agents would allow their charges to make use of this right as long as there was a single buffalo alive in the vicinity, and his present conviction was that the buffalo had ceased to range there and that the right had thus expired.

The fears of Pope and Sherman were realized in 1873 when hunting parties from a number of different tribes appeared in western Kansas. There were about 900 Omaha Indians on the Saline River, but at least they were accompanied by their agent. The Sioux and their bitter enemies, the Pawnee, were in the area as well, and the dangers of this situation became obvious when a clash occurred between the two tribes. This incident finally caused the Commissioner of Indian Affairs to ask the Secretary of the Interior to abrogate the old hunting privilege for the Sioux because their "wanton and murderous attack" on the Pawnee had violated the Treaty of 1868. He also suggested that Indians be forbidden to wander off their reservation without the authority of their agent. This was done, but it did not satisfy Pope, because agents continually gave such permission. When the Sioux left their reservation to hunt in Nebraska after they had been warned not to, Commissioner Smith angrily asked that the army be called in to force them back to the reservation. He preferred that they be taken prisoner, but left the use of force up to the military.[28] Although humanitarians usually insisted that the army wanted an Indian war, the soldiers carried out the task peacefully.

Following the murder of the surveyors, relationships with the Southern Cheyenne were tense. Large numbers of them moved to the headwaters of the Washita River and refused to come near the agency. Whiskey traders continued to deal with this dissident group despite attempts by the military to stop it. Agent Miles was concerned enough that he requested a guard for the agency. A guard was supplied although Pope suggested that the agency be moved to the vicinity of Camp Supply where the army could keep a better watch over the tribe.

Despite fears that the Cheyenne might revolt, hostilities were avoided. The situation was dangerous, however—so dangerous that the Cheyenne had no interest in sending their chiefs to Washington. After a visit by the Commissioner of Indian Affairs and the Secretary of the Interior, however, a delegation of Cheyenne chiefs did visit Washington. While the chiefs were in Washington, a party of about 200 Cheyenne moved into southeastern Colorado looking for the Ute. They passed west of Fort Lyon and moved up as far as the tracks of the Kansas Pacific Railroad at River Bend. Pope learned of this soon after their departure, ordered the troops in the region to intercept them and induce them to return to the reservation, and instructed his field commanders to use force only as a last resort. A company of the Eighth Cavalry near Spanish Peaks was ordered to move to the Purgatory River to intercept the Cheyenne if they moved west toward the mountains, while others patrolled the valley of the Arkansas River. Due to the failure of Major James Biddle at Fort Lyon to carry out his orders, the Indians were allowed to pass west of the fort, which resulted in a mass exodus from the settlements and cries of alarm from the government of Colorado.

Pope bitterly complained of the practice of allowing Indians to leave the reservation with or without permits from the agents. But because the Indians were not hostile and did no more than steal a few cooking utensils and kill some cattle, Pope had no intention of causing a conflict. Sheridan believed that they had killed nothing more than "two chicken cocks in order to get their tail feathers," and concurred with Pope that hostilities should be avoided. The Secretary of the Interior, however, thought otherwise; he wanted the Indians killed or captured. Pope found this somewhat ironic, for when the Cheyenne had been attacked near old Fort Bascom in February, the Indian Bureau and the Interior Department had severely criticized the army for making an unprovoked attack. Now the army, which Indian Bureau officials always claimed wished Indian wars, was in a position to have one and rejected the opportunity. Pope's reply to the Secretary of the Interior was that if the government wanted the Cheyenne punished, the Indian Bureau had only to consent to their arrest when they returned to the reservation and that this would avoid unnecessary bloodshed.[29]

During the autumn of 1873, hostilities were avoided

with the Cheyenne, but conflict between army officers and members of the Indian Bureau continued, with Pope as usual in the middle of the debate. By late 1873 Pope had sent a constant stream of protests against the practice of allowing Indians to wander off their reservations and go where they pleased. In keeping with this, he also urged the cessation of giving permits to hunt off the reservation, and he believed that this should be applied to all Indians and not just to the wild tribes, for the presence of a hunting party of peaceful Indians among the settlements caused the same alarm as a war party. Sheridan took up the fight as well. With the steady growth of western settlement it was becoming more and more apparent that the Indians must be kept on the reservations. He urged that a rigid rule be made and enforced which forbade their absence from the reservation, and that if disregarded, the military would seek them out on the reservation and punish them.[30]

The Quakers, in spite of their concern for the lives of the Indians, seemed to be unconcerned about the lives of the settlers. Hoag had urged that the "humane policy" be continued despite the continuance of raiding activities, and Tatum's successor, John Haworth, was in basic agreement. "I may say our prospects for the future are very encouraging," Haworth reported, "and I firmly believe if good faith is kept with these people, that the day will come when they will cease to be a burden to the Government, will become self-sustaining—with the spear turned into the pruning-hook, the art of war no longer learned, and the sweet name of Jesus spoken and loved by man. . . ."[31] In the autumn of 1873 no spears were turned into pruning hooks nor would they be. Lone Wolf, who had demanded a reservation stretching from the Rio Grande to the Missouri River, was not planning to give up the art of war, nor did the noted raider, White Horse, who had boasted of his role in the murder of the Lee family, plan to speak "the sweet name of Jesus."

Despite the attitude of Hoag and other Quakers, officials in Washington began to realize that the situation was serious. The Commissioner of Indian Affairs found it necessary to request a military force at each of the Sioux agencies, and he suggested that all Indians be required to remain on the reservations. He found the conduct of the Comanche "especially flagrant" and decided that they must be punished. He had no desire to punish the innocent, but had come to the conclusion that there was no alternative to calling in the army. The reservation could not remain a refuge for thieves and murderers. Secretary of the Interior Columbus Delano agreed and spelled out the Peace Policy as it had been meant to operate: when the Indians refused to go to the reservations and continued to raid, they were to be punished and driven back to the reservation. And there they must remain, for in no other way could assimilation be carried out or the Peace Policy enforced. [32]

CHAPTER NINE

"Attack any hostile Indians"

The Quaker interpretation of the Peace Policy had been in effect on the southern plains for several years with few results by 1873. Fresh graves and burned and abandoned cabins along the Texas frontier attested to its failure, and in the autumn of 1873 the Secretary of the Interior and the Commissioner of Indian Affairs began to talk of implementing the Peace Policy as it had been meant to be enforced. Not until July 1874, however, a month after the attack on the trading establishment at Adobe Walls in the Texas Panhandle made it evident that war had broken out, was the army given a free hand to deal with the hostiles.

The winter of 1873-74 had been a time of discontent for the wild tribes of the southern plains. In late December 1873, Agent John Miles reported that Satanta was stirring up trouble and talking of war. The Kiowa and Comanche continued to strike at the Texas frontier, and the Southern Cheyenne joined them. Troops in the Department of Texas were on the alert, and on February 4, 1874 Lieutenant Colonel George Buell and a detachment of Negro troopers of the Tenth Cavalry surprised a Comanche raiding party and killed eleven warriors. Kiowa raiding parties were out as well. In April, Lone Wolf led a raid into Texas seeking revenge for the death of his son. The Department of Texas, warned of the chief's activity, sent a detachment of the Fourth Cavalry in search of him. They trailed the chief and his warriors for 240 miles until their mounts were so worn that they abandoned the chase.

Other problems added to the turmoil. The whiskey and the arms trade, which continued unabated, was having its effect. In the spring of 1874 the southern tribes were better armed than ever before. James Haworth of the Kiowa-Comanche Agency noted that his Indians had acquired many of the latest model pistols and large supplies of ammunition.[1]

The slaughter of the great southern buffalo herd added to the discontent. Development of the hide market in the East was causing the systematic destruction of the herds, and when the buffalo began to disappear from the central plains, the hunters moved south into the Texas Panhandle. In 1873 over 750,000 hides were shipped on the Atchison, Topeka and Santa Fe Railroad alone, and it is estimated that over 7.5 million buffalo were killed from 1872 to 1874.[2]

The activities of white horse thieves operating from Kansas and Texas added to the troubles, and Indian agents were, of course, powerless to stop this. Horse stealing by white or Indian could lead to bloodshed, and in the spring of 1874 it did. A party of young Cheyenne warriors traveled into Kansas in pursuit of a band of thieves. They took some stock to replace their stolen ponies, but before they could return to the reservation they were met by a company of cavalry, and in the ensuing clash Little Robe's son was wounded. By June the chiefs could no longer control the young men, and depredations by the Southern Cheyenne increased.[3]

Throughout the spring the agents worked hard to keep their charges at peace. On March 2, James Haworth reported that two Comanche raiding parties were out, but he had hopes that the Kiowa would remain peaceful. They claimed that they had not been involved in any raids, and their word was good enough for the agent. On April 20, he reported "good feelings among my Indians." There was some grumbling, he admitted, but he was satisfied that with sufficient rations to supply their needs he could control them.[4]

In May a delegation of Quakers, accompanied by Hoag and his clerk, visited the Kiowa-Comanche Agency to counsel the Indians to remain at peace, but their words had little effect. Haworth was beginning to fear trouble, for he had heard stories of a new and powerful medicine man, but he was confident that the Indians still wanted peace. He was much concerned when he received reports that troops in the Department of Texas had authority to pursue raiders onto the reservations and to kill or capture them. He admitted that he could see no alternative to this, but he hoped that "out of all our trials and troubles and tribulations and conflicts the Lord can and may deliver us. My hope is not given out," he wrote, "though I confess our outlook is discouraging at present. . . ." His hopes were soon dashed. In mid-July he was warned that a large body of Comanche and Southern Cheyenne warriors were on their way to the agency to compel the friendlies to join them. He reported to Superintendent Hoag, "I confess I hardly know what kind of an opinion to express, only that at present writing the sky looks considerably hazy."[5]

The sky looked considerably hazy, indeed. War had already begun on the southern plains. Cheyenne warriors had struck at the camps of buffalo hunters in the Texas Panhandle and had battled with a detachment of the Sixth Cavalry between Fort Dodge and Camp Supply. On June 27, Comanche, Southern Cheyenne, and Kiowa warriors gathered around the trading post of Adobe Walls to exterminate that nest of hunters and traders.

The battle of Adobe Walls spectacularly signaled the existence of hostilities. The leader of that attack was a new Kwahadi medicine man named Isatai. Tales of his supernatural powers had spread rapidly through the Indian camps, causing great excitement among the southern tribes. Reputedly able to control the elements and raise the dead, Isatai, it was said, could also produce great quantities of cartridges from his stomach and could deflect the bullets of the soldiers from the warriors. His fame was such that he was soon in a position to urge a general war. In late May he ordered the Comanche to assemble for a sun dance, something that the tribe had never done before. Large numbers of Cheyenne and a few Kiowa appeared, and amid great quantities of liquor, Isatai harangued the warriors. The decision was thus made to wipe out the white hunters and traders at Adobe Walls.

A hangout for buffalo hunters, Adobe Walls consisted of several stores and a saloon. Located on the north bank of the Canadian River and in the general area where Kit Carson had battled with the Comanche in 1864, Adobe Walls was a trading center that supplied both white hunters and Indians with arms, ammunition, liquor, and other supplies. It was a lucrative but dangerous business, for trade with the Indians was illegal without a license from the Indian Bureau.

On the morning of June 27 several hundred warriors swarmed into Adobe Walls, and the twenty-eight men at the trading center jumped to the alert. Although the battle raged most of the day, the booming Sharp's rifles in the hands of experienced buffalo hunters kept the Indians at bay. By mid-afternoon the hostiles broke off the attack, but the Indian war had begun in earnest.[6]

From his headquarters at Fort Leavenworth, Pope followed and reacted to each event as it occurred. With the first scattering of raids in Kansas he strengthened his defensive lines by sending additional men into the field. He attempted, as he had in previous years, to throw a line of troops around the northern and western boundaries of Indian Territory in an effort to contain the hostiles. Troops were guarding the routes of the Kansas Pacific and the Atchison, Topeka and Santa Fe railroads, and cavalry camps were established near Fort Hays and at Grinnell Station east of Fort Wallace. Department of the Missouri soldiers were in the field, and they were on the move as they searched for hostiles and sought to turn them back to the reservations. Some cavalry was in motion near old Fort Bascom and along the Purgatory and Arkansas rivers in the west, while others patrolled the southern boundary of Kansas. With panic spreading along the Kansas frontier, Pope informed Governor Thomas Osborn of the disposition of his troops in an attempt to allay the fears of the settlers. "There was never in my experience," he wrote to Osborn, "a frontier so fully guarded as the frontier of Kansas. . ." but Kansans did not feel safe.[7]

Pope, willing to do everything in his power to protect the settlements as well as all white men engaged in legitimate occupations, was not willing to protect the whiskey sellers and illegal traders whom he considered largely responsible for the outbreak of hostilities. When he received through Governor Osborn a request for aid at Adobe Walls, Pope flatly refused to send troops. Trading firms from Dodge City had gone into the Texas Panhandle to sell liquor and to trade with buffalo hunters and "ruffians" and had committed violent outrages upon the Indians, thereby endangering the lives of the peaceful settlers, he said. The operations of these traders were illegal, and they would get no sympathy from him. "They have justly earned all that may befall them," he informed Governor Osborn, "and if I were to send troops to the locality of these unlawful trading establishments, it would be to break them up and not to protect them."[8]

On July 10, Pope sent Sheridan information regarding the disposition of his troops. He had, Pope reported, a cordon of troops from Fort Union, the Raton Mountains, and the Purgatory and Arkansas rivers across the southern boundary of Kansas. The Cheyenne, Kiowa, and Comanche were still raiding northward in small parties, but Pope was confident that he could protect the frontier settlements. "Certainly," he wrote, "we shall act vigorously and use everything we have."

Pope believed that he could provide adequate protection for the roads and settlements within his command, but he wanted to do more than to remain on the defensive. He wanted to strike at the hostiles on the reservations. The Indian Bureau still refused to authorize this, and Pope urged Sheridan to use his influence to obtain approval for an offensive movement in Indian Territory.[9]

Pope, ready to take the offensive, realized that the only effective way to deal with the hostiles was to attack them on the reservations. When he was unable to secure authority for such a move from Hoag and when Sheridan became critical of his lack of action, Pope asked that his position be clarified. He wanted to attack without warning. If the friendly Indians were ordered to gather at the agencies before an attack were made, Pope wrote to Sheridan, the hostiles would also go there and then commence raiding when the troops had passed. Pope suggested that the most effective way of dealing with the hostiles was a winter campaign.[10]

The correspondence between Pope and Sheridan resulted in confusion and misunderstanding, which caused sharp words and bad feelings for a time. Pope wanted instructions to clarify his position, but Sheridan received the impression that Pope was opposed to all offensive measures and preferred to remain on the defensive. Sheridan criticized Pope and wrote to Sherman, "He is so taken with the idea of a defensive line that he does not see the absurdity of using Cavalry in that way."

Sheridan was somewhat indecisive himself and vacillated between Sherman's belief in immediate action and Pope's request to delay the campaign until winter when the Indians would be helpless. Sheridan, probably remembering his successes during the winter of 1868, was also thinking of a winter campaign, and like Pope he stressed the need for an understanding with the Interior Department to permit military operations on the reservations.[11]

On July 20 the Secretary of War informed Sherman that the hostiles could be pursued and punished wherever found, and on the following day Sheridan ordered Pope to put the Sixth Cavalry in motion. Sherman approved of the order and advised Sheridan to make every Kiowa and Comanche "knuckle down." Sherman was confident that when the Indians learned that raids would result in punishment they would soon tire of it. "I agree with you perfectly," he wrote, "that defensive war is always bad, and until these Reservation Indians know that every time they go out, they will be followed back, we cannot guard the frontier with five times the forces we have there."[12]

Although the order to launch the attack was given, misunderstanding continued. When one of Sheridan's dispatches criticizing Pope appeared in the newspapers, Pope complained. Sheridan caustically replied that he had the right to criticize officers under his command, and he castigated Pope for not moving sooner. It was his opinion that

184

Pope should have sent relief forces to the beleaguered hunters and traders at Adobe Walls, for no matter "what may have been the character of these men, they were in distress," and they had a legal right to hunt and trade in the region because it was not on a reservation. "You should have used the troops for the protection of life and property," he wrote, "wherever it might have been"[13]

Sheridan disregarded the fact that the trading center at Adobe Walls was involved in unlicensed and illegal trade with the Indians, but before Pope could reply, Sherman stepped in to calm the rising tempers of his subordinates. Pope was disturbed, but he was more disturbed at the tone of Sheridan's dispatch than by its contents. Pope had never been an advocate of defensive operations against the Indians, and he did not suggest this now. He did, however, want permission to invade the reservations and seize the hostiles at the agencies, and he did believe that military operations would be more effective during the winter months.

Sheridan was hasty in his judgment of his departmental commander, and he was overly harsh in his criticisms. Pope had merely offered suggestions, while Sheridan had vacillated. Even after the Interior Department had approved military operations on the reservations, Sheridan admitted that he did not expect much from a summer campaign. General Pope was ignorant of the situation in the Department of Texas where most of the hostile activity occurred, and he did not realize the extent of the outbreak. As divisional commander, Sheridan had both departments under his command. He received reports from both Pope and General C. C. Augur of the Department of Texas, and he was in a position to make decisions. He also should have kept his subordinates informed of events in the adjoining departments. Despite the harsh words between Pope and

185

Sheridan, there was virtually no difference in their views, and the rancor quickly passed.[14]

By the time the conflict between the two officers was settled, all cause of disagreement had disappeared. The Interior Department had finally made its decision: the hostiles were to be punished, and the army was freed from restrictions against military action on the reservations. The discussions between the War Department and Interior Department came to a close, and on July 20 authority was given to punish guilty Indians wherever found. The friendly Indians were required to congregate at the agencies for enrollment, and all males capable of bearing arms were required to answer a daily roll call. All others would, after a suitable time, be treated as hostile.

At the request of the Interior Department, these orders went into effect July 20, but action already had been taken by others in anticipation of this. Soon after the first outbreak of hostilities, Superintendent Hoag, acting on his own volition to protect his Indians, had sent his clerk, Cyrus Beede, to the Cheyenne Agency to collect the friendlies. Lieutenant Colonel John Davidson of the Tenth Cavalry, the post commander at Fort Sill in the Department of Texas, issued a similar order on July 17 because of depredations in the vicinity of the post. To distinguish the friendlies from the hostiles, he ordered the friendlies to camp on the east side of Cache Creek where he could keep them under surveillance.[15]

Pope was disappointed that the authority given by the Interior Department was not more sweeping, and he feared that the hostiles would gather at the agencies to be enrolled in order to avoid punishment. "Certainly," he wrote to Sheridan, "by giving such notice in advance, we are practically disarming ourselves and frustrating the very object we have in view. . . .If we make treaties with the tribe, at least to the extent of pointing out the criminals, if they cannot control or punish them themselves." Pope feared that the act of calling the friendlies to the agencies would give warning to the hostiles and allow them to flee and scatter or claim to be friendly. "What chance," he wrote, "would the police of New York have if all the people of their vilest districts were to be notified when the police force was about to move upon them and all those who wanted protection must assemble in certain buildings and localities where they would be unmolested, or disperse for the occasion? We are placed with the Reservation Indians precisely in this position," he continued. Pope also insisted upon and received the right to go to the agencies and seize any of the criminals who had taken refuge there. [16]

Pope's predictions were in part fulfilled. Hoag's call for all the friendlies to come to the agencies brought most of the Kiowa in, and although Haworth regarded them as friendly, their reliability was open to question. The Quaker officials of the Central Superintendency were quite upset that the army was enforcing the order from the Secretary of the Interior, and they attempted to protect the Indians and undermine the power of the military. Haworth wrote to Beede, "Matters here have assumed a fearful shape. So far as this agency is concerned I might say the peace policy is at an end for the present. . . ." Beede hurried to the agency and protested Davidson's announcement that the enrollment of the friendlies was complete and that no new names would be added except on proof of innocence and on the condition that the men be disarmed, dismounted, and held as prisoners of war.

As General Pope had predicted, some of the hostiles attempted to join the friendly camp. Lone Wolf, Big Bow, and other hostile Kiowa were in the camp of the friendlies to be enrolled, and Beede urged that this be permitted. He argued that Agent Haworth was the proper man to decide which Indians were entitled to enrollment, especially when the military commander was "an enemy of the peace policy or at any rate manifests no sympathy with the workers thereunder." He urged that Haworth be allowed to enroll others who were still at large, because he feared that a "petulant, vindictive General" would involve all the Indians in hostilities. Hoag also requested that the agent be allowed to let the Kiowa and Comanche come in, and urged that Davidson be removed from his command. The Quakers frantically worked to maintain control of the situation and avoid war, but their attempt to undermine the function of the military and the order from the Secretary of the Interior was crushed by Davidson. The harassed post commander announced, "I will not abate one jot or tittle of his [Commissioner of Indian Affairs'] requirements," and he forbade the issue of rations to the Kiowa until they had been disarmed, dismounted, and placed under military control.[17]

The dangers inherent in the attitude of the Quakers soon became apparent. Big Red Food of the Comanche decided that it was time to make peace and avoid punishment. He did not like the requirement that he give up his arms and become a prisoner of war, so he went to the Wichita Agency at Anadarko to enroll. The situation there was inflammatory. Big Red Food and other hostile Comanche were there, and Lone Wolf was also in the vicinity causing trouble. When Davidson was notified of the dangers, he immediately moved out with four companies of Buffalo Soldiers. Big Red Food agreed to surrender to Davidson, but then attempted to escape, and a battle began. Although Davidson's Negro troopers were under fire from front and rear and were hampered by friendlies in their line of fire, they held their ground and the hostiles withdrew. The battle at Anadarko served notice that the government was determined to punish the hostiles, and it helped to separate the friendlies from the hostiles. When news of the battle reached the Kiowa-Comanche Agency, the Indians all fled, but the peaceful ones soon returned.[18]

The hostiles were now scattered across the western reaches of Indian Territory and the Staked Plains, and it was up to the army to punish them and drive them back to their reservations. Pope and Augur faced a difficult task. The strategy called for several strong columns to invade the Indian country. When Pope received word that he could enter the reservations, he sent orders to his officers in the field: "You will attack any hostile Indians whom you may meet either in or out of the Indian country." He also ordered Colonel Nelson Miles of the Fifth Infantry into the field.

The strategy for the Indian war was similar to that of Pope's earlier campaigns against the Sioux. Six separate commands were put into operation from the Department of the Missouri and the Department of Texas. Miles, eager to build his reputation and willing to use influential connections to further his career, was rapidly completing preparations to strike southward from Fort Dodge with eight companies of cavalry and four companies of infantry. Major William Redwood Price was ordered to lead four companies of the Eighth Cavalry from their summer camp near old Fort Bascom and move down the Canadian River to act in conjunction with Miles. Lieutenant Colonel Thomas H. Neill operated in the vicinity of the Cheyenne Agency at Darlington and captured all Indians who attempted to seek refuge there. Ranald S. Mackenzie, the brilliant young commander of the Fourth Cavalry, was ordered to march northward from Fort Concho on the Colorado River in Texas with eight companies of cavalry and five companies of infantry. Lieutenant Colonel George P. Buell and Lieutenant Colonel Davidson were to strike westward from Fort Griffin and Fort Sill with columns consisting largely of Negro troopers from the Ninth and Tenth Cavalry.

The strategy was remarkably effective although few Indians were killed. Invading the Indian country from every direction, five strong columns maintained a steady pursuit as the hostiles fled before them. Several brisk engagements were fought as Miles and Mackenzie scoured the country along the eastern edge of the Staked Plains.

As Pope sought to get his troops into action and keep them supplied, he was forced to deal with the eager Colonel Miles who wanted all the glory for himself. Miles' expedition numbered over 700 fighting men, but the colonel was not satisfied even though Pope had stripped his department to provide that many men. When Miles found his movements restricted by lack of supplies, he insisted that he be given more wagons and mounts despite the fact that he knew they were not available, Pope criticized him caustically. Pope, who had given Miles everything available and was establishing a supply depot in the Indian country for the expedition, was annoyed with Miles' requests and especially with his use of newspaper correspondents accompanying his command to make it appear that he was being hampered by his departmental commander. [19]

Pope was gratified by Miles' accomplishments, but like other men associated with the able but vain Miles, he did not appreciate Miles' attitude. Miles appeared at times more concerned with winning victories to enhance his reputation than with terminating the Indian war. He had large hostile groups behind him, but he wanted to continue the pursuit southward, apparently from a desire to defeat the Indians before they were driven into the grasp of Mackenzie, his rival for a general's star.

While Pope sought to provide overall direction to the troops operating from his Department of the Missouri, he was hindered by the lack of information regarding troop movements from Augur's department, but he kept his cavalry in motion. The campaign continued throughout the summer and autumn. On September 28, Mackenzie dealt the hostiles their severest blow. At daybreak his command picked its way down the steep side of Palo Duro Canyon and surprised a large hostile camp. The capture of their horse herd and winter supplies was a spectacular victory, and Mackenzie made sure that the Indians were permanently dismounted by destroying approximately 1,050 animals.

September and October passed, but still the persistent soldiers were in the field. Brief fire fights erupted sporadically as the harassed Indians attempted to elude the troops and sought a place of refuge. But there was no place to hide, no escape, and no relief. With no time to hunt or to rest the horses, the Indians were hungry and their mounts were poor. Discouraged and beaten and with winter approaching, the hostiles gradually straggled in to their agencies. The pursuit had been relentless, the pressure too great. The strategy that Pope had used with little success on the northern plains in 1863 and 1865 had been tried again, and the results exceeded all expectations. The resistance of the powerful tribes of the southern plains was broken completely. [20]

As the Indian campaign progressed, military men began to ask what was to be done with the Indians once they were defeated and captured. When Satanta and Big Tree were captured near the Cheyenne Agency, there was no problem. According to the agreement made at the time of their release from the Texas penitentiary, they were returned to prison. The disposition of the other Indians was not so easy, but military men wanted a prompt decision by government officials. [21]

Sheridan suggested that all those who had committed murder or engaged in horse stealing during the past two years be tried by a military commission, their horses sold at auction, and the proceeds invested in cattle for the tribe. The ringleaders, he said, should be confined at Fort Snelling, Minnesota, far from their homeland. Sherman, who had followed the campaign closely, was doubtful of the long-term results of the war and wished that the troops had managed to kill more braves. He expected that once they were disarmed and unhorsed and confined to the reservations under military surveillance they would behave for a time, "at least until the Quakers manipulate them a while longer." [22]

The Interior Department accepted the proposal that the hostiles be tried by a military commission, but the disposition of the remainder of the tribes remained the subject of lively discussion. Pope soon made his views known. He, like Sherman, did not expect the Indians to be given harsher punishment than before and believed that after "waxing fat at the agencies" they would forget their defeat and be ready for war again. Pope did not want another Indian war. Halfway measures had been used in the past, he said, but should not be used again. Calling attention to some of his earlier statements on Indian policy, Pope once again recommended that the tribes be moved to some place remote from their homeland, to the east of the Great Plains. They should be disarmed and dismounted and strictly controlled, he insisted. The government would have to support them, he acknowledged, but the profits from the sale of their lands would more than compensate for this expense. This was, he believed, the only solution to recurrent Indian wars.[23]

Pope and Sherman both feared that the Indians would remain subdued for only a short time, and there were indications that they might soon be proved right. Although military operations continued during the winter and into the spring, they were on a small scale, and some of the Indians were becoming troublesome again. Cheyenne Agent Miles informed his colleague at Fort Sill that the Indians "had grown Saucy" and were sending out raiding parties. They were after horses, he said, but "of course would not hesitate to *lift hair.*"[24]

Despite indications of renewed hostilities, the continuation of military operations proved effective. One by one small bands surrendered, and in late February 1875 word was received that Stone Calf was bringing the main Southern Cheyenne village toward the agency. On March 6 the destitute Cheyenne surrendered, and Agent Miles wrote, "A more wretched and poverty-stricken community than these it would be difficult to imagine."[25] Lone Wolf and Red Otter of the Kiowa had surrendered in February; the infamous White Horse capitulated in April, and in June Colonel Mackenzie rounded up the Kwahadi of the Staked Plains and brought the Indian war to a close.

With the surrender of Lone Wolf and Stone Calf, plans were made to select the ringleaders for confinement. The transfer of Fort Sill to the Department of the Missouri placed both the Kiowa-Comanche and Cheyenne-Arapaho agencies within Pope's command, and he gave the orders to have the leaders rounded up and sent eastward for special punishment. Colonel Mackenzie at Fort Sill accomplished this with little difficulty, but Lieutenant Colonel Neill at the Cheyenne Agency was less fortunate. While the warriors were being placed in irons, one of them broke and ran. A guard fired, killing the escapee. But the shots caused such a panic in the camp that the warriors fled to a nearby sandhill where they had secreted weapons. Although troops moved in and attacked immediately, they were repulsed by the well-armed Cheyenne who held an excellent defensive position.

During the night the Indians escaped and fled northward. Troops started in pursuit, and although most of the escapees soon returned to the agency, many of the worst criminals managed to flee across the Arkansas River. Their escape was not complete, however, for Lieutenant Austin Henely and a detachment of the Sixth Cavalry hurried from Fort Lyon to Fort Wallace by rail and picked up their trail. At daybreak on April 23 he surprised the fugitives and nearly destroyed them all.[26]

The brief outbreak at the Cheyenne Agency demonstrated that the Indians were still dangerous. The ringleaders would soon be on their way to Fort Marion, Florida for confinement, but General Pope was concerned about the remainder of the tribes. What was to be done with them? When Stone Calf surrendered in April, Pope asked that the government state its policy toward the defeated Indians. The appropriation act for these tribes prohibited issue of any kinds of goods or supplies to those who had been hostile, yet they were completely destitute and would have to be fed and clothed.

While the bureaucrats talked, Pope acted. The extermination of the race was "abhorrent to humanity" and unbecoming to a civilized and Christian nation, he believed, and he informed Sheridan that unless otherwise directed, he would order Neil to march the Cheyenne to Fort Leavenworth and place them on the military reservation on the east side of the Missouri River opposite the post.

There was ample room and good ground and timber. Supplies would be inexpensive and close at hand, and above all, he said, the danger of a Cheyenne war in the future would be eliminated. Placed under military control, the Southern Cheyenne could be civilized and Christianized. "Certainly," he wrote, "they can never again depredate, nor be depredated on, and the Indian question, as far as the tribe of Cheyenne is concerned, will be finally settled."[27]

Pope's proposal was discussed in Washington, and President Grant soon gave his approval. But presidential approval did not end the debate nor settle the issue. Quakers, Indian Bureau officials, and humanitarians realized the implications of the plan and, as they were totally opposed to military control of the Indians, began to gather support for a different disposition of the Southern Cheyenne. In time they were successful in preventing Pope's proposals from being carried out. Securing an appropriation from Congress, the Indian Bureau decided to purchase part of the Quapaw Reservation in the northeastern portion of Indian Territory for the Southern Cheyenne. They too were thwarted, however. Pope was opposed to this location because it was too close to their homeland, and the citizens of southeastern Kansas protested virulently and effectively. In the end the decision was made to leave the Cheyenne on their old reservation.[28]

CHAPTER TEN

"The old
'hand to mouth way' "

The Indian campaign of 1874 did not settle the Indian problem on the southern plains although it did teach the Kiowa, Comanche, and Southern Cheyenne respect for the power of the government. The defeat of the three warlike southern tribes brought peace to the region, but Pope feared that hostilities might begin again. During the remainder of his tour of duty in the Department of the Missouri, he did his utmost to keep the peace and in so doing once again found himself embroiled in a major controversy with the officials of the Indian Bureau.

Even before the conclusion of the military campaign, Pope began to criticize the Indian Bureau. In October 1874 while military operations were at their height, Commissioner of Indian Affairs Edward P. Smith gave permission to 400 Pawnee to hunt buffalo in Indian Territory. Pope protested immediately. To send unsuspecting Indians into an area where troops were under orders to attack all Indians who were not at the agencies was unthinkable. "When it is considered," he wrote, "that the Indian Territory is everywhere now the theatre of active hostilities, and that troops, as well as hostile bands of Indians, are to be met anywhere, this action of the Indian Department seems most extraordinary." It was "extraordinary," but as time passed, such decisions no longer surprised the protesting general. [1]

With the arrival of winter Pope became increasingly concerned about the conditions at the Indian agencies at Fort Sill and Darlington. The peaceful Indians were nearly starving, and when Pope met with Sheridan in December to discuss the military campaign, he discussed their condition and raised the question of treatment of the friendly Indians. Sheridan was appalled. "The peaceful Indians have behaved so admirably," he wrote, "that they should not be allowed to suffer." [2]

The friendly Indians did suffer because the Indian Bureau was unable to care for them, a situation not limited to the agencies at Fort Sill and Darlington. All across the West the Bureau was confronted with the specter of starving Indians. Early in January 1875 agents throughout the Central Superintendency were forced to give the Indians permission to leave the reservations to hunt so that they could feed themselves. Because he could not feed them, Agent Haworth sent some Kiowa and Comanche out to hunt, and soon thereafter Superintendent Hoag gave permission to the Osage tribe to follow suit.

Pope responded angrily to these developments because the Kiowa and Comanche were permitted to hunt while the peaceful Arapaho, who had remained at the agency during hostilities, were starving. He was not surprised that the Arapaho were dissatisfied and feared that they might be forced to depredate to avoid death by starvation. It was a question, he said, of whether they would die of hunger on the reservation or at the hands of soldiers, militia, or citizens off the reservation. There was no doubt, he wrote, that the peaceful Indians should be kept at the agencies and fed sufficiently during the campaign. The friendlies were in a serious condition, he explained, and "in their cases, certainly, keeping the peace has paid badly."[3]

As time passed, the problem intensified. Jonathan Richards of the Wichita Agency was forced to send his Indians on a hunt despite protests by the military; and far to the north in Sioux country, Custer reported that Indians at the Standing Rock Agency had been on half rations for two months and would soon be without any.

Sending hunting parties into the war zone was extremely dangerous, since troops were likely to strike them at any time. There was also the possibility that the hunters might join their hostile comrades. In fact, when the Cheyenne and Arapaho were sent on a hunt west of the agency in January 1875, they did meet the main group of hostile Cheyenne and camped with them, but only for a time.

As the new year progressed and large groups of hostiles continued to surrender, the problem of feeding them reached crisis proportions. In February, Pope received orders from Washington to cease issuing supplies to Indians who had surrendered as prisoners of war, but he protested that if he did not feed them, they would starve. He could arm them and send them into the war zone, he commented, but he did not think the government desired this. When Stone Calf and the Southern Cheyenne surrendered, Pope pointed out that as prisoners of war humanity demanded they be fed and clothed until the question of their future status was settled.[4]

The question of feeding and caring for the Indians remained a major issue during the time that General Pope commanded the Department of the Missouri. Pope insisted that it was the duty of the Indian Bureau to care for the Indians, but the Bureau was failing in this task as it had failed to enforce the Peace Policy before the outbreak of hostilities in 1874.

Officials of the Interior Department were not pleased

with Pope's criticisms. Commissioner Smith complained that Pope gave the wrong impression when he said that the Indians were forced either to starve or be hostile. The blame, Smith said, rested with Congress because sufficient funds had not been appropriated. Congress had, in fact, repeatedly refused to deal with specific problems regarding Indians and Indian policy, but the Interior Department had also failed to meet its responsibilities. The department had made no preparation for the return of peace, and steps that were taken to secure funds to care for the Indians were inadequate.[5]

Conditions at agencies in the Central Superintendency did not improve. In April, Colonel Edward Hatch reported that Indians at Fort Sill complained that they were suffering from hunger. He investigated and found the complaint accurate. He explained that the ration had been established when the Indians were in a position to supplement it by hunting, and no provision for issuing a full ration had been made. There was no flour or sugar, and the beef was "shamefully bad." Beef was issued on the hoof, but the animals often broke down before they had been driven the few miles to the camps. Conditions were abominable at the Wichita Agency where the agent was absent and the Indians were killing their horses for food, and they were little different at Darlington where Agent Miles reported that he had four head of cattle but no sugar, coffee, bacon, tobacco, or salt for over 3,000 Indians.[6]

Pope endorsed Hatch's report and immediately forwarded it through channels to Washington in an attempt to stir up some action. He did not expect the Indians to stay on the reservation and starve. "So long as this maladministration of affairs with these Indians exists," he wrote, "the military authorities cannot be, and will not consent to be, held accountable for any outbreak which may occur on their part." The Indian Bureau did not permit these charges to pass unchallenged, and Agent Haworth questioned the validity of the report. Despite the fact that the acting agent had told Hatch the only available beef was "unfit for food" but was all he had, Haworth insisted that the Indians had received ample rations and that the beef was of good quality. He admitted that the regular ration was inadequate and that he lacked flour and sugar, but he also said, "at my agency I do not think that there has been any severe suffering."[7]

It was inconceivable to Pope that Indians should be forced to suffer once they had been driven to the reservations, and he feared that starvation would cause a renewal of the war. "Who can blame them," he wrote, "if, rather than starve to death and see their women and children suffering the pangs of hunger and in slow process of starvation, they break away and get food for them in any manner and as soon as they can." When no improvement occurred, he wrote directly to Sherman and urged the War Department to assume the government's obligation to feed the Indians.[8]

Indian agents in the field also reported the lack of supplies and begged for action. In September 1875 the only food available at Darlington was beef, but the Commissioner of Indian Affairs was remarkably unconcerned. The Indians, he said, had no treaty claims on the government for supplies, and what they did receive was "gratuity." Since the Indians were thoroughly humbled, the Commissioner had no fears that they would go on the warpath. The Secretary of the Interior, however, lacked the confidence of the Commissioner and requested that the army give the agents any supplies they could spare. The whole problem led Sherman to propose that "if the military commanders can have control over the supplies needed by these Indians as they now have over their persons, I am convinced by a recent visit that a condition of peace can be maintained."[9]

Pope kept a watch over affairs in Indian Territory, and he was constantly startled and angered by what he discovered. In November 1875 Agent Miles sent his charges on a buffalo hunt and asked the army to supply the Indians with ammunition. "I would be glad to know where and from whom these Indians procured the fire arms. . ." he told Superintendent Hoag. "Is it the purpose of the Indian Bureau to furnish to these Indians another supply of fire arms to replace those surrendered to the troops, and thus enable them again to commence a war which has only just been brought to a close?" Pope protested vehemently and said that the Indians could kill what buffalo they needed with bows and arrows. If arms and ammunition were furnished by the Indian Bureau, "that Bureau must alone be responsible for the consequences."[10]

Pope's protests that the Indians were suffering produced no results, but the southern tribes managed to avoid starvation by spending the winter months on a hunting expedition although game was scarce. Pope also recognized the fact that failure to feed the Indians delayed their assimilation, for while they were absent on hunts, teachers, missionaries, and farmers could not work with them.

The dangers inherent in this situation became apparent in 1876 when Pope feared that hunger might cause the Southern Cheyenne to join the Sioux. "It is very unfortunate," he wrote to Enoch Hoag's replacement, William Nicholson, "that at this time and in the face of the troubles with the Northern Indians, the Indian Bureau should be unable to buy or otherwise to supply these Southern Indians with food absolutely needed to keep them from starving."[11]

As war swept the northern plains during 1876, Pope was especially concerned with the situation at the Darlington and Fort Sill agencies, for he did not have enough troops to handle emergencies. After the Custer massacre, eighteen companies of cavalry and ten companies of infantry were hurriedly called north, and although Pope was given some artillery companies as replacements, his forces were seriously weakened.

Pope was not the only man to make an issue of the failure to care for the Indians. Although they did not appreciate the tone of his complaints and criticisms, the agents at Darlington and Fort Sill echoed Pope's complaints. They sent their charges out to hunt; they seized cattle by forced sale; and they welcomed supplies received from sympathetic army officers. But their efforts were not enough to prevent hunger. [12]

Supplies of various commodities were either short or missing most of the time, and agents were forced to allow the Indians to leave the reservations to hunt. Hunting parties were often absent for six months at a time, and in November 1877, Agent Miles reported that 3,400 of the 5,000 Indians at Darlington were hunting in the western part of Indian Territory. Game on the southern plains was disappearing so rapidly, however, that the hunters themselves often suffered from hunger. Pope reported that the Cheyenne and Arapaho managed to eke out a bare subsistence during a six-month hunt in 1877, but that on their return the supplies ostensibly for the entire year were barely sufficient to furnish them with half rations for the remaining six months. [13]

Year after year, the agents repeatedly declared that rations were inadequate and begged for a larger appropriation, but Congress refused to provide funds. In 1881 the Kiowa-Comanche agent reported that the yearly appropriation provided supplies for only eight months and that the Indians went hungry for two to three days each week. In 1882 the agent wrote, "There is no doubt that there is actual suffering among these Indians, that they are without anything to eat during a part of each week." The Indian Bureau was forced, however, to issue orders to the Southern Cheyenne, Arapaho, Kiowa, and Comanche agents that the beef ration must be reduced by one-third. [14]

That last order brought Pope into the struggle once more, and he angrily warned Washington, "The Indians cannot live on this amount of beef." Rations were barely sufficient to prevent starvation, and to reduce them further was unthinkable. "Are they expected to suffer the pangs of hunger in the midst of plenty without complaining?" he asked. "Will they refrain from satisfying their absolute needs by levying by force, or otherwise, on the herds around them?" Pope fully expected the Indians to slaughter beef from cattle herds in and around the reservations to provide their families with food, and he requested orders to clarify the duty of the army on this matter. Were the troops "to be used to compel these hungry wretches to submit to hunger and suffering in such a manner and for such reasons?" he asked. Pope's anger was aroused. "I can state with full conviction that I have never known a case in which Indians have been so plainly or so unnecessarily driven to do wrong," he wrote. He had no desire to order his troops to perform the "hateful duty" of forcing the Indians to starve. It was "unreasonable and indefensible," he said, that five thousand peaceful Indians should be driven to hostilities by the lack of food costing such an insignificant sum, and "almost any responsibility ought to be assumed to prevent it." [15]

Pope had a deep and honest concern for the welfare of

the Indians, and as no department in Washington seemed willing to assume the responsibility for preventing trouble, he knowingly exceeded his authority to provide a temporary solution. "Indians, like white men, are not reconciled to starve peacefully," he declared, and ordered the post commander at Fort Reno to supplement the rations for the Southern Cheyenne and Arapaho for one week. He also arranged for cattlemen who had large herds in the vicinity of the agency to furnish beef on a weekly basis without guarantee of payment. All Pope could promise was that he would use every influence to see that they were paid. A similar arrangement was made by the Kiowa-Comanche agent, and another crisis passed without depredations and bloodshed. [16]

When Indians were absent from the reservations for long periods of time, the process of assimilation was retarded. In 1876, Agent Haworth had protested, "If Congress fails to furnish the necessary means and the old 'hand to mouth way' has to be continued, no matter how good the management or how faithful and earnest those who work among them may be, they can accomplish but little." Haworth's successor very quickly reached the same conclusion. Some of the Indians had acquired herds of cattle, but when hungry, they slaughtered their cattle to feed their families despite the protests of the agent. He attempted to stop this practice by prohibiting the traders from purchasing any hides which did not have the brand of the Indian Department, but the Indians were quite ingenious in circumventing this. One tribesman, who learned to read and write while a prisoner in Florida, simply forged the brand. [17]

To keep the Indians, especially tribes with warrior traditions such as the Kiowa and Comanche, on the edge of subsistence was a dangerous practice. There was, however, surprisingly little trouble in the years following the hostilities of 1874 and 1875. The military campaign impressed upon the Indians the power of the government and its determination to keep them on the reservations and punish them for their crimes, but the precautionary measures which Pope took also helped to prevent trouble. He maintained strong garrisons in Indian Territory and constructed new military posts at strategic locations. Fort Reno near the Cheyenne-Arapaho Agency, Fort Elliott in the Texas Panhandle, and a cantonment on the North Fork of the Canadian River did much to control the Indians.

In preparing for any emergencies, Pope also gave orders to his post commanders in Indian Territory to supersede the agents and take any action necessary to prevent an outbreak. His primary desire was to disarm and dismount the Indians, but this he was unable to accomplish because they had to supplement their meager rations by hunting. If the Indians were well fed, they could be disarmed and required to remain near the agency, and thus be in a position for assimilation. The fact that the Indians were forced to hunt, however, kept Pope and his troops constantly on the alert. "No man can tell," he said, "whether they will hunt buffalo or people." Pope did urge that the warriors be given muzzle-loading muskets in exchange for their rifles. Muskets were adequate for hunting, and he saw no reason why the Indians should have large quantities of the newest repeating rifles. [18]

Hunger, when added to other causes of discontent, could be serious as the case of the Northern Cheyenne, who had been removed to Indian Territory in 1877, demonstrated. Pope gave orders that the Northern Cheyenne be disarmed and dismounted before they were turned over to the agent at Darlington, but this order was suspended because of promises made to them before they had been sent south. The Northern Cheyenne had many reasons for discontent: short rations, sickness, and the desire to return to their homeland. In September 1878 Dull Knife led about 300 Indians from the reservation and began the long flight to the north. When Pope learned of the escape, he ordered his troops in pursuit. But his department had been stripped of cavalry during the Sioux war in 1876, and infantry units and the few available cavalry troops were unable to prevent their escape.[19]

The Northern Cheyenne who remained in the Indian Territory continued to be troublesome and dissatisfied, constantly threatening that they, also, might attempt to return to the north. Pope, on the one hand, ordered the troops at Fort Reno to seize the warriors at the first hint of flight, but, on the other hand, he also suggested that the government permit them to return home. They disrupted life at the agency and hindered the progress of the other Indians, but the Indian Bureau insisted that they remain at Darlington.

In 1881 this decision was reversed, but only part of the tribe, those under Little Chief, was permitted to move to the Sioux Reservation at Pine Ridge. In 1883 the remainder of the tribe followed, and the disturbing influence of the Northern Cheyenne was finally removed.

Time and again during the 1870s and the early 1880s Pope pondered over the disposition of his troops, studied the Indian problem, and worked for improvement in the government's treatment of the Indian. On the frontier for years, he had watched policies change, suggested numerous reforms that had been disregarded, and still saw no solution. He exhibited a humane attitude and a desire for justice for the Indian, and he earnestly sought to improve their lot and prevent suffering. His primary goal, like that of the humanitarians and the officials in the Indian Bureau, was assimilation, and he offered knowledgeable suggestions as to how this could best be accomplished, but his words made no impact. The Indian Bureau and its humanitarian supporters had made up their minds that the Indians must become farmers and ignored the advice and criticism of the men in the field—like Pope—who offered wiser solutions.

General Pope was an expert on the plains region, having led exploratory and survey parties across the region in the 1850s and having served long years in the West before, during, and after the Civil War. He had always had strong doubts regarding the prospects of agriculture in the dry and barren plains region, and although he watched the settlers surge westward after the Civil War and observed them spreading along the river valleys in Kansas, he still doubted that farming would be successful without water.

At the conclusion of the military campaign of 1875, Pope proposed that the Indians, the Southern Cheyenne in particular, be moved eastward where they could be fed at low cost. He pointed out that the savings in transportation costs alone would enable the government to feed them adequately. Sheridan at first opposed the proposals, but when he understood the relationship of hunger to hostilities, he changed his mind. In 1876 he saw starvation drive many of the reservation Sioux into the hostile camp, and with the conclusion of the Sioux war he fought to have the Sioux reservations located on the Missouri River where transportation costs would be insignificant. [20]

Pope never ceased making suggestions to improve the lot of the Indians, and with his knowledge of the plains and the character of the nomadic Indians, he opposed their conversion into farmers. "These Indians cannot be made self-supporting within any calculable time," he reasoned, "and the sooner that fact is recognized the sooner will the management of them be made to conform to the commonest dictates of humanity." The process of teaching them to support themselves and of preparing them to take their place in white society would be long and difficult, he maintained, and the first step should be to convert them into a pastoral people rather than into farmers.[21]

The Indian tribes, he further explained, were not "precisely alike" and should not be treated as such. "Among tribes so diversely employed we must of course expect to find diversity of life, of habits, and of ideas," he wrote, "and it seems to me essential to any success in civilizing the wild tribes, that a careful study of such matters be made for each tribe, so as best to determine the kind of occupation most suitable, and which would be least at variance with former habits of life." The nomadic plains tribes had a strong warrior tradition, and they were hunters with no interest in agriculture. "It would be (as, indeed it has been found) as difficult to force the nomadic Indians. . .to undergo the daily toil of such plowing and hoeing and reaping as are necessary for the cultivation of a farm," he said, "as it would be to force an Arab or a Tartar to adopt so artificial a mode of life."

Teach them to be stock raisers, he urged, and the first significant step toward assimilation would be accomplished. Those reservations that are unsuited for agriculture could support large herds of animals, and the Indians would soon discover that herding was profitable. In time, he pointed out, they would be able to support themselves, and in so doing would develop an understanding of property ownership which they lacked.[22]

For several years, officials in the Indian Bureau failed to grasp the wisdom of Pope's suggestions, and humanitarian groups in the East never did take cognizance of Pope's experience or heed his advice. The humanitarians were determined to transform warriors who had fought under such great chiefs as Lone Wolf, Stone Calf, Dull Knife, and Red Cloud into peaceful farmers and landowners, and they expected to accomplish this in a few years. The politicians who ran the Interior Department and the Indian Bureau concurred in these views, and for over two decades they fought for legislation which would authorize the allotment of land to individual Indians.

With a notable lack of success, the Indian agents on the reservations did their best to teach the nomadic tribes to become farmers. As time passed, they agreed with Pope. James Haworth, for example, commented in his 1877 annual report, "Five years' experience and observation satisfy me that this is not a good agricultural district, and cannot be relied upon for farming. . . ." As drought and crop failures followed year after year and the Indians who tried their hand at farming gave up in disgust, Haworth's successors and the agents at Darlington echoed his views. "The Indians, as also myself," reported John Miles in 1881, "have become completely discouraged in their efforts to obtain a living from the cultivation of the soil." A year earlier the Kiowa-Comanche agent had remarked that he was convinced that even experienced farmers would have been discouraged after the past three seasons. [23]

The problem was not limited to the agencies in Indian Territory, but was common to all the reservations on the semi-arid high plains. Explorers labeled the Great Plains the "Great American Desert," and after years of repeated crop failures it is probable that most of the agents in the region would have agreed. The outspoken agent at Pine Ridge, V. T. McGillycuddy, had some hard words to say about farming on the high plains. "White men well trained in farming have tried to till the soil in this vicinity in Northern Nebraska and have lost all the money invested, and have not produced enough to pay for the seed. I can confidently venture to state that, if the experiment were tried of placing 7,000 white people on this land, with seed, agricultural implements, and one year's subsistence, at the end of that time they would die of starvation, if they had to depend on their crops for their sustenance."[24]

Pope's ideas on how best to teach the Indians to be self-supporting and how to prepare them for assimilation were not heeded despite similar recommendations from the Indian agents in the field, but the termination of hostilities on the southern plains in 1875 presented Pope with an opportunity to test his theory on a small scale. During the campaign and with the surrender of the hostiles, the army confiscated large numbers of the Indians' ponies. Some were given to Indian scouts who served with the troops; some were returned to their owners, and some were sold at auction. Since the ponies did not sell at their true value, the income from these sales did not amount to much, but the use which Pope made of this money was significant. Some of the funds were used to purchase supplies for the Indians while they were held by the army as prisoners of war, and he turned some over to the U.S. Treasury Department. At the Kiowa-Comanche Agency, however, Pope and Mackenzie also put some of the money to yet another use. About 10,000 animals taken from the hostile bands of the Kiowa and Comanche had brought in about $29,000, and approximately $3,500 of that sum was turned over to the Treasury Department. The remainder, $25,500, was used to purchase livestock for the two tribes.

Mackenzie, who had come under Pope's command with the addition of Fort Sill to the Department of the Missouri, purchased several thousand sheep in New Mexico Territory and distributed them to the Indians in 1875. This experiment was disastrous because the warriors discovered they did not like mutton and the women had no inclination to become weavers. In the following year Mackenzie purchased cattle rather than sheep, and the Indians willingly began to care for their livestock. The experiment was a remarkable success. Agent Haworth praised the army for its work and, noting the "peculiar fitness of the Indians for stock-raising," secured even more cattle for the tribal herd. Although the army made a start in teaching the Indians to become stockmen, it was on a small scale. Despite the desire of the agents to expand the herd, little was done to purchase a sufficient number of cattle to prevent the warriors from having to slaughter their animals in time of need. The agents attempted to impress upon them the value of maintaing their herds, but when hungry women and children cried, the Indians thought only of feeding their families. [25]

When Pope left the Department of the Missouri to command the more prestigious Division of the Pacific in 1883, the condition of the Indians had improved little. During the thirteen years which Pope served in the Department of the Missouri, he waged a continuous battle with the Indian Bureau over the treatment of the Indians. In the early years of the 1870s Pope sought to make the Indians uncomfortable when they were absent from the reservations and to have them punished for their crimes. At the conclusion of hostilities in 1875 he struggled to make them comfortable when they were on the reservations. He begged and borrowed to provide them with food, and he spent nine years writing letters of criticism and suggestions.

CHAPTER ELEVEN

"That old
philanthropic humbug"

During the years from 1870-83 that General John Pope commanded the Department of the Missouri, he was concerned with the Indian problem throughout the far-flung reaches of his command. For thirteen years he dealt with the peaceful Cherokee and the troublesome Warm Springs and Mescalero Apache as well as the Cheyenne, Kiowa, and Comanche. In subsequent years he commanded the Division of the Pacific, and although the region and the Indian tribes were different, the problems were basically the same. What was to be done with the Indians? How were they to be controlled? How were they to be prepared for assimilation? Would the government develop a carefully planned, long-range policy, or would it continue to act only when necessity demanded? These were the questions which concerned him.

The Cheyenne, Kiowa, and Comanche occupied much of Pope's attention during the 1870s, but similar problems existed in the mountain and desert country in the western part of his department, and as the years progressed they became increasingly serious. Here again the Indian Bureau appeared to lack knowledge and seemed unable to act wisely. Pope protested against what he considered stupid policies and offered his suggestions while the settlers raised a cacophony of protest.

212

During his years in the West, Pope opposed the repeated removals of various Indian tribes, but officials of the Indian Bureau were slow in recognizing the wisdom of his views. Removals continued to be carried out and invariably caused trouble and bloodshed. This proved especially true of the Apache of New Mexico Territory. The Apache had been hostile from the time of their first contact with the white man. They fought the Spaniards and the Mexicans, and following the acquisition of the Southwest in the Treaty of Guadalupe Hidalgo they fought the Americans. They were, Pope said, "the most squalid, cowardly, thieving Indians I know," but these opinions were mild compared with those held by New Mexicans, who feared that the Apache were making sections of the territory "like unto the valley of the shadow of death" and insisted that these "gorgons of the mountains" be "hunted to their holes."[1]

Concomitant with the removal policy was the failure of the reservation system. Indian agencies were scattered throughout the territory, but the government had not provided reservations for the vast majority of the tribes, and when reservations were created, they rarely were used by the Indians except as a place of refuge. Lacking permanent homes, the Indians roamed the countryside. In 1871, for example, a new agent for the Mescalero Apache found only 27 Indians in the vicinity of the agency. Not until 1873 was a reservation created for the tribe.

The Mescalero, who had an agency near Fort Stanton, and the Warm Springs Apache, who had their agency at Cañada Alamosa on the west side of the Rio Grande in southern New Mexico, were the most troublesome Indians in the territory, and as deaths and thefts multiplied, the settlers called for help. Suffering was greatest in the southwestern portion of the territory despite the concentration of military posts in that region. These Indians are "picking off our best citizens," one settler asserted, "and Congress laughs at our calamities, and the friends of the savages shed maudlin tears, in New York City, over the wrongs that the 'Noble Red Men' suffer."[2]

The thin line of troops scattered throughout the territory was ineffective in protecting life and property, and although there were demands for new military posts and additional soldiers, the people of the territory understood the problems that the understaffed army faced and often praised the troops for their efforts. There was, however, talk of buying Henry rifles and dealing with the Indians themselves. If the army could not maintain peace, the people were ready to "take it into our own hands and kill them, without regard to 'Uncle Samuel' and his handful of soldiers."[3]

New Mexicans aimed their criticisms at eastern humanitarians, their political supporters, and anyone who considered an Apache a "noble red man." One citizen asked, "Why don't the Peace Commission come out here and sit a while? The wet-rag Miss Nancy milk-sops would learn something about Indians if they would only come out this way. They are now like persons who never came into contact with fluid but are setting themselves up as teachers of swimming." Another irate citizen commented that a hungry Apache was as voracious as a black beetle and as dangerous as "the sweetest mannered man that ever cut a throat or scuttled a ship." He admitted that there were those who denied this and believed that the Indians were "as gentle as sucking doves" if left alone, but he questioned the validity of their point of view. "I know very little of the dusky sons myself, having my scalp entire," he said, "but the gentleman with the peeled skull. . .says that the American Indian is not exactly the paragon that some, who never saw him, paint him.'"[4]

Judging from the editorials and letters in the *Daily New Mexican* and other territorial newspapers, New Mexicans in the early 1870s agreed with the stated goals of the Peace Policy. They wanted the Indians placed on reservations and kept there. When raids continued, however, the frontiersmen demanded that the Indians be exterminated.[5]

In the summer of 1871 the government decided to settle the Apache trouble in New Mexico and Arizona territories. The massacre of a group of peaceful Apache at Camp Grant, Arizona, shocked the government into action, and Vincent Colyer, secretary of the Board of Indian Commissioners, was sent to the Southwest to establish reservations for the various Apache bands and to end the Indian troubles in that region.

New Mexicans had already singled out Colyer scornfully, calling him "this braying donkey," this "puritanical Collyer [sic]", and they did not welcome his visit to the territory. Under the headline, "Humbug," the *Daily New Mexican* announced, "We regret to learn that that old philanthropic humbug, Vincent Colyer, is about to inflict another visit upon our unfortunate Territory." Let us have more soldiers and fewer men of the Colyer stripe, the editors said. "We want no commissioner who does not know the difference between a war dance around a scalped victim, suspended over a slow fire, and a religious ceremony," they wrote. They preferred that he travel from Mesilla to Tucson without a military escort and without letting the Indians know that he was a peace messenger, and they were willing to wager that "his scalp will prove the occasion of one of the finest religious demonstrations ever witnessed in the Apache nation." [6]

Vincent Colyer toured the Southwest with a military escort and established reservations for the Apache bands in Arizona and New Mexico territories. New Mexicans were willing to give the reservation system a fair trial, and Pope was pleased that reserves were finally created, but events quickly demonstrated that the Apache problem had not been solved.

The reservation selected by Colyer for the Warm Springs Apache was in the Tularosa Valley in western New Mexico, but it proved an immediate failure although the army cooperated fully with the Indian Bureau. Pope ordered his district commander, Colonel Gordon Granger, to personally attend the removal of the 1,600 Indians from Cañada Alamosa to Warm Springs, but the Indians were so opposed to leaving Cañada Alamosa that only 450 made the journey.[7]

In the following year General Oliver O. Howard, the courageous one-armed "Christian Soldier," who had headed the Freedman's Bureau, visited the Southwest. Armed with extensive powers, Howard attempted to solve the Apache problem. The general managed to convince Cochise to move his Chiricahua Apache to the newly established Tularosa Reservation, but he accomplished little else besides irritating and angering Pope and General George Crook of the Department of Arizona. When Howard visited the Tularosa Reservation, he realized that the Indians would not remain there. He halted the military movements which were designed to force the Indians to the reserve and gave the tribesmen passes to return to Cañada Alamosa. When Pope learned of this development, he reacted so furiously that he was reprimanded for his "strong condemnation" of the high-ranking general. Howard had, in effect, caused the abandonment of the Tularosa Reservation, and Pope protested because the

Apache were roaming the countryside. These developments meant that the new post at Tularosa was worthless and that Fort McRae near Cañada Alamosa would have to be reoccupied. Pope argued that the government must be consistent and that a policy must be decided upon and carried out, but policies toward the Warm Springs Apache were anything but consistent.[8]

The Tularosa Reservation was continued even though the Apache used it mainly as a place of refuge. In 1874 the Indians were moved to a new reservation at Ojo Caliente, which was virtually identical with their location before Colyer had arrived. The agent, Benjamin Thomas, noted some difference in the Indians at the time of this removal. During the past year, he said, they had changed "from a condition to be compared with that of very wild beasts of prey, with many of the vices of human beings superadded, to that of uncivilized, indolent, cruel human beings. . . ." He was pleased with this development because "they have not offered, on any occasion during the year, to shoot the agent or any of the employees." This was an improvement, for during the previous year agency employees had been constantly threatened and forced to dodge flying arrows.[9]

In succeeding years the condition of the Warm Springs Apache changed very little, and because of depredations, Pope urged that they be disarmed and dismounted. Since there was no game in the area, the Indians had no need for firearms, "except to shoot other people," but no action was taken on Pope's suggestion. In 1877 Agent John Clum of the San Carlos Reservation in Arizona, captured Geronimo at Ojo Caliente and, acting on orders from the Indian Bureau, removed all the Indians from Ojo Caliente to San Carlos. This experiment at concentration did not work because the Warm Springs Apache absolutely refused to remain at San Carlos. They broke away, were rounded up by

217

the army and sent back despite Pope's warning that they had an "invincible objection" to returning and that they would break out again. Pope's predictions soon came true. [10]

Victorio, chief of the Warm Springs band, broke away several times and occupied the attention of troops in the District of New Mexico. The badly undermanned Ninth Cavalry had, since 1875, been responsible for the safety of the entire district, and the Ninth's weary black troopers chased Victorio and other renegades all over southern New Mexico. Searching for a solution to this problem, Pope unsuccessfully sought permission to pursue the Indians into Mexico and once more recommended military control of hostiles. In September 1879 Victorio broke away from the Mescalero Reservation, taking a number of Mescalero with him, and shortly after, Pope secured the cooperation of the Interior Department in the use of military force to control the Mescalero. In April 1880 the Ninth Cavalry, assisted by additional troops from the Department of Texas, succeeded in disarming and dismounting the Mescalero and in separating Victorio from them. This effort plus constant pursuit eventually forced Victorio into Mexico where he was killed by troops under Colonel Joaquin Terrazas.[11] Pope not only blamed the Indian Bureau for the troubles with the Warm Springs Apache but also found ample opportunity to criticize the entire managment of Indian affairs in New Mexico.

The Cimarron Agency in northeastern New Mexico offers another example of Pope's struggle with short-sighted Indian Bureau policies. The agency was located on private land on the Maxwell Grant. When the grant was sold in 1870, settlers moved in and demanded that the Jicarilla Apache and Muache Ute who were located there should be removed. Although the agency was discontinued in 1876, the Indians were not removed until 1878. Over the objections of Pope, who realized that it would probably require force to make the Jicarilla leave their old agency, the Jicarilla were taken to the Mescalero Reservation near Fort Stanton, and the Muache Ute were moved to the Southern Ute Agency in Colorado.

Force was not needed to make the peaceful Jicarilla leave the Cimarron Agency, but only a few of them went to the Mescalero Reservation. The majority gradually made their way to the Abiquiu Agency in the northern part of the territory where other members of the tribe were located. The Indian Bureau and the army spent several years gathering up the Jicarilla who repeatedly returned to their old homes. In 1883 the Indian Bureau once more had the Jicarilla removed to the Mescalero Reservation, but finally in 1887, the Bureau consented to their return to northern New Mexico and established a reservation for them just south of the Colorado-New Mexico boundary.

The treatment of the Jicarilla Apache in the 1870s and 1880s was just one example of the Indian Bureau's inconsistent policies that Pope so often questioned. Other difficulties also developed during these years in other regions of Pope's department. One of the long-term problems was that of white intrusion on the Indian reservations. Although this had long been a chronically irritating issue, it became acute in the late 1870s and the 1880s when the Boomer Movement to open the "Oklahoma District" in Indian Territory to white settlers reached it peak.

Throughout the 1870s Pope had sent his soldiers to expel white squatters from the various Indian reservations in his department, and in 1871 he finally admitted that this was "the most difficult and vexatious" question he faced. At that time he asked the War Department to define the duties and authority of the army in relation to the intrusion issue and pointed out the dangers in allowing the problem to continue. Wrongs were being committed against the Indians on their own reservations, and he explained it was certain that "the Indians will not be slow to do the same to the whites."

Pope believed that the "troublesome and complicated" question of intrusion could not be settled by military authorities and that it was "beyond the management, or even the comprehension" of the average Indian agent. The army could, and did, remove squatters, but this often resulted in court proceedings that invariably favored the settlers.

With reservation boundaries often unmarked and with local courts prejudiced in favor of the squatters, intrusion was indeed a "troublesome and complicated" question, and Pope was not at all sure what role the army should play. He believed that the situation had passed beyond the "legitimate province" of the army, and he considered the Indian agents as "helpless and useless" in meeting it. Indian agents were as a rule "not characterized by much wisdom or knowledge of law or good policy," and Pope did not wish to have his soldiers violating the law simply because the agents requested action. When squatters were removed by troops at the request of Indian agents, it was the Army which suffered, for the soldiers not only endured the condemnation of the frontier population, but were also subject to legal action. Pope therefore requested "careful and detailed" instructions to provide for the adjudication of the problem by legal means, and he further suggested that the civilized tribes in Indian Territory should have an organized civil government.[12]

When the Boomer Movement began, thousands of prospective settlers headed for Indian Territory under the leadership of men like David Payne who were determined to open the land for settlement. The situation was so serious in 1879 that President Rutherford B. Hayes issued a proclamation on April 26, warning white invaders of Indian reservations that they would be expelled by force. Sherman considered the danger great enough to suggest that either Pope or Sheridan be present on the border, but neither proclamations nor threats stopped David Payne.[13]

The Hayes proclamation did bring an outburst from another leader of the Boomer Movement, Charles Carpenter, who had been involved in illegal invasion of the Indian reservations in the Black Hills some years earlier. The bombastic Carpenter announced that he did not care a "fig" for "General Bull Run Pope," who would enforce the President's order, and he challenged the general to settle the matter by "the Western Code." Carpenter proclaimed that "Bull Run Pope" might arrest him, "but unless he cuts a better figure on the frontier than he did at Bull Run there will be a hellitisplit retreat, and it won't be Carpenter's expedition." Despite his words Carpenter declined to test Pope's powers; others, however, were not so hesitant.

Nearly a year later, on February 12, 1880, President Hayes reaffirmed his policy with a new proclamation against the invasion of Indian Territory by white settlers, but David Payne disregarded it. On several occasions Payne led his followers into the forbidden area, and each time Pope strengthened army patrols in the region. Each time Payne and his followers were arrested, tried, and fined. Since the Boomers were without funds, however, they were released without paying their fines. Pope repeatedly asked for more effective legislation and penalties for such men, at the same time doing everything in his power to keep intruders off Indian lands. He insisted that "some adequate punishment for these offenders should be provided," but Congress refused to act, and eventually the Boomers succeeded in opening Indian Territory to settlement.[14]

White intrusion on Indian lands existed in varying degrees throughout the West, and it was one of several factors that disrupted the government's relations with the Ute Indians of Colorado. The Ute were always remarkably peaceful in their relationships with the whites, but the white man wanted their land. Governor Edward McCook, ex officio Superintendent of Indian Affairs for Colorado Territory, remarked in 1871, "I believe that God gave us the earth, and the fullness thereof, in order that we might utilize and enjoy his gifts. I do not believe in donating to these indolent savages the best portion of my Territory. . . ." [15]

The people of Colorado Territory concurred and demanded that the Ute lands be opened for agriculture and mining. Colorado was rich in gold and silver, and the miners refused to be stopped by reservation boundaries. The mountains must be opened, Coloradans believed. They talked of opening the area "by force of arms" and said, "an Indian has no more right to stand in the way of civilization and progress than a wolf or bear." They considered the Ute a "bragging, stealing, vagabondish, miserable" people, and gradually the government met the demands of the Coloradans by releasing more and more land through a series of treaties with the Ute Indians.[16]

The Indians were alarmed at the failure of the government to meet its treaty obligations, and when trouble threatened, Pope stepped in to maintain peace. Aware that the Ute were peaceful, he wanted to avoid war, and in 1871 when the Ute refused to go to their new reservation, he suggested that they be given an opportunity to air their grievances and that the Indian Bureau attempt to satisfy them before force was used. Again in 1873 when difficulties between the Ute and the settlers increased, Pope suggested that the Superintendent of Indian Affairs visit the Ute in person to listen to their requests and to calm their fears. [17]

Although military forces in the Department of the Missouri were occupied with the Apache of New Mexico and with the hostile tribes of the southern plains, Pope did his best to expel intruders from Ute lands and to quiet the people of Colorado. Fort Garland at the base of the Sangre de Cristo Mountains in the San Luis Valley was the only military post in the mountains of Colorado, which reflects the peaceful nature of the Ute, but as white pressure increased in the mid-1870s, Pope began to send cavalry patrols into South and Middle Parks and along the San Juan River. He also recommended that a new post be established in the San Juan region to replace Fort Garland.

With the continued development of the mining industry in southwestern Colorado, Pope became more insistent that the government decide what to do with the Ute. Although they had three separate and widely scattered agencies in western Colorado, the Ute rarely remained on their lands. Pope explained that a large military force would be required to keep them on the reservation, but troops were not available. Since white men were "not likely to be deterred by the imaginary line of an Indian reservation" in their hunt for gold, he expected trouble.

It was evident to Pope that the situation in western Colorado was becoming critical. He was especially concerned because the Ute agencies were so scattered and isolated, for he lacked manpower to place troops at each of them. As the region was "wholly irresistible" to whites, he said, it was "next to impossible" to prevent intrusion on Indian lands, nor was it possible to leave the Ute where they were without constant collisions and outrages by both whites and Indians. The safety of both races required a change of location. Pope repeatedly recommended that the Ute agencies be consolidated in a region where they would be left alone.[18] The area along the Colorado-New Mexico border drained by the Chama, Navajo, and Blanco rivers seemed ideal. It was not valued as a mining region but was accessible to the railroad. Equally important was the fact that Pope would then need only one military post to watch all the Ute. This was an important consideration because of the widespread need for troops, and the point was driven home in 1878 when troops were requested at the Uncompahgre Agency. Pope normally had one company of cavalry at Fort Garland, but even that unit was unavailable because it was being used to control the Jicarilla Apache in New Mexico.[19]

Officials of the Indian Bureau were certainly in favor of concentration and believed that if all the Indians were collected on a few reservations conditions would improve. In February 1878, the Indian Bureau planned to move the Ute to Indian Territory, but before the move was made Congress acted to require the location of all the Ute at the White River Agency in an isolated region of northwestern Colorado. Pope was dismayed by this choice. He doubted that the large Uncompahgre and southern Ute bands would peacefully move to so remote a region. White River, he said, "is the worst point I know for an Indian Agency and Military Post involving the maximum of expense with the minimum of goods." For once the Indian Bureau agreed with the critical general, for the Commissioner of Indian Affairs remarked that it was a mystery why White River had been selected by Congress.[20]

Pope's suggestions were accepted in part in 1878 when the Southern Ute were offered and accepted a reservation in the area along the Colorado-New Mexico border that he had chosen. But agreements were not reached with the other Ute bands. Colonel Edward Hatch, commander of the Ninth Cavalry and of the District of New Mexico, participated in the Ute Commission of 1878 and represented his commanding officer's views. In addition, Pope conferred with Agent Nathan Meeker at White River and with Colorado officials and personally selected the site for a new military post at Pagosa Springs. Patrols were also increased, and Captain Francis S. Dodge, who was scouting in Middle Park, was instructed to proceed to the White River Agency if danger should arise there. Despite these precautions, however, the Uncompahgre Ute killed Meeker and other agency employees and pinned down the relief column sent from Fort Fred Steele under Major Thomas Thornburgh.

The Meeker massacre presented an unusual situation, for although the agency was in the Department of the Missouri, the only adequate military force in the vicinity was in the Department of the Platte under General George Crook. Thornburgh's command, in fact, came from Crook's department, and the first information of the uprising came through Crook's headquarters. It was Crook, therefore, who dispatched Colonel Wesley Merritt and a large force to White River while troops from Pope's command were concentrated in southern Colorado.

The Ute outbreak at White River and fear of a general Indian war came at an unusually inopportune time, for Pope faced numerous other dangers. He was deeply concerned about continued activity by Oklahoma Boomers and their potential impact on the tribes in Indian Territory. At the same time he was forced to keep a watchful eye on the discontented Northern Cheyenne who might emulate Dull Knife and return to the north. In addition, there were numerous trouble spots in New Mexico Territory where many Jicarilla Apache were wandering about and where the Navajo were demonstrating increasing displeasure with their agent, Galen Eastman. More serious was Victorio's return to the warpath in September 1879 and the support he received from the Mescalero Apache. It is not surprising, therefore, that Pope was perturbed when he learned of hostilities in Colorado.

Pope rushed troops to White River and permitted Colonel Edward Hatch to participate in a new commission organized to negotiate with the Ute. Pope feared for the lives of the commissioners, a concern shared by Ouray, chief of the Uncompahgre Ute and a member of the commission, and told Ranald S. Mackenzie, who commanded Pope's troops in Colorado, "If Hatch escapes alive from the trap he is in, I shall be rejoiced."[2][1] Bloodshed was avoided, however, because of the influence of Ouray, the work of the commissioners, and the massing of troops in Colorado. Once agreements were made for the removal of the White River and Uncompahgre Ute, Pope took great precautions to prevent trouble. Mackenzie was given ample strength to carry out the removal of the Uncompahgre Ute, and Pope himself proceeded toward the scene although the Apache war in southern New Mexico caused him to stop at Fort Garland where he was in contact with the telegraph. Mackenzie, operating with a relatively free hand, managed the removal with great skill.

Troops in the Department of the Missouri, occupied with the Ute and other problems, were in no position to deal with fresh hostilities elsewhere. But when the large and powerful Navajo tribe threatened hostilities, Pope was forced to deal with the situation. He did not want to let Galen Eastman, the Navajo agent at Fort Defiance, New Mexico, create a crisis similar to the one Meeker had produced at White River. Eastman, like Meeker, was the type of agent who attempted to force the Indians in his charge to do what he wanted, and he managed only to arouse their hostility. He attempted to "control them in their amusements" and force them to conform to his religious beliefs by withholding their supplies. Pope protested immediately at the first threat of trouble. He would not judge whether Eastman was a saint or a sinner, he wrote, but he predicted that if he were retained, there might be another Meeker massacre. When the situation worsened, Pope acted immediately. He sent Colonel George P. Buell and all the military forces in southern Colorado to Fort Wingate by forced march; he then deposed Eastman and placed Captain Frank Bennett of the Ninth Cavalry in temporary charge of the agency. Bennett, who had previously served as Navajo agent, was liked and respected by the Indians, and under his regime the danger quickly subsided. [22]

When Pope placed Bennett in charge of the agency, he begged that a new agent be chosen who knew the Indians and who was able to hold their confidence. He was shocked and disappointed when the Indian Bureau reinstated Eastman as the Navajo agent. Eastman was "a psalm-singing hypocrite whom Navajoes despised and whom they tried to kill," and troubles commenced again with his return. When it appeared that a full-scale war had broken out with the Apache in Arizona in August, Pope feared that the angry Navajo might join the Apache, and again he acted without delay. He sent Captain Bennett back to the agency in hopes that his influence might restrain the Navajo, while Mackenzie and four companies of the Fourth Cavalry were hurriedly withdrawn from the task of removing the Uncompahgre Ute from Colorado and sent to Fort Wingate. [23]

The Eastman affair demonstrated one of the major problems that the Indian Bureau faced throughout the West because Congress was largely responsible for the quality of the agents in the field. Even the religious denominations found it difficult to secure able men for $1,500 a year, which was less than the salary of a village postmaster or a third-class clerk in Washington. Virtually everyone connected with the Indian problem urged that salaries be raised. The Secretary of the Interior, the Commissioner of Indian Affairs, army officers, and the agents themselves begged for higher salaries, but Congress refused to consider the matter. It is little wonder that graft was rampant in the Indian service and that there was a great turnover at the agencies.

The Indian Bureau had always been plagued by inept agents. For example, in 1862 at the time of the Sioux outbreak in Minnesota, Lucius Walker, the Chippewa agent, believed that his Indians were planning to go to war. He abandoned the agency and fled to Fort Ripley and then continued toward St. Paul. During his flight, he encountered William Dole, the Commissioner of Indian Affairs, but by then he was almost incoherent. Soon after he left the startled and confused commissioner, the distracted agent ended his life with a pistol shot. [24]

In 1871 there were difficulties at the Los Pinos Ute Agency in Colorado, and the Ute were demanding the removal of their agent. A special agent of the Indian Bureau investigated and reported that the agent was merely eccentric rather than insane as rumored. The agent had walked from Denver to the agency, a distance of about 300 miles. The Ute, unconcerned whether the agent was insane or eccentric, wanted him removed, and Ouray, the great Ute chief, promised to go all the way to Washington to see the President about the matter if necessary. [25]

Indian agents were often absent from their posts for long periods of time, and to Pope it appeared that they were always absent when most needed. During the winter of 1874-75 the Mescalero Apache agent, who apparently was afraid of his Indians, was absent, and he had left his son, "a mere boy," in charge. Later when a group of citizens attacked the Mescalero and stole some horses, the agent refused to give the army any assistance. "In fact he took no apparent interest in the matter nor showed any disposition to act," the post commander at Fort Stanton reported. Pope and his officers requested that a reliable man be appointed, but the Indian Bureau supported that agent, and he remained in office. [26]

While Pope commanded the Division of the Pacific in 1884, he again was forced to deal with troubles resulting from activities of an Indian agent. The agent at the Yakima Reservation was tyrannical and brutal. In an attempt to force the Indians to send their children to school, the agent seized parents, placed them in irons, and fed them on bread and water. When army officers investigated the situation, the agent angrily informed them, "My word is law. I will punish any man on the Reservation as I see fit to do." Pope again requested that a wiser and more reasonable man be sent as agent for the Yakima, but his advice was ignored. [27]

CHAPTER TWELVE

"The army
gets the cuffs
from both sides"

On a clear spring day in 1886 an aging and thickset soldier said his good-bys and turned his back upon the Presidio of San Francisco. Major General John Pope, commander of the Division of the Pacific, had watched his last review and given his final order. Having reached the mandatory retirement age, the greying veteran was mustered out. As the new civilian made the long train ride eastward, he again was impressed with the development of the American West. Mountain, desert, and plain were settled; railroads crisscrossed the vast stretches of country; towns and cities stood where buffalo once had roamed. The frontier was passing; rolling grasslands of the Great Plains and high mountain valleys of the Rockies and the Sierras felt the bite of the plow and rang with the sound of the axe and the hum of mining machinery.

Nearly a quarter of a century had passed since the debacle at Bull Run on those hot August days in 1862. The intervening years, almost all spent in the West, had been interesting and rewarding. As the train chugged eastward—topping the crest of the high Sierras, crossing the Nevada and Utah deserts and the Wyoming high country, and rolling across the high plains—Pope passed through the regions which had been under his command. With the exception of Texas every section of the American West had been within his command at one time or another, and all the major Indian tribes—the Sioux and Cheyenne, the Kiowa and Comanche, the Ute and Apache—battled with his soldiers at various times. Even now, as he left the West and its future behind, General George Crook was attempting to settle the Apache problem in the Department of Arizona, which had been within Pope's last command.

As the train crossed through what had once been the undisputed domain of the American Indians, there was no doubt who owned it now, for the frontiersman's mines, ranches, and farms dotted the countryside. And the mighty Indian warriors, once lords of their country, were now located on reservations. Although the Indian wars had come to an end, the Indian problem had not been solved.

Geronimo still terroriized Arizona Territory, but he had few followers. He was fighting a guerrilla war, but Pope was confident that George Crook would soon bring peace, for the Apache feared and respected Crook. Pope was confident that if anyone could capture Geronimo and his raiders, Crook could. The Ghost Dance craze and the Battle of Wounded Knee in Dakota were still in the future, but the major Indian tribes of the West had been conquered. The Indian "wars" were passing into memory and were already entering the fanciful writings of the dime novelists.

The dime novels and the tales of the Indian campaigns did not relate the feats of men like John Pope. They dealt with the dashing and ambitious George Armstrong Custer, the boastful William Fetterman, and the eager Nelson A. Miles. Pope had not personally led colorful cavalry charges against the Indians. As a senior officer and a departmental and divisional commander, he was not well known to the average citizen who thrilled to such stories as Custer's exploits or Chief Joseph's tragic flight with the Nez Percé. But Pope, though unknown by the people, was recognized and respected by influential men throughout the West.

Well-known field officers had fought the campaigns that Pope had planned; Sully and Sibley, Connor and Dodge, Custer, Miles, Mackenzie, Grierson, and Crook had all executed his orders. The famous and the little known, the political generals, the ambitious and the able Indian fighters—all had carried out his instructions. Ambitious officers such as Nelson A. Miles, who was married to the niece of General Sherman and Senator John Sherman, often irritated Pope, while others like Mackenzie received his praise and support. Miles, for example, sent a stream of glowing reports to Sherman and constantly sought more important commands. In 1879 Sherman, speaking of Miles, remarked to Phil Sheridan, "I know no way to satisfy his ambitions but to surrender to him absolute power over the whole Army with President & Congress thrown in." When Miles was promoted to brigadier general and given the Department of the Columbia, both Sherman and Pope were upset that Ranald Mackenzie had been passed over. Sherman's explanation to Pope was that President Hayes had been determined to create a vacancy for Miles on the openly expressed theory that the army was not grateful enough to the Republican Party.[1]

Like Pope, the officers of the regular army—Sherman, Sheridan, Crook, Miles, Mackenzie, and others—were not exterminationists, although the humanitarians often claimed that they were. Generally, military men in the West agreed that the American Indians could not be allowed to stand in the way of the white man's civilization. The West would be settled and the Indians pushed aside—that the army officers well realized. Pope, recognizing that the red man would lose his land and his freedom in the white settlement of the West, wished that it could be accomplished as painlessly as possible. He and other officers who were devoted to preventing hostilities attempted to influence Federal Indian policy each time a major issue arose. They supported the reservation system; they favored the Peace Policy when it was enforced—which was rarely—; they protested when the Indians were not well cared for, and they tried to protect the Indians from unscrupulous traders and hypocritical agents. Neither Pope nor his fellow officers believed in indiscriminately killing Indians, but they did insist that the Indians remain on their reservations and that warriors be punished for their crimes. The army may have been organized for war, as the humanitarians claimed, but it was devoted to maintaining peace.

In the years after the Civil War increased interest was shown in the Indian problem, and many individuals offered various solutions and schemes. A Georgia banker offered to sell the government a coastal island where all the Indians could be located. This, he believed, would end the conflict between the races. Another interested citizen suggested the purchase of Lower California. He was confident that Mexico would be willing to sell the territory for a small sum, and once the transaction had been completed, a great wall like the wall of China could be erected across the peninsula and all the Indians placed south of the wall. [2]

Despite these and other proposals, the Indian Bureau, the humanitarians, and the army agreed that the goal of Federal policy should be acculturation. There was little opposition to the idea that the Indians should be placed on reservations and then be civilized, educated, and Christianized for assimilation into white society.

Despite agreement on final goals and despite the common belief that Indians must eventually be treated as individuals, Pope and other army officers differed with the

Indian Bureau as to how this should be accomplished. Humanitarians and officials of the Interior Department, determined to convert the Indians into peaceful, landowning farmers, believed that property ownership would provide the incentive for the Indian to civilize himself. Nowhere is this belief better exemplified than by the Sioux agent at Devil's Lake, who reported that once the Indians became landowning farmers they would sing at their work:

> We'll have a little farm, a horse, a pig, and cow,
> And she will mind the dairy and I will guide the plow.[3]

Pope agreed that the Indians must become property owners, but his appraisal of the situation was far more sophisticated than that of the humanitarians. He recognized that some of the tribes were ready to become individual landowners, but he did not believe that the warlike tribes of the plains were ready for this step. Nor did he believe that reservations on the high plains were suitable for agriculture, and he repeatedly stated that warriors who had battled with Miles and Mackenzie in 1874 and 1875 were not prepared to become farmers. The Indian tribes were varied, he said, and should be directed to some enterprise that was suited to their traditions. He recommended that the horse Indians become cattle herders, and he and Mackenzie provided some tribesmen with livestock in 1875 and 1876. Although the Indian agents praised this experiment, Washington officials were determined to convert the warriors into farmers and persisted in this determination in spite of crop failures year after year.

Throughout his entire career in the West, Pope never ceased to criticize and make recommendations regarding the treatment of the American Indian. As early as 1862, soon after he assumed command of the newly created Department of the Northwest, he began a debate with the officials of the Interior Department on Federal Indian policy that was to continue for nearly a quarter of a century. Although rejected at the time, many of his suggestions were carried out in later years.

Pope attacked the treaty system as unrealistic and unworkable; he demanded the cessation of the payment of money annuities to the tribes; he attempted to strengthen and enforce trade regulations; and he insisted that graft and corruption among traders be checked. During the 1870s these recommendations were implemented. In 1871 the treaty system was abolished, and the fiction that the Indian tribes were independent nations was abandoned. In time the Indians were given annuity goods rather than money, and in 1873 the Indian Bureau employed inspectors to investigate corruption and ensure that the Indians received the quality and amount of goods allotted to them.

The Quaker Policy of President Grant attempted to improve the Indian Service along the lines suggested by Pope, and it also fulfilled his hope that religious groups of various denominations recognize their opportunities for missionary work among the Indians. Certainly Pope and Sully contributed their influence to the creation of the Quaker Policy, for Pope had been in constant communication with Grant during 1865 and made his views known.

In 1864 Pope recommended that the semi-civilized tribes should be moved eastward away from the disruptive frontier environment. Although this suggestion was never adopted, he did not abandon it; and in 1875 he almost succeeded in having the defeated Southern Cheyenne moved to the military reservation at Fort Leavenworth. Pope believed that the frontier environment was detrimental to the civilization of the Indians, and he knew that the cheating of the red man and the intrusion on their lands could only lead to bloodshed. His desire to have the Indians fed and cared for as inexpensively as possible also influenced his thinking. The refusal of Congress to appropriate sufficient funds to feed the Indians and the failure of the Indian Bureau to see that contracts were fulfilled caused the Indians to suffer. Pope argued that if the tribes were moved eastward, the reduction in transportation costs would enable the government to feed them better and thus keep them near their agencies where the process of assimilation could begin.

Transportation costs for carrying goods to remote agencies were great, and the failure of contractors to deliver the full amount and stipulated quality of annuity goods and supplies on time was common. The Indian Bureau never improved its contract system although Indian agents repeatedly reported that the Indians suffered because goods did not arrive on expected dates. In 1877, John Miles of the Cheyenne-Arapaho Agency reported that for the first time the annuity goods were issued in the autumn, when they were due, only because the Indians themselves had transported the goods from the railroad depot.[4]

The cost of feeding the Indians at remote agencies was so great that in 1866 when Sherman visited the Navajo Agency at Bosque Redondo near Fort Sumner, New Mexico and found the army feeding the Navajo as prisoners of war, he remarked, "I think we could better send them to the Fifth Avenue Hotel to board, at the cost of the United States."[5]

Along with his suggestion to move the semi-civilized Indians away from the frontier, Pope also recommended that the army be given control of the wild tribes. Pope first raised the transfer issue in the 1860s, inaugurating a debate that continued for several decades. Army officers were in overwhelming agreement that control of Indian affairs should be transferred to the War Department where it had originally been. Army officers recognized that force was a vital part of a successful Indian policy. They deplored their lack of authority on the reservations and attributed the failings of the system to divided authority and responsibility. General Crook once testified that two things were required to govern the Indians—absolute honesty and authority to control them.[6] Pope and other officers believed that army control would reduce corruption, raise the caliber of the agents, and ensure that the Indians were well cared for. Their plan would have placed army officers in control of the wild tribes, but military agents would have continued to employ teachers, farmers, and missionaries while leaving civilian agents, who were responsible to the Secretary of War, to carry on the work with the more civilized tribes.

Congress debated the transfer issue for two decades and collected volumes of testimony, but each time humanitarians were able to block passage of the transfer bill. They argued that army officers lacked the training and experience to serve as Indian agents. Officers were trained for war, the humanitarians protested, and were not suited for teaching Indians and instructing them in agriculture. Although historians have often agreed with these sentiments, there is evidence to indicate that military agents could have improved the situation.

The officers who served in the small frontier army after the Civil War were not a group of rash young men. Many had spent long years on the frontier and knew more about the Indian character than many a petty eastern politician who had secured his appointment through political patronage. These officers, under orders from superiors, were always subject to court-martial for rash and foolish actions or for malfeasance in office and several who served as temporary agents did an excellent job. Captain Frank Bennett, whom Pope placed in temporary control of the Navajo Reservation during the crisis of 1880, had previously served as the Navajo agent in the 1860s, while Lieutenant Jesse Lee, who was placed in charge of the reservation for the Brulé Sioux in 1877 had also acted as an Indian agent from 1869 to 1871. In 1886, Lee again fulfilled the duties of Indian agent at the Cheyenne-Arapaho Reservation although he then held the rank of captain.[7] Both officers were notably successful.

The army was in an unenviable position throughout the post-war period, and Pope and other officers recognized this. Lacking the authority to undertake military action on the reservations, the army was unable to prevent raids before they occurred or to punish Indian criminals on the reservations. The army was rarely free from criticism, for pleasing both frontiersmen and humanitarians was impossible. When troops did attack Indians who were off the reservations and when they were given the authority to deal with hostiles wherever found, they were castigated by the Indian Bureau and the humanitarians. The officials of the Central Superintendency, for example, in the summer of 1874 attempted to undermine and remove the commanding officer of Fort Sill and sought to prevent him from enforcing orders from the Secretary of the Interior to enroll friendly Indians.

In 1870 the army, acting at the request of the Interior Department, undertook a winter campaign to punish the Blackfeet Indians of Montana, but when Colonel E. M. Baker struck a Piegan camp, the humanitarians condemned the soldiers, claiming that mostly women and children had been killed. Easterners were horrified by the "Baker Affair," but westerners offered only praise.

The frontiersmen did not always praise the army, however. General Sherman aptly defined the position of the army when he said, "There are two classes of people, one demanding the utter extinction of the Indians, and the other full of love for their conversion to civilization and Christianity. Unfortunately the army stands between and gets the cuffs from both sides."[8]

Westerners did not spare the soldiers, but they saved most of their abuse for the Indian Bureau and eastern sentimentalists. "But why prolong this folderol?" asked the *Daily New Mexican* in criticizing the use of civilian instead of military agents for the Indians. "Why keep up the Indian agency business when everybody knows . . . that they are as powerless as new born infants in a hornets nest without the aid of the soldiers," the paper exclaimed. "Why not transfer the entire management of Indians to the military, where it of right belongs, and where it should have been placed had it not been for a sickly sentimentality, a desire to make more political offices, so as to expend as much as possible of the public money."[9]

The frontier press alternately ridiculed and damned the humanitarians. Under the title, " 'RECONCILED'— SPOTTED TAIL'S TRIBUTE OF GRATITUDE," the *Daily New Mexican* contributed this doggerel:

> Great Father, we love you; our numbers are few.
> And our poor tribe is melting away like the dew;
> We wish to be friends with the pale face, and live
> On whatever lands that his bounty will give;
> But if I'm not chosen to Congress next fall,
> We'll scalp every man, woman and child of you all.[10]

Westerners listened closely to the words of humanitarians who influenced policies. "We don't attach much consequence to this gentleman as an expounder of the Indian question," commented the *Omaha Republican* following a speech by Wendell Phillips. "His brain seems to be as fuddled on this subject as upon that of the currency; but we regard him as one of that dangerous class of literary triflers, called public lecturers, who make a comfortable living by catering to the popular demand for senationalism, and who seek to portray the Indian as arrayed in the garments of heaven and the poor western settler as clothed in the livery of hell."[11]

Although frontiersmen supported the transfer issue and demanded that the army be enlarged rather than reduced, they damned the soldiers when they failed to punish raiding parties and were unable to keep Indians on their reservations. When the army did not meet their expectations, the settlers talked of taking care of the Indians themselves. During the Modoc War in 1873, A. G. Boone of Colorado offered to take a regiment of Coloradans to California and promised that they would end the war inside of ninety days. The editor of the *Boulder County News* heartily approved of this offer and predicted, "If the government were to offer a reward of a thousand dollars for each Modoc scalp, they would gather to the front, and in less than a month there would not be a hostile Modoc on earth who was not bald headed." The ingredients of a successful Indian policy, announced the *Sentinel* of Monroe, Wisconsin, "consist of Spencer rifles, plenty of powder and lead, and volunteer troops, who are not usually proceeded [sic] by brass bands while looking for 'Injuns.' "[12]

Statements such as these were common. If troops killed Indians, they drew the wrath of the humanitarians; and if the troops failed to kill Indians, they received the scorn of the frontiersmen. The army faced an impossible task; although given the duty of keeping peace on the plains, the army was repeatedly reduced in size and limited in authority by Congress.

Pope, Crook, Sherman, and other officers had a more

realistic approach to the Indian problem, but except on rare occasions, they were unable to implement their views. In many ways military men were more humane than the humanitarians, and this was certainly true of Pope. Recognizing that relationships between the two races had reached a crisis stage during the Civil War years, he sought to prevent hostilities and to save the Indians from extermination. Pope insisted that they be fed and cared for when they were placed on reservations, and he sought approval for policies that would protect the red man from suffering at the hands of unscrupulous whites.

The sweeping reforms of the Indian system that Pope and others desired were not achieved, but Pope played an important role in relationships with tribes within his commands. The sheer volume of his policy statements ensured widespread distribution of his views, while collection of testimony by congressional committees familiarized congressmen with his views. His proposals reinforced the beliefs of his superiors if, indeed, they did not influence them, and his recommendations were known throughout the departments of War and of the Interior. Indeed, several congressmen made similar statements during the post-war period. Pope's influence was felt to its greatest degree, however, in the everyday relationships with the Indians. It is here that his understanding of the Indian problem and his concern for the Indian's future is most evident. He provided an important force for moderation in a critical area.

Moreover, military men of Pope's era were placed in an ambiguous situation. The so-called Indian wars in the West were not really wars so much as they were military campaigns, police actions, or limited wars, and there are many comparisons between the so-called Indian wars and modern guerrilla fighting in the underdeveloped countries of the world today. Troops conducted search-and-destroy missions although few Indians were destroyed; they employed native scouts and allies; and in some areas their task was more difficult because of the proximity of a foreign sanctuary. To some degree soldiers also acted as pacification teams, encouraging the Indians to become farmers or stockmen and at times providing them with livestock, implements, and instruction.

In the final analysis the Indian problem was a racial problem, for the American Indians became a racial minority. Many military men and government officials agreed that the natives must ultimately be assimilated into white society. Although Pope accepted this goal, he was not sure that assimilation was possible; and, so far, time has shown him correct in this belief. Over a hundred years have passed since Pope went West to command the Department of the Northwest, and Indians are still a minority problem. Acculturation has been slow, and the Indian problem has not been solved. The adoption of Pope's proposals would not have provided the solution, but in all probability they would have reduced the problem and prevented some of the hostilities.

Notes

CHAPTER ONE

1. T. Harry Williams, *Lincoln and the Radicals* (Madison: University of Wisconsin Press, 1941), pp. 141-48.

2. Charles J. Kappler (ed.), *Indian Affairs: Laws and Treaties,* 57th Cong., 1st sess., *Senate Document No. 452,* vol. 2, pp. 590-98. Kenneth Carley, *The Sioux Uprising of 1862* (St. Paul: The Minnesota Historical Society, 1961), p. 12.

3. Carley, pp. 11-22. William W. Folwell, *A History of Minnesota* (St. Paul: Minnesota Historical Society, 1924), vol. 2, pp. 212-41. Folwell gives a full discussion of the causes of the outbreak.

4. Carley, pp. 16-22.

5. Ramsey to Stanton, Aug. 21, 1862, *The War of the Rebellion: A Compilation of the Official Records of the Union and the Confederate Armies* (Washington, D.C.: Government Printing Office, 1880-1901), Series I, vol. 13, p. 590. Hereafter cited as *Official Records.*

6. Kirkwood to Stanton, Sept. 8, 1862; Paddock to Stanton, Sept. 9, 1862; Nicolay to Stanton, Aug. 27, 1862; Ramsey to the President, Sept. 6, 1862: ibid., pp. 599-600, 617, 620-21.

7. Good accounts of the second Bull Run campaign can be found in Kenneth Williams, *Lincoln Finds a General* (New York: The Macmillan Co., 1949), vol. 1; and T. Harry Williams, *Lincoln and His Generals* (New York: Alfred A. Knopf, 1952), pp. 119-24. The latter work is very critical of Pope. For a clear understanding of the campaign, see Vincent J. Esposito, *The West Point Atlas of American Wars* (New York: Frederick A. Praegar, Inc., 1959), vol. 1, pp. 54-64.

8. Stanton to Pope, Sept. 6, 1862, General Orders No. 128, War Department, *Official Records,* Series I, vol. 13, pp. 617-18.

9. Pope to Sibley, Sept. 17, 1862, ibid., pp. 648-49.

10. Ibid.

11. Sibley to Pope, Sept. 19, 1862; Schofield to Halleck, Sept. 18, 1862: ibid., pp. 650-52.

12. Stanton to Halleck, Sept. 23, 1862; Stanton to Pope, Sept. 23, 1862; Halleck to Pope, Sept. 23, 1862: ibid., pp. 658-59, 662-63.

13. Pope to Stanton, Sept. 25, 1862; Pope to Halleck, Sept. 23, 1862; Pope to Halleck, Sept. 25, 1862: ibid., pp. 663-64, 668-69.

14. Paroled Union troops are not to be confused with the Galvanized Yankees (Confederates in Union prison camps who volunteered to fight Indians rather than remain prisoners). The Third Minnesota Infantry, which played an important role in the Battle of Wood Lake in September, is an example; they surrendered at Murfreesboro, Tennessee and were paroled.

15. The released were 107 whites and 162 half-breeds. The battle actually occurred near Lone Tree Lake, which the guide had mistaken for Wood Lake.

16. Pope to Halleck, Oct. 9, 1962, *Official Records,* Series I, vol. 13, p. 722.

17. Pope to Sibley, Sept. 28, 1862, ibid., pp. 685-86.

18. Pope to Halleck, Oct. 10, 1862; Ramsey to Lincoln, Nov. 10, 1862; Pope to Lincoln, Nov. 11, 1862: ibid., pp. 724, 787-88. Pope to Lincoln, Nov. 12, 1862, Abraham Lincoln Papers, XCII, Division of Manuscripts, Library of Congress, Washington, D.C. Pope sent the list of names by telegraph at a cost of $400 to the government.

19. *Annual Report of the Secretary of the Interior, 1862,* 37th Cong., 3rd sess., *House Executive Document No. 1,* pt. 2 (Serial 1157), vol. 177, pp. 213-14. Wilkinson et al. to Lincoln, 37th Cong., 3rd sess., *Senate Executive Document No. 7* (Serial 1149), pp. 2-4.

20. Memorial of the Citizens of St. Paul to President Lincoln, ibid., pp. 4-6.

21. *Yankton Dakotian,* Dec. 9, 1862.

22. Carley, pp. 64-65. Folwell, vol. 2, pp. 200-05.

23. Pope to Kelton, Feb. 18, 1863; Halleck to Pope, Mar. 23, 1863: *Official Records,* Series I, vol. 22, pt. 2, pp. 117-18, 176.

24. Agent Thomas Galbraith to Superintendent Clark Thompson, Jan. 27, 1863, *Annual Report of the Secretary of the Interior,* 1863, 38th Cong., 1st sess., *House Executive Document No. 1* (Serial 1220), pp. 382-412. Folwell, vol. 2, pp. 256-58.

25. Secretary of the Interior Caleb Smith to Cyrus Aldrich, Chairman of the Committee of Indian Affairs, Dec. 16, 1862, 37th Cong., 3rd sess., *House Report No. 13* (Serial 1173), pp. 1-4.

26. *St. Paul Pioneer,* Oct. 23, 1862, quoted in Folwell, pp. 11, 242.

27. *St. Paul Press,* quoted in the *Yankton Dakotian,* Nov. 11, 1862.

28. P. Chouteau Jr. and Co. to Dole, Dec. 2, 1862; Feather Tied to His Hair et al. to agent, July 25, 1862: *Annual Report of the Secretary of the Interior, 1862* (Serial 1157), pp. 515-17.

29. Charles Primeau, agent in charge of Fort Pierre, to the Commissioner of Indian Affairs, June 20, 1862, ibid., pp. 517-19.

30. Henry Reed (Blackfoot agent) and La Barge, Harkness & Co. to Dole, Jan. 14, 1863; Latta to Dole, Mar. 7, 1863: *Annual Report of the Secretary of the Interior, 1863* (Serial 1182), pp. 282-84. *Yankton Dakotian,* Jan. 1, 1863.

31. Pope to Sibley, Feb. 17, 1863, *Official Records,* Series I, vol. 22, pt. 2, pp. 115-16.

32. Pope to Sibley, Feb. 20, 1863, ibid., pp. 119-20.

33. Pope to Kelton, April 4, 1863, ibid., pp. 198-99.

34. Halleck to Pope, April 11, 1863, ibid., p. 211. Alvin C. Gluek, Jr., "The Sioux Uprising: A Problem in International Relations," *Minnesota History,* vol. 34 (winter 1955), pp. 317-19. Gluek points out that the Sioux were unwelcome guests in Canada. Despite Halleck's reply, Pope continued to request authority to pursue the hostiles across the international boundary, Pope to Halleck, May 19, 1863, *Official Records,* Series I, vol. 22, pt. 2, pp. 288-89.

35. Doane Robinson, "A History of the Dakota or Sioux Indians," *South Dakota Historical Collections,* 1904, vol. 2, p. 318. Gabriel Renville was the son-in-law of Scarlet Plume, a Sisseton chief.

36. Board of Commissioners, *Minnesota in the Civil and Indian Wars, 1861-1865* (St. Paul: The Pioneer Press Co., 1890), provides good accounts of Sibley's expedition of 1863. Doane Robinson, pp. 317-25.

37. Pope to Sully, Aug. 5, 1863; Pope to Sully, Aug. 25, 1863; Pope to Sully, Aug. 31, 1863: *Official Records,* Series I, vol. 22, pt. 2, pp. 434, 496-97, 502-03. It was reported that the river was lower than it had been in thirty years.

38. For the battle reports of Sully and his officers, see ibid., pt. 1, pp. 555-611. See also Board of Commissioners, pp. 457-560, 520-24, 670-71. Sully destroyed 300 lodges and about 400,000 to 500,000 pounds of meat.

39. Erling T. Jorstad, "The Life of Henry Hastings Sibley" (unpublished doctoral dissertation, University of Wisconsin, 1957), pp. 116-18. Folwell, vol. 1, pp. 240, 260, 317-18, 369-72.

40. Pope to Halleck, Nov. 20, 1862, ibid., vol. 12, pt. 3, p. 826.

41. Pope to Kelton, July 13, 1863, ibid., vol. 22, pt. 2, 371-72. Sibley, writing of the Hatch appointment, said, "The whole thing I regard as a miserable scheme got up by Rice & others who hate Gen. Pope, and do not love me, & who wish to annoy & humiliate us both. I have contempt for the whole humbug inventors & all." Diary of Henry H. Sibley, June 6–Sept. 13, 1863. Sibley Papers Corresp., AS564, Box 16, Minn. Historical Society, St. Paul.

42. Halleck to Pope, July 17, 1863; Pope to Halleck, July 18, 1863: *Official Records,* vol. 22, pt. 2, pp. 380-82.

43. Pope to Halleck, July 21, 1863, ibid., pp. 385-86.

44. Pope to Stanton, Aug. 29, 1863, ibid., pp. 493-95.

45. Miller to Pope, Aug. 24, 1863, ibid., p. 495.

46. Pope to Halleck, July 27, 1863, ibid., pp. 403-05.

47. The *Yankton Dakotian,* Oct. 13, 1863.

48. Henry A. Boller, *Among the Indians: Eight Years in the Far West,*

1858-1866, ed. Milo M. Quaife (The Lakeside Classics edition, Chicago: R. R. Donnelley & Sons, Co., 1959), p. 358.

49. Halleck to Pope, Oct. 10, 1863, *Official Records,* Series I, vol. 22, pt. 2, p. 633.

CHAPTER TWO

1. Francis P. Prucha, *American Indian Policy in the Formative Years* (Cambridge: Harvard University Press, 1962), pp. 1-4. William T. Hagan, *American Indians* (Chicago: University of Chicago Press, 1961), chapter 3.

2. *Annual Report of the Secretary of the Interior, 1863,* 38th Cong., 1st sess., *House Executive Document No. 1* (Serial 1182), 420-27. *House Report No. 13,* 37th Cong., 3rd sess. (Serial 1173), pp. 1-4. Dakotans had mixed feelings about the establishment of the Crow Creek Reservation, but some were happy to have it because it would mean more military posts, more troops, and thus a new market for their goods, *Yankton Dakotian,* May 19, 1863.

3. Pope to Kelton, Oct. 21, 1863, *The War of Rebellion: A Compilation of the Official Records of the Union and Confederate Armies* (Washington, D.C.: Government Printing Office, 1880-1901), Series I, vol. 22, pt. 2, pp. 671-72. Hereafter cited as *Official Records.* William W. Folwell, *A History of Minnesota* (St. Paul: Minnesota Historical Society, 1924), vol. 2, pp. 260, 439-41.

4. Folwell, vol. 2, pp. 439-41.

5. Diary of Charles W. Johnson quoted in Board of Commissioners, *Minnesota in the Civil and Indian Wars, 1861-1865* (St. Paul: The Pioneer Press Co., 1890), p. 319.

6. Sully to Asst. Adjt. Gen., Dept. of the Northwest, Nov. 22, 1864, *Official Records,* Series I, vol. 41, pt. 4, pp. 651-52.

7. Pope to Kelton, July 13, 1863, ibid., vol. 22, pt. 2, pp. 372-73.

8. Charles Mix, acting commissioner, to Secretary of the Interior Usher, July 2, 1863; Salomon to Usher, July 10, 1863; Pope to Salomon, July 3, 1863: *Annual Report of the Secretary of the Interior, 1863* (Serial 1182), pp. 477-83.

9. Pope to Kelton, July 21, 1863; L. Barnes et al. to Salomon, July, 1863: ibid., pp. 484-85, 490-93. Gov. Lewis of Wisconsin to Stanton, July 11, 1865, *Official Records,* Series I, vol. 48, pt. 2, pp. 1225-26.

10. *Annual Report of the Secretary of the Interior, 1862,* 37th Cong., 3rd sess., *House Executive Document No. 1* (Serial 1157), pt. 2, pp. 10-11.

11. Pope to Halleck, Sept. 23, 1863, *Official Records,* Series I, vol. 22, pt. 2, pp. 569-70.

12. Henry B. Whipple, *Lights and Shadows of a Long Episcopate* (New York: The Macmillan Co., 1912), p. 249.

13. Pope to Stanton, Feb. 6, 1864, *Official Records,* Series I, vol. 34, pt. 2, pp. 259-63.

14. Ibid., p. 261.

15. Ibid.

16. Ibid., pp. 260-63.

17. Ibid., pt. 3, pp. 565-67. Pope to C. A. Dana, Asst. Secretary of War, Sept. 9, 1864, ibid., vol. 41, pt. 3, pp. 123-24.

18. Ibid., pp. 125-26.

19. Halleck to Pope (confidential), Apr. 4, 1864, ibid., vol. 34, pt. 3, p. 159.

20. Annual Report of Agent Burleigh, Oct. 21, 1864, *Annual Report of the Secretary of the Interior, 1864,* 38th Cong., 2nd sess., *House Document No. 1* (Serial 1220), pt. 2, pp. 429-30.

21. Dole to Usher, Apr. 6, 1864, *Annual Report of the Secretary of the Interior, 1864,* 38th Cong., 2nd sess., *House Document No. 1* (Serial 1220), pt. 2, pp. 573-74.

22. Ibid., p. 574.

23. Ibid.

24. *Annual Report of the Secretary of the Interior, 1854,* 33rd Cong., 2nd sess., *House Executive Document No. 1* (Serial 777), pp. 40-41. *Annual Report of the Secretary of the Interior, 1858,* 35th Cong., 2nd sess., *House Executive Document No. 2* (Serial 997), pp. 80-81.

25. *Annual Report of the Secretary of the Interior, 1862* (Serial 1157), p. 11.

26. Ibid., p. 179. Whipple, pp. 519, 521-24.

27. Whipple, p. 144.

CHAPTER THREE

1. Annual Report of William Dole, Annual Report of John Hutchinson, Sept. 23, 1863, *Annual Report of the Secretary of the Interior, 1863,* 38th Cong., 1st sess., *House Executive Document No. 1* (Serial 1182), pp. 141, 270-73.

2. Pope to Sibley, Jan. 18, 1864; Pope to Kelton, Feb. 6, 1864: *The War of the Rebellion: A Compilation of the Official Records of the Union and Confederate Armies* (Washington, D.C.: Government Printing Office, 1880-1901), Series I, vol. 34, pt. 2, pp. 109-10, 256-59. Hereafter cited as *Official Records.*

3. Sully to Sibley, Mar. 28, 1864; P. Chouteau & Co. to Halleck, Mar. 26, 1864: ibid., pp. 743-44, 766-67.

4. Pope to Kelton, Jan. 12, 1864; Halleck to Pope, Jan. 17, 1864: ibid., pp. 69, 100.

5. Pope to Sibley, May 28, 1864, ibid., pt. 4, p. 102.

6. Helen M. White (ed.), *Ho! For the Gold Fields* (St. Paul: Minnesota Historical Society, 1966), pp. 2, 6, 8, 106.

7. Pope to Stanton, Feb. 6, 1864, *Official Records,* Series I, vol. 34, pt. 2, p. 258.

8. Pope to Sully, Mar. 25, 1864, "Circular to Emigrants," Mar. 14, 1864, ibid., pp. 608-09, 735.

9. Pope to Sully, May 26, 1864, ibid., pt. 4, p. 59.

10. Grant to Halleck, Aug. 13, 1864, ibid., vol. 41, pt. 2, p. 680.

11. Halleck to Pope, Feb. 8, 1864; Pope to Stanton, Mar. 30, 1864: ibid., vol. 34, pt. 2, pp. 275, 745.

12. Pope to Halleck, Mar. 30, 1864, ibid., pp. 792-93.

13. Duff to Rawlins, July 2, 1864, ibid., vol. 41, pt. 2, pp. 29-30.

14. Pope to Halleck, Aug. 17, 1864, ibid., p. 754.

15. Halleck to Grant, Aug. 17, 1864, ibid., p. 739.

16. Pope to Halleck, Sept. 17, 1864, ibid., p. 237.

17. Pope to Sibley and Sully, Mar. 15, 1864; Pope to Halleck and Stanton, Mar. 25, 1864: ibid., vol. 34, pt. 2, pp. 622-25, 688.

18. Latta to Dole, Aug. 27, 1863: *Annual Report of the Secretary of the Interior, 1863* (Serial 1182), pp. 288-89. Annual Report of William Dole, *Annual Report of the Secretary of the Interior, 1864,* 38th Cong., 2nd sess., *House Executive Document No. 1* (Serial 1220), pt. 2, pp. 169-72.

19. Report of Special Agent Henry Reed, Dole to De Smet, Mar. 21, 1864; De Smet to Dole, Aug. 23, 1864: *Annual Report of the Secretary of the Interior, 1864* (Serial 1220), pp. 416, 419-20, 424-26.

20. David L. Kingsbury, "Sully's Expedition Against the Sioux in 1864," *Collections of the Minnesota Historical Society,* vol. 8, 1898, p. 455.

21. Reports of Sully and his officers are in *Official Records,* Series I, vol. 41, pt. 1, pp. 131-74. See also Board of Commissioners, *Minnesota in the Civil and Indian Wars, 1861-1865* (St. Paul: The Pioneer Press Co., 1890), pp. 387-94.

22. Sully to Asst. Adjt. Gen., Dept. of the Northwest, Aug. 13, 1864, *Official Records,* Series I, vol. 41, pt. 1, pp. 144-48.

23. *Frontier Scout* (Fort Union, Dakota Territory), July 27, 1864.

24. White, pp. 115-16.

25. Sully to Asst. Adjt. Gen., Dept. of the Northwest, Oct. 7, 1864, *Official Records,* Series I, vol. 41, pt. 3 pp. 698-701.

26. Sully to Asst. Adjt. Gen., Dept. of the Northwest, Aug. 18 (?), 1864, ibid., pt. 1, pp. 148-49. Sully to Pope, Aug. 18, 1864, ibid., pt. 2, p. 768.

27. Sully to Pope, Aug. 18, 1864, ibid., pt. 2, pp. 767-78.

28. Sully to Asst. Adjt. Gen., Dept. of the Northwest, Oct. 7, 1864, ibid., pt. 3, pp. 698-701.

29. Sully to Asst. Adjt. Gen., Dept. of the Northwest, Nov. 22, 1864, ibid., pt. 4, pp. 651-52.

30. Grant to Halleck, Nov. 30, 1864, ibid., p. 716.

31. Grant to Halleck, Nov. 28 and 30, 1864; Grant to Lincoln, Dec. 7, 1864: ibid., pp. 702-716-17, 785.

CHAPTER FOUR

1. Pope to Sully, Mar. 25, 1864; Pope to Sibley, May 18, 1864; Pope to Halleck, Nov. 17, 1864: *The War of the Rebellion: A Compilation of the Official Records of the Union and Confederate Armies* (Washington, D.C.: Government Printing Office, 1880-1901); Series I, vol. 34, pt. 2, p. 735; pt. 3, p. 662; vol. 41, pt. 4, p. 600. Hereafter cited as *Official Records.*

2. Good accounts of the Sand Creek massacre and preceding events can be found in Stan Hoig, *The Sand Creek Massacre* (Norman: University of Oklahoma Press, 1961); and Donald J. Berthrong, *The Southern Cheyennes* (Norman: University of Oklahoma Press, 1963), chapters 8 and 9.

3. Livingston to Mitchell, Jan. 8, 1865; Moonlight to Charlot, Jan. 11, 1865: *Official Records,* Series I, vol. 48, pt. 1, pp. 463, 491.

4. Halleck to Grant, Jan. 11, 1865; George Reynolds on behalf of the proprietors of the Santa Fe Mail Co. to Charlot, Jan. 16, 1865; Rumfield et al. to Stanton, Jan. 14, 1865: Sanders to Stanton, Jan. 14 and 17, 1865; Usher to Stanton, Jan. 12, 1865: *Official Records,* Series I, vol. 48, pt. 1, pp. 486, 498-99, 522, 549-50.

5. Curtis to Evans, Jan. 12, 1865, ibid., pp. 503-04. Curtis did order an investigation, but his reluctance is demonstrated in a letter to Moonlight on Jan. 13, 1865, when he said, "I suppose a commission of officers better be ordered . . . " ibid., p. 511.

6. Curtis to Halleck, Jan. 12, 1865; Curtis to Evans, Jan. 12, 1865: ibid., pp. 502-03.

7. Livingston to Dodge, Feb. 9, 1865, ibid., pp. 793-94. Eugene F. Ware, *The Indian War of 1864,* ed. Clyde Walton (New York: St. Martin's Press, 1960), pp. 363-79, provides an eyewitness account of the attack.

8. Pope to Dodge, Feb. 9, 1965, *Official Records,* vol. 48, pt. 1, p. 795.

9. Ibid., pp. 807-08.

10. Pope to Halleck, Feb. 8, 1865, Div. of the Missouri, Letters Sent, Records of the War Department, U.S. Army Commands, National Archives, Washington, D.C., General Order No. 80, Department of the Missouri, Mar. 28, 1865, *Official Records,* p. 1285.

11. Colfax to Stanton, May 24, 1865, ibid., pt. 2, p. 589.

12. Pope to Dodge, Feb. 8, 1865, Dept. of the Missouri, Telegraphs Sent, Records of the War Department, U.S. Army Commands, National Archives, Washington, D.C. See D. Alexander Brown, *The Galvanized Yankees* (Urbana: University of Illinois Press, 1963), for a history of these troops. Pope already had members of the new regiments on the Upper Missouri.

13. Pope to Halleck, Mar. 9 and 10, 1865, *Official Records,* Series I, vol. 48, pt. 1, pp. 1131, 1140. Pope also requested the use of three regiments of Cherokee Indians which were stationed at Fort Gibson near present-day Mus-

kogee, Oklahoma, Pope to Halleck, Mar. 3, 1865, ibid., p. 1069.

14. George E. Hyde, *Spotted Tail's Folk: A History of the Brulé Sioux* (Norman: University of Oklahoma Press, 1961), pp. 102, 105. The bodies of the dead chiefs were still hanging near the fort two months later, Diary of Capt. B. F. Rockafellow, Sixth Michigan Cavalry in LeRoy R. and Ann W. Hafen (eds.), *Powder River Campaigns and Sawyer's Expedition of 1865* (Glendale, Calif.: Arthur H. Clark Co., 1961), p. 167. Moonlight reported, "I concluded to tie them up by the neck with a trace chain, suspended from a beam of wood, and leave them there without any foothold." Report of Col. Moonlight, May 27, 1865, *Official Records,* Series I, vol. 48, pt. 1, pp. 276-77.

15. Hyde, *Spotted Tail's Folk,* pp. 102-05. Report of Capt. John Wilcox, June 21, 1865, *Official Records,* Series I, vol. 48, pt. 1, pp. 322-24.

16. Report of Col. Moonlight, June 21, 1865, *Official Records,* Series I, vol. 48, pt. 1, pp. 325-28.

17. Conner to Potter, July 3, 1865; Connor to Dodge, July 3, 1865; Connor to Cole, July 4, 1865; Connor to Walker, July 28, 1865: ibid., pp. 1045, 1049, 1131. Pope to Dodge, Aug. 11, 1865, ibid., pt. 1, p. 356.

18. Pope to Sherman, Aug. 17, 1865; Dodge to Pope, Aug. 2, 1865: ibid., pt. 2, p. 1190, 1157.

19. Mitchell to Dodge, Mar. 16, 1865; Dodge to Connor, Apr. 6, 1865: ibid., p. 42; ibid., pt. 1, p. 1194.

20. Price to Connor, July 31, 1865, ibid., p. 1145. Capt. H. E. Palmer's account of the Connor expedition in Hafen and Hafen, p. 107. The Sixteenth Kansas had been in trouble before; the men of Company D shot one of their officers in February and threatened to burn down the town of Council Grove, Kansas, *Official Records,* Series I, vol. 48, pt. 1, pp. 796-97.

21. Connor to Dodge, July 7, 1865; Connor to Dodge, July 15, 1865: ibid., pt. 2, pp. 1063, 1084.

22. Pope to Dodge, Aug. 11, 1865; Pope to Dodge, Sept. 2, 1865: ibid., pt. 1, pp. 352-53, 355-56.

23. Charles H. Springer, "Campagne [sic] against the Sioux Indians While Lieutenant Commanding Company 'B' 12th Missouri Volunteer Cavalry," unpublished diary in Cobb Collection, University of Colorado Library.

24. Report, Cole to Grant, Feb. 10, 1867, *Official Records,* Series I, vol. 48, pt. 1, pp. 366-80. Report, Walker to Price, Sept. 25, 1865, reproduced in Hafen and Hafen, pp. 92-100. H. D. Hampton, "The Powder River Indian Expedition, 1865," *Montana, The Magazine of Western History,* vol. 14 (autumn 1864), pp. 12-14.

25. Price to Dodge, Aug. 14, 1865, *Official Records,* Series I, vol. 48, pt. 2, p. 1188. Capt. H. E. Palmer's account of the Conner expedition in Hafen and Hafen, pp. 130-35.

26. See J. W. Vaughn, *The Battle of Platte Bridge* (Norman: University of Oklahoma Press, 1963), for an account of this affair. Fort Connor, which was

located on the Powder River north of present-day Sussex, Wyoming, was renamed Fort Reno on Nov. 11, 1865.

27. Ford to Charlot, Jan. 8, 1865, *Official Records,* Series I, vol. 48, pt. 1, p. 462.

28. Leavenworth to Ford, Feb. 20, 1865; Halleck to Dodge, Feb. 23, 1865; Ford to Dodge, Mar. 3, 1865: ibid., pp. 923-24, 960, 1078-79. Stanton to Pope, Apr. 29, 1865, ibid., pt. 2, pp. 243-44.

29. Doolittle to Harlan, May 31, 1865; Doolittle et al. to President Andrew Johnson, June 11, 1865: ibid., pt. 2, pp. 857, 868.

30. Dole to Harlan, June 12, 1865, ibid., pp. 869-70.

31. Dodge to Pope, June 13, 1865; Sacket to Brig. Gen. Hardie, June 14, 1865; Ford to Dodge, June 14, 1865: ibid., pp. 871-72, 883-84.

32. Doolittle to Seward and Stanton, July 19, 1865; Sanborn to Dodge, Aug. 3, 1865: ibid., pp. 1094, 1162.

CHAPTER FIVE

1. Col. Charles Dimon to Lt. Col. Edward Ten Broeck, Act. Asst. Adjt. Gen., Dist. of Iowa, Jan. 24, 1865, *The War of the Rebellion: A Compilation of the Official Records of the Union and Confederate Armies* (Washington, D.C.: Government Printing Office, 1880-1901), Series I, vol. 48, pt. 1, pp. 636-37. Hereafter cited as *Official Records.* Dimon was a protégé of Gen. Benjamin Butler and was a colonel of the First United States Volunteers, a regiment of Galvanized Yankees.

2. Pope to Sully and Sibley, Feb. 1, 1865, ibid., pp. 719-20.

3. Sibley to Curtis, Mar. 26, 1865; Curtis to Sibley, Apr. 3, 1865: ibid., pp. 1264-65; pt. 2, p. 26.

4. Sibley to Major C. S. Charlot, Asst. Adjt. Gen., Dept. of the Northwest, Apr. 4, 1865; Sibley to editor of the *Press and Pioneer* (St. Paul), May 5, 1865: ibid., pp. 30-31, 327-99.

5. Curtis to J. M. Bell, Asst. Adjt. Gen., Div. of the Missouri, May 8, 1865; Curtis to Bell, May 11, 1865: ibid., pp. 358-59, 412-13.

6. Sibley to Pope, May 8, 1865; Curtis to Bell, May 11, 1865: ibid., pp. 358-59. Folwell, vol. 2, pp. 349-50. Most of the murderers were caught. Several were tracked down by Sisseton scouts of the army, and one of them pleaded for mercy on the grounds that he was a good Indian and a member of the church. The scouts "took the ground that if so he was in a proper frame of mind to go to the happy hunting grounds, and he went." Sibley to Charlot, May 26, 1865, *Official Records,* vol. 48, pt. 2, p. 616.

7. Sibley to Curtis, May 15, 1865; Sibley to Charlot, May 17 and 21, 1865: ibid., pp. 456, 486, 532-33.

8. Bell to Curtis, May 18, 1865; Pope to Curtis, May 20, 1865: ibid., pp. 501, 524-25.

9. Pope to Grant, May 22, 1865; Pope to Pleasonton, May 22, 1865; Pope to Sully, May 22, 1865: ibid., pp. 539-40, 556-58.

10. Pope to Sully, May 23, 1865; Sully to Curtis, May 25, 1865; Sully to Pope, May 26, 1865: ibid., pp. 579, 600, 617-18.

11. Dimon to Sully, June 2, 1865, ibid., pp. 304-05; Dimon to Cram, April 29, 1865; Dimon to Sully's headquarters, Apr. 3 and 14, 1865; Dimon to Sully, May 26, 1865: Charles Dimon Papers, Yale Univ. Library, New Haven, Conn.

12. Hubbard to Pope, May 26, 1865, *Official Records,* Series I, vol. 48, pt. 2, p. 618.

13. Pope to Grant, June 2, 1865, ibid., pp. 731-32.

14. Miller to Curtis, June 2, 1865, ibid., pp. 741-42.

15. Curtis to Pope, June 3, 1865; Curtis to Sully, June 5, 1865: ibid., pp. 763, 789.

16. Adams to Olin, June 27, 1865, ibid., pp. 1013-14.

17. Sully to Sawyer, July 22, 1865; Sully to Asst. Adjt. Gen., Dept. of the Northwest, July 30 and Aug. 8, 1865; Olin to Carnahan, June 28, 1865: ibid., pp. 1022-24, 1109-10, 1136-37, 1172-74. The *Frontier Scout* (Fort Rice), Aug. 17, 1865, includes a report of the expedition by "Medicus" which is critical of Pope. "If he [Sully] is sent here to fight Indians let him have the privilege of going where the Red-Skins are, and not tie him down with orders from Head Quarters, a thousand miles away, telling him to fight the Indians, but to be sure and not go where they are! Much which might be accomplished this year, will not be, simply on account of such 'hand-tying orders.' "

18. *Yankton Dakotian,* Nov. 17, 1863.

19. Ibid., Jan. 6, 1864.

20. Ibid., July 7, 1863.

21. Ibid., Dec. 8, 1863. Howard R. Lamar, *Dakota Territory, 1861-1889* (New Haven: Yale Univ. Press, 1956), pp. 102-03.

22. Sully to Pope, June 14, 1865, *Official Records,* Series I, vol. 48, pt. 2, p. 877.

23. Pope to Edmunds, May 8, 1865; Pope to Edmunds, May 10, 1865: ibid., pp. 357, 392.

24. *Yankton Union and Dakotaian,* May 12, 1865.

25. Ibid., May 20 and 27, 1865.

26. Ibid., May 27 and July 1, 1865.

27. Ibid., July 8, 1865. Capt. Sylvester Bagg was Sully's quartermaster.

28. Ibid., Sept. 2, 1865.

29. Pope to Sully, June 2, 1865; Pope to Hubbard, June 3, 1865; Pope to Harlan, June 9, 1865; Harlan to Pope, July 6, 1865: *Official Records,* Series I, vol. 48, pt. 2, pp. 742, 764-65, 933-35, 1056. Harlan to Cooley, July 11, 1865: *Annual Report of the Secretary of the Interior, 1865,* 39th Cong., 1st sess., *House Executive Document No. 1* (Serial 1248), pt. 5, pp. 385-86.

30. Pope to Grant, May 9, 1865; Pope to Grant, May 18, 1865: *Official Records,* Series I, vol. 48, pt. 2, pp. 367, 492-94.

31. Pope to Grant, June 19, 1865, ibid, p. 933.

32. Pope to Grant, May 23, 1865; Pope to Bowers, June 3, 1865; Pope to Grant, June 14, 1865: ibid., pp. 567, 751-52, 879-82. Connor reported the extent of travel through Fort Kearny, Connor to Dodge, June 26, 1865, Dept. of the Missouri, Telegrams Received, Records of the War Department, U.S. Army Commands, National Archives.

33. Pope to Grant, May 23, 1865; Grant to Pope, May 17, 1865: *Official Records,* Series I, vol. 48, pt. 2, pp. 565-68, 480.

34. Pope to Grant, June 14, 1865, ibid., pp. 879-82.

35. Ibid., pp. 879-82.

36. Grant to Pope, June 15, 1865; Harlan to Pope, July 6, 1865: ibid., pp. 892, 1056-57.

CHAPTER SIX

1. General Orders N. 44, War Department, Mar. 21, 1865, *The War of the Rebellion: A Compilation of the Official Records of the Union and Confederate Armies* (Washington, D.C.: Government Printing Office, 1880-1902), Series I, vol. 48, pt. 1, p. 1225. Hereafter cited as *Official Records.*

2. Pope to Sherman, Oct. 28, 1865, Letters Sent, Dept. of the Missouri, Records of the War Department, U.S. Army Commands, National Archives, Washington, D.C. Hereafter cited as L.S., D.Mo. Sherman to Grant, Nov. 6, 1865, William T. Sherman Papers, Division of Manuscripts, Library of Congress, Washington, D.C.

3. Pope to Harlan, Aug. 21, 1865, *Annual Report of the Secretary of the Interior, 1865,* 39th Cong., 1st sess., *House Executive Document No. 1* (Serial 1248), pt. 5, p. 580.

4. See ibid., pp. 699-719, for the report of the treaty negotiations.

5. Pope to President Andrew Johnson, Oct. 27, 1865; Pope to Harlan, Oct. 27, 1865: L.S., D.Mo.

6. Pope to Bent, Oct. 30, 1865; Bell to Dodge, Dec. 27, 1865: ibid.

7. Captain Gordon to Asst. Adjt. Gen., District of Kansas, Mar. 5, 1866, *Annual Report of the Secretary of the Interior, 1866,* 39th Cong., 2nd sess., *House Executive Document No. 1* (Serial 1284), p. 277.

8. Taylor to Thomas Murphy, Central Superintendency, Oct. 1, 1866, ibid., pp. 280-82.

9. The Commissioner of Indian Affairs announced that treaties had been made with 16,020 Indians representing the Two Kettle, Lower Brulé, Miniconjou, Hunkpapa, Yanktonai, Sans Arc, Upper Yanktonai, Oglala, and Blackfeet bands, ibid., p. 4.

10. George Hyde, *Red Cloud's Folk* (Norman: University of Oklahoma

Press, 1937), p. 136. Hyde describes these treaties as "a cracker-and-molasses peace."

11. Maynadier to Cooley, Jan. 25, 1866, *Annual Report of the Secretary of the Interior, 1866* (Serial 1284), pp. 204-06. Pope to General Frank Wheaton, District of Nebraska, Aug. 23, 1865: *Official Records,* Series I, vol. 48, pt. 2, pp. 1206-08.

12. Hyde, *Red Cloud's Folk,* pp. 138-40. James C. Olson, *Red Cloud and The Sioux Problem* (Lincoln: University of Nebraska Press, 1965), pp. 30-38. Report of E. B. Taylor and Colonel Maynadier, Annual Report of Superintendent Taylor, Oct. 1, 1866: *Annual Report of the Secretary of the Interior, 1866* (Serial 1284), pp. 208-09, 210-13. The Indian Bureau later blamed Carrington's arrival for the failure of the treaty but was aware of his orders and made no protest at the time.

13. Report of Special Agent E. B. Chandler to Superintendent H. B. Denman, Jan. 13, 1867, 39th Cong., 2nd sess., *Senate Executive Document No. 15* (Serial 1277), pp. 6-7. Chandler described the treaty as "little better than a farce."

14. Pope to Maynadier, June 14, 1866, L.S., D.Mo.

15. *Rocky Mountain News* (Denver), Aug. 3, 1866.

16. Carson and Bent to Pope, Oct. 27, 1865, Dept. of the Missouri, Letters Received, 1865, File C185, Records of the War Department, U.S. Army Commands, National Archives, Washington, D.C. This document now appears in *Colorado Magazine,* vol. 46 (Winter 1969), pp. 55-68.

17. Ibid.

18. Sherman to Grant, Nov. 6, 1865, Sherman Papers.

19. Pope to Sherman, Mar. 3, 1866, L.S., D.Mo. This document now appears in *Kansas Historical Quarterly,* vol. 35 (Winter 1969), pp. 345-72.

20. Sherman to Pope, Mar. 5, 1866; Sherman to Cooke, Mar. 28, 1866, Div. of the Missouri, Letters Received, 1866-68, Special File; Sherman to Rawlins, Mar. 6, 1866, Div. of the Mississippi, Letters Sent, 1865-66; Grant to Sherman, Mar. 14, 1866, Dept. of the Missouri, Letters Received, File A44; all in Records of the War Department, U.S. Army Commands, National Archives, Washington, D.C.

21. Pope to Governor W. R. Marshall of Minnesota, Mar. 7, 1866; Pope to S. L. Spink, Secretary of Dakota Territory, Mar. 8, 1866: L.S., D.Mo.

22. General Order No. 27, Dept. of the Missouri, Feb. 28, 1866; Sherman to Major George Leet, Feb. 16, 1871: 40th Cong., 1st sess., *Senate Executive Document No. 2* (Serial 1308), pp. 1-4.

23. Olson, pp. 41-47; Hyde, *Red Cloud's Folk,* pp. 140-48. Commissioner of Indian Affairs Lewis V. Bogy blamed the army for the Fetterman massacre. He said that the Indians did not want war and were on a friendly visit to the fort. He ignored the reports of his own officials and blamed the army for restricting the sale of arms and ammunition to the Indians although the military orders enforced his own stated policy. Bogy to the Secretary of the

Interior, Feb. 2, 1867, in letter from the Secretary of War on. . .massacre. . .at Fort Phil Kearny, 39th Cong., 2nd sess., *Senate Executive Document No. 15* (Serial 1277), pp. 2-4.

24. Robert G. Athearn, *William Tecumseh Sherman and the Settlement of the West* (Norman: University of Oklahoma Press, 1956), pp. 172-83.

25. George Bird Grinnell, *The Fighting Cheyenne* (Norman: University of Oklahoma Press, 1956), pp. 268-75; Donald J. Berthrong, *The Southern Cheyennes* (Norman: University of Oklahoma Press, 1963), pp. 289-99; and Douglas C. Jones, *The Treaty of Medicine Lodge* (Norman: University of Oklahoma Press, 1966), include a number of eyewitness accounts of the treaty council.

26. Carl Coke Rister, *Border Command: General Phil Sheridan in the West* (Norman: University of Oklahoma Press, 1944), chapters 8 and 9; Clarence Reckmeyer, "The Battle of Summit Springs," *Colorado Magazine,* vol. 6, no. 6 (November 1929), pp. 211-20; James T. King, *War Eagle: A Life of General Eugene A. Carr* (Lincoln: University of Nebraska Press, 1963), pp. 112-18.

C H A P T E R   S E V E N

1. Henry Whipple, *Lights and Shadows of a Long Episcopate* (New York: The Macmillan Co., 1912), pp. 136-37.

2. James D. Richardson, *A Compilation of the Messages and Papers of The Presidents* (New York: Bureau of National Literature and Art, 1910), vol. 5, pp. 3333, 3338.

3. Robert W. Mardock, "The Humanitarians and Post-Civil War Indian Policy" (unpublished doctoral dissertation, University of Colorado, 1958), pp. 28-32, 34, 49-50.

4. Ibid., pp. 59-63, Henry E. Fritz, *The Movement for Indian Assimilation, 1860-1890* (Philadelphia: University of Pennsylvania Press, 1963), pp. 72-75.

5. The Roman Catholic Church did not participate in the creation of the Quaker Policy and later criticized the work of other denominations. It claimed that a majority of the agencies should be filled by Roman Catholics. Peter J. Rahill, *The Catholic Indian Missions and Grant's Peace Policy, 1870-1884* (Washington, D.C.: The Catholic University Press, 1953), defends the Catholics while Fritz, chapter 4, condemns them. See also F. N. Blanchet to E. S. Parker, July 8, 1871, Board of Indian Commissioners, Letters Received, National Archives, Washington, D.C.

6. Pope to Grant, Jan. 26, 1867, John Pope, *General Pope's Reports and Letters on Indian Affairs* (n.p., n.d.), p. 10.

7. Robert Utley, "The Celebrated Peace Policy of General Grant," *North Dakota History,* vol. 20, no. 3 (July 1953), pp. 126-27. Fritz, pp. 80-81.

8. Utley, p. 126.

9. *Daily New Mexican* (Santa Fe), July 27, 1871.

10. *Boulder County News* (Colo.), June 8, 1870.

11. The New York *Herald,* quoted in the *Boulder County News* (Colo.), June 8, 1870.

12. The Denver *Tribune,* quoted in the *Boulder County News* (Colo.), June 15, 1870.

13. Pope to Custer, May 20, 1870; Pope to Lt. Col. George Hartsuff, Asst. Adjt. Gen., Div. of the Missouri, May 23, 1870; Pope to Nelson, May 17, 1870: Dept. of the Missouri, Letters Sent, Records of the War Department, U.S. Army Commands, National Archives, Washington, D.C. Hereafter cited as L.S., D.Mo. Annual Report of General Pope, *Annual Report of the Secretary of War, 1870,* 41st Cong., 3rd sess., *House Executive Document No. 1* (Serial 1446), pt. 2, pp. 6-7. Camp Supply had been founded in 1868 during Sheridan's campaign on the south central plains.

14. Pope to Hartsuff, June 3, 1870, L.S., D.Mo.

15. Pope to Hartsuff, July 11, 1870, ibid. Annual Report of Lawrie Tatum, *Annual Report of the Secretary of the Interior, 1870,* 41st Cong., 3rd sess., *House Executive Document No. 1* (Serial 1449), pt. 4, p. 726.

16. Pope to Hartsuff, June 1, 1870, L.S., D.Mo.

17. Pope to Hartsuff, June 1, 1870; Pope to Nelson, June 8, 1870: ibid.

18. Pope to Hartsuff, June 8, 1870, L.S., D.Mo.

19. Tatum to Hoag, June 18, July 1 and 5, 1870, Field Office Files, Kiowa-Comanche Agency, Records of the Bureau of Indian Affairs, National Archives, Washington, D.C. Hereafter cited as Kiowa File. Pope to Hoag, July 2, 1870, L.S., D.Mo.

20. Pope to Gov. James Harvey, July 11 and Aug. 5, 1870, L.S., D.Mo.

21. Annual Report of Lawrie Tatum, *Annual Report of the Secretary of the Interior, 1870* (Serial 1449), pp. 724-27. Annual Report of General Pope, *Annual Report of the Secretary of War, 1870* (Serial 1446), p. 10.

22. Lawrie Tatum, *Our Red Brothers and the Peace Policy of President Ulysses S. Grant* (Philadelphia: John C. Winston & Co., 1899), pp. 42-45. Wilbur S. Nye, *Carbine and Lance: The Story of Old Fort Sill* (Norman: University of Oklahoma Press, 1943), pp. 116-17.

23. Pope to Adj. Gen. of the Army, Nov. 2, 1870, L.S., D.Mo.

24. Ibid.

25. Pope to Brig. Gen. E. D. Townsend, Adj. Gen. of the Army, Dec. 30, 1870, L.S., D.Mo.

26. Annual Report of General Pope, *Annual Report of the Secretary of War, 1870* (Serial 1446), pp. 7-10, 18-19.

27. Pope to Parker, Jan. 4, 1871; Mitchell to Davidson, Feb. 13, 1871: L.S., D.Mo. Parker to Pope, Feb. 14, 1871, Dept. of the Missouri, Letters Received, 1871, File 16.

28. Pope to Porter, secretary to President Grant, Feb. 20, 1871, L.S., D.Mo.

29. Pope to Sherman, Mar. 1, 1871, L.S., D.Mo.

256

30. Pope to Sherman, Mar. 7, 1871, ibid.
31. Pope to Townsend, Mar. 7, 1871, ibid.
32. Ibid.
33. Pope to Hartsuff, Mar. 15, 1871, L.S., D.Mo.
34. Sherman to the Secretary of War, Mar. 25, 1871, Dept. of the Missouri, Letters Received, 1871, File M240.
35. Robert G. Athearn, *William Tecumseh Sherman and the Settlement of the West* (Norman: University of Oklahoma Press, 1956), pp. 288-89. Carl C. Rister, *Border Command: General Phil Sheridan in the West* (Norman: University of Oklahoma Press, 1944), pp. 172-73.
36. Athearn, pp. 288-90. Nye, *Carbine and Lance,* pp. 125-30. Rister, *Border Command,* pp. 174-76.
37. Sherman to General J. J. Reynolds, May 18, 1871, Sherman Papers. Athearn, p. 290.
38. Sherman to Mackenzie, May 19, 1871; Sherman to Col. Wilbain Wood, Fort Gibson, May 19, 1871: Sherman Papers.
39. Sherman to Pope, May 24, 1871; Sherman to Townsend, May 24, 1871: Carl Coke Rister, "Documents Relating to General W. T. Sherman's Southern Plains Indian Policy, 1871-1875," *Panhandle-Plains Historical Review,* vol. 10 (1937), pp. 50-55. Tatum to Hoag, May 25, 1871, Kiowa File.
40. Tatum to Grierson, May 27, 1871, Sherman Papers. Tatum to Hoag, May 28, 1871, Kiowa File.
41. Mizner to Sherman, June 9, 1871, Sherman Papers. Pope to Sheridan, June 5, 1871, L.S., D.Mo.
42. Tatum to Sherman and Grierson, May 29, 1871, Sherman Papers. William H. Leckie, *The Military Conquest of the Southwest Plains* (Norman: University of Oklahoma Press, 1967), p. 154. Robert G. Carter, *On the Border with Mackenzie* (New York: Antiquarian Press, Ltd., 1961; first published, 1935), pp. 99-102.
43. Sherman to Mackenzie, May 29, 1871, Sherman Papers.
44. Parker to Delano, June 19, 1871 in Delano to the Secretary of War, June 20, 1871. Dept. of the Missouri, Letters Received, 1871, File M498/2.
45. Carter, *On the Border with Mackenzie,* describes Mackenzie's campaign in chapter 6. William Leckie, *The Buffalo Soldiers: A Narrative of the Negro Cavalry in the West* (Norman: University of Oklahoma Press, 1967), pp. 64-65.

CHAPTER EIGHT

1. Tatum to Hoag, Sept. 16 and 26, 1871, Nov. 4, 1871, Field Office Files, Kiowa-Comanche Agency, Records of the Bureau of Indian Affairs, National Archives, Washington, D.C. Hereafter cited as Kiowa File.
2. Wilbur S. Nye, *Carbine and Lance* (Norman: University of Oklahoma Press, 1943), pp. 152-54.
3. Pope to Col. James Fry, Asst. Adjt. Gen., Div. of the Missouri, June 5,

1872; Pope to Sheridan, May 22 and 25, 1872: Dept. of the Missouri, Letters Sent, Records of the War Department, U.S. Army Commands, National Archives, Washington, D.C. Hereafter cited as L.S., D.Mo.

4. Pope to Hoag, May 25, 1872, L.S., D.Mo.

5. Pope to Hoag, May 22, 1872; Pope to Sheridan, May 22 and 25, 1872; Pope to Gov. James Harvey, June 3 and July 26: L.S., D.Mo.

6. Tatum to Hoag, June 5 and July 1, 1872, Kiowa File. Tatum reported that the Kiowa had killed about forty people and taken several hundred captives, Tatum to Hoag, Aug. 6, 1872, ibid.

7. Tatum to Hoag, Aug. 6, 1872, Kiowa File, Annual Report of L. Tatum, *Annual Report of the Secretary of the Interior, 1872,* 42nd Cong., 3rd sess., *House Executive Document No. 1* (Serial 1560), pt. 5, pp. 631-32.

8. Annual Report of L. Tatum, Report of the peace commission sent under the general council of the Indian Territory, *Annual Report of the Secretary of the Interior, 1872* (Serial 1560), pp. 579-82, 631-32.

9. Report of Capt. Henry Alvord, Oct. 10, 1872, ibid., pp. 513-14. Edward Parrish became ill and died at the Kiowa Agency.

10. Ibid., pp. 513-18.

11. Ibid., pp. 521-23, 525-27.

12. Annual Report of E. Hoag, ibid., pp. 1610-13.

13. Annual Report of L. Tatum, ibid., pp. 631-32. Tatum to Hoag, Nov. 1, 1872, Kiowa File. Thomas Battey, *Life and Adventures of a Quaker Among the Indians* (Boston: Lee and Shepard, 1875), p. 138.

14. Pope to Gov. James Harvey, Dec. 4, 1872, L.S., D.Mo.

15. Annual Report of Gen. Pope in *Annual Report of the Secretary of War, 1872,* 42nd Cong., 3rd sess., *House Executive Document No. 1* (Serial 1558), pt. 2, pp. 45-48.

16. Satanta offered to control the Kiowa, Comanche, Southern Cheyenne, Arapaho, Kiowa-Comanche, and Wichita tribes. Hoag to Commissioner Clum, Feb. 11, 1873, Central Superintendency, Letters to the Commissioner of Indian Affairs, 1871-74, Records of the Bureau of Indian Affairs, National Archives, Washington, D.C. Lawrie Tatum, *Our Red Brothers and the Peace Policy of President Ulysses S. Grant* (Philadelphia: John C. Winston & Co., 1899), pp. 132-33.

17. Tatum, p. 160.

18. Haworth to Hoag, Apr. 7 and 9, 1873, Kiowa File.

19. Hoag to Secretary of the Interior Columbus Delano, Apr. 19, 1873, Central Superintendency, Letters to the Commissioner of Indian Affairs, 1871-74.

20. Annual Report of E. Hoag, *Annual Report of the Secretary of the Interior, 1872* (Serial 1560), pp. 610-13.

21. Haworth to Hoag, June 9, 1873, Kiowa File.

22. *Daily Herald* (San Antonio), Apr. 3, 1873, quoted in William Leckie,

The Military Conquest of the Southern Plains (Norman: University of Oklahoma Press, 1963), p. 175.

23. Thomas Battey was with the Kiowa and recorded that they were excited, armed, and determined to rescue the chiefs if they were not released. Battey, pp. 201-04.

24. Sherman to Grierson, Sept. 28, 1872, Benjamin H. Grierson Papers, Newberry Library, Chicago, quoted in Robert G. Athearn, *William Tecumseh Sherman and the Settlement of the West* (Norman: University of Oklahoma Press, 1956), p. 296. Sherman to Davis, Feb. 16, 1874; Davis to Sherman, Feb. 7, 1874: Sherman Papers.

25. Annual Report of John Miles, *Annual Report of the Secretary of the Interior, 1873*, 43rd Cong., 1st sess., *House Executive Document No. 1* (Serial 1601), pt. 5, pp. 588-90. Pope to Hoag, Feb. 15, 1873, L.S., D.Mo. Donald Berthrong, *The Southern Cheyennes* (Norman: University of Oklahoma Press, 1963), pp. 372-74.

26. Annual Report of Gen. Pope, *Annual Report of the Secretary of War, 1872* (Serial 1558), pp. 48-50. *Daily New Mexican* (Santa Fe), Sept. 1, 1870.

27. Pope to Townsend, Apr. 8, 1873, L.S., D.Mo.

28. Sherman to Sheridan, May 2, 1873, Headquarters of the Army, Letters Sent, Records of the War Department, U.S. Army Commands, National Archives, Washington, D.C. Commissioner of Indian Affairs Smith to Delano, Sept. 18 and Nov. 14, 1873; Acting Commissioner Clum to Delano, Sept. 19, 1873: Records of the Bureau of Indian Affairs, Report Books, vol. 23, pp. 244-45, 251, 360-61.

29. Pope to Fry, Oct. 10, 1873; Pope to Biddle, Nov. 3, 1873: L.S., D.Mo. Annual Report of Gen. Pope, *Annual Report of the Secretary of War, 1873*, 43rd Cong., 1st sess., *House Executive Document No. 1* (Serial 1598), pt. 2, p. 46. *Boulder County News* (Colo.), Nov. 17, 1873.

30. Annual Report of Gen. Sheridan, *Annual Report of the Secretary of War, 1873* (Serial 1597), pp. 39-42.

31. Annual Report of James Haworth, *Annual Report of the Secretary of the Interior, 1873* (Serial 1601), pp. 587-88.

32. Annual Report of Columbus Delano; Annual Report of Edward Smith: ibid., pp. iii-vii, 371-76. Agent Miles also requested a company of cavalry to protect life and property at the Cheyenne-Arapaho Agency, Williams to Commanding Officer of Camp Supply, Nov. 6, 1873, L.S., D.Mo.

CHAPTER NINE

1. Haworth to Hoag, Apr. 20, 1874, Field Office Files, Kiowa-Comanche Agency, Records of the Bureau of Indian Affairs, National Archives, Washington, D.C. Hereafter cited as Kiowa File. William Leckie, *The Military Conquest of the Southern Plains* (Norman: University of Oklahoma Press, 1963), pp.

186-88. Wilbur S. Nye, *Carbine and Lance: The Story of Old Fort Sill* (Norman: University of Oklahoma Press, 1943), pp. 187-200.

2. Carl Coke Rister, "The Significance of the Destruction of the Buffalo in the Southwest," *Southwestern Historical Quarterly,* vol. 33 (July 1929), pp. 47-48. Carl Coke Rister, *Fort Griffin on the Texas Frontier* (Norman: University of Oklahoma Press, 1956), pp. 165, 193. Rister reports that one hunter took 1,000 pounds of lead and five kegs of powder on one hunt in 1877 and killed 4,900 buffalo.

3. Annual Report of John Miles, *Annual Report of the Secretary of Interior, 1874,* 43rd Cong., 2nd sess., *House Executive Document No. 1* (Serial 1639), pt. 5, p. 541.

4. Haworth to Commissioner Smith, Mar. 2, 1874; Haworth to Hoag, Apr. 20, 1874; Haworth to Cyrus Beede, Apr. 25, 1874: Kiowa File.

5. Haworth to Beede, June 13, 1874; Haworth to Hoag, July 14, 1874: Kiowa File.

6. Recent studies indicate that only 250 to 300 warriors were involved in the attack. Donald Berthrong, *The Southern Cheyennes* (Norman: University of Oklahoma Press, 1963), p. 385.

7. Pope to Osborn, July 1, 1874; Dunn to Osborn, July 8, 1874: Dept. of the Missouri, Letters Sent, Records of the War Department, U.S. Army Commands, National Archives, Washington, D.C. Hereafter cited as L.S., D.Mo.

8. Dunn to Osborn, July 8, 1874, L.S., D.Mo.

9. Pope to Sherman, July 8, 1874; Pope to Sheridan, July 10, 1874: L.S., D.Mo.

10. Pope to Sheridan, July 16, 1874, L.S., D.Mo.

11. Sheridan to Sherman, July 16 and 18, 1874, Div. of the Missouri, Letters Sent, Records of the War Department, U.S. Army Commands, National Archives, Washington, D.C.

12. Sherman to Sheridan, July 23, 1874, Sheridan Papers (Sherman-Sheridan Correspondence), Division of Manuscripts, Library of Congress, Washington, D.C.

13. Sheridan to Pope, Aug. 21, 1874, Div. of the Missouri, Letters Sent.

14. Sherman to Sheridan, Sept. 12, 1874, Sheridan Papers (Sherman-Sheridan Correspondence). Pope to Sherman, Sept. 16, 1874, William T. Sherman Papers, Division of Manuscripts, Library of Congress, Washington, D.C. Sheridan to Pope, July 24, 1874, enclosed in Sheridan to Pope, July 21, 1874, Dept. of the Missouri, Letters Received, File M438/2, Records of the War Department, U.S. Army Commands, National Archives, Washington, D.C.

15. Annual Report of Enoch Hoag, *Annual Report of the Secretary of the Interior, 1874* (Serial 1639), p. 521.

16. Pope to Sheridan, July 22, 1874, L.S., D.Mo.

17. Haworth to Beede, July 29 and Aug. 6, 1874; Beede to Hoag, Aug. 8, 1874 (enclosing Capt. G. K. Sanderson to Haworth, Aug. 5, 9, and 10, 1874); Sanderson to Haworth, Aug. 12, 1874, Kiowa File.

18. William Leckie, *The Buffalo Soldiers: A Narrative of the Negro Cavalry in the West* (Norman: University of Oklahoma Press, 1967), pp. 120-23. Satanta was present at the battle, and some of the enrolled Kiowa were involved in the fighting.

19. Pope to Miles, Aug. 5, Sept. 18 and 20, 1874, L.S., D. Mo.

20. There are many accounts of the war of 1874-75, the so-called Red River War. Nye, *Carbine and Lance,* makes use of Kiowa informants. Leckie, *The Buffalo Soldiers,* concentrates on the Ninth and Tenth Cavalry, the Negro regiments. Ernest Wallace's *Ranald S. Mackenzie on the Texas Frontier* (Lubbock: West Texas Museum Association, 1964) is a recent study of an outstanding Indian fighter. Sherman was pleased with the conduct of the troops. "They go in with the relish that used to make our hearts glad in 1864-5," he wrote. Sherman to Sheridan, Sept. 12, 1874, Sheridan Papers (Sherman-Sheridan Correspondence).

21. Satanta's health failed rapidly, and in 1878 the dying warrior committed suicide by jumping through an upper story window of the jail.

22. Sheridan to Secretary of War W. W. Belknap, Div. of the Missouri, Letters Sent. Sherman to Sheridan, Oct. 30, 1874, Sheridan Papers (Sherman-Sheridan Correspondence).

23. Smith to Delano, Nov. 20, 1874, Indian Office Report Books, vol. 24, pp. 193-94, Records of the Bureau of Indian Affairs, National Archives, Washington, D.C. It is an interesting commentary on the attitudes of army officers and the Indian Bureau that Sheridan and Pope wanted to send the families with the prisoners while the Indian Bureau refused. Pope to Drum, Jan. 5, 1875, L.S., D.Mo.

24. John Miles to Haworth, Jan. 21, 1875, enclosed in Davidson to Asst. Adjt. Gen., Dept. of Texas, Jan. 26, 1875, Dept. of the Missouri, Letters Received, File T593.

25. Annual Report of John Miles, *Annual Report of the Secretary of the Interior, 1875,* 44th Cong., 1st sess., *House Executive Document No. 1* (Serial 1680), pt. 5, p. 771.

26. Fort Sill was transferred to the Dept. of the Missouri in Mar. 1875. Henely killed more Cheyenne in one battle than all the troops had killed during the campaign of 1874-75, Berthrong, pp. 401-05.

27. Pope to Drum, Feb., 25, 1875, L.S., D.Mo.

28. Commissioners Smith to Delano, July 3, 1875, Indian Office Report Books, vol. 26, pp. 339-41. Annual Report of the Commissioner of Indian Affairs, *Annual Report of the Secretary of the Interior, 1875* (Serial 1680), p. 541.

CHAPTER TEN

1. Pope to Townsend, Oct. 27, 1874, Dept. of the Missouri, Letters Sent, Records of the War Department, U.S. Army Commands, National Archives, Washington, D.C. Hereafter cited as L.S., D.Mo.

2. Sheridan to Whipple, Act. Adjt. Gen., Dept of the Missouri, Dec. 27, 1874, Div. of the Missouri, Letters Sent, Records of the War Department, U.S. Army Commands, National Archives, Washington, D.C.

3. Pope to Drum, Jan. 6, 1875, L.S., D.Mo.

4. Pope to Townsend, Feb. 20, 1875; Pope to Drum, Feb. 23, 1875: L.S., D.Mo.

5. Smith to the Secretary of the Interior, Feb. 26, 1875, Indian Office Report Book, vol. 25, p. 512, Records of the Bureau of Indian Affairs, National Archives, Washington, D.C.

6. Hatch to Asst. Adjt. Gen., Dept. of the Missouri, Apr. 10, 1875, Dept. of the Missouri, Letters Received, File S117, Records of the War Department, U.S. Army Commands, National Archives, Washington, D.C. John Miles to Hoag, Apr. 9, 1975, Field Office Files, Cheyenne-Arapahoe Agency, Records of the Bureau of Indian Affairs, National Archives, Washington, D.C. Hereafter cited as Cheyenne File.

7. Pope endorsement, Apr. 17, 1875; Haworth to Hoag, May 31, 1875, enclosed in Acting Secretary of the Interior B. Conner to the Secretary of War, June 21, 1875, Dept. of the Missouri, Letters Received, File M907.

8. Pope to Drum, May 12, 1875; Pope to Sherman, Aug. 31, 1875: L.S., D.Mo.

9. Acting Agent Covington to Commissioner Smith, Sept. 14, 1875, Cheyenne File, Smith to the Secretary of the Interior, Sept. 11, 1875, Indian Office Report Books, vol. 26, pp. 521-24. Acting Secretary of the Interior Connor to Secretary of War, Sept. 21, 1875, Dept. of the Missouri, Letters Received, File M1268/3. Annual Report of Gen. Sherman, *Annual Report of the Secretary of War, 1875,* 44th Cong., 1st sess., *House Executive Document No. 1* (Serial 1674), pt. 2, p. 34.

10. Pope to Hoag, Nov. 20, 1875, L.S., D.Mo.

11. Annual report of J. A. Smith, *Annual Report of the Secretary of the Interior, 1876,* 44th Cong., 2nd sess., *House Executive Document No. 1* (Serial 1749), pt. 5, pp. 382-83. Pope to William Nicholson, June 6, 1876, L.S., D.Mo.

12. John Miles to Nicholson, Apr. 12, 1876, Cheyenne File. Miles seized 198 head of cattle on Apr. 11 by a forced sale.

13. John Miles to Commissioner Hayt, Nov. 30, 1877, Cheyenne File. Annual Report of Gen. Pope, *Annual Report of the Secretary of War, 1877,* 45th Cong., 2nd sess., *House Executive Document No. 1* (Serial 1794), pt. 2, p. 61.

14. Annual Report of P. B. Hunt, *Annual Report of the Secretary of the Interior, 1881,* 47th Cong., 1st sess., *House Executive Document No. 1* (Serial 2100), pt. 5, pp. 126-27.

15. Pope to Williams, Apr. 3 and 17, 1882, L.S., D.Mo.

16. Ibid.

17. Annual Report of James Haworth, *Annual Report of the Secretary of the Interior, 1876* (Serial 1749), p. 457. Annual Report of P. G. Hunt, *Annual*

Report of the Secretary of the Interior, 1879, 46th Cong., 2nd sess., *House Executive Document No. 1* (Serial 1910), pt. 5, pp. 171-72.

18. Pope to Gov. Pitkin of Colo., Mar. 31, 1879; Pope to Whipple, Dec. 18, 1878: L.S., D.Mo.

19. Ibid., Oct. 10, 1878, L.S., D.Mo. The 46th Cong., 2nd sess., *Senate Report No. 708* (Serial 1899) is a complete collection of testimony and documents regarding the Northern Cheyenne.

20. Pope to Drum, June 8, 1877, L.S., D.Mo. Annual Report of Gen. Sheridan, *Annual Report of the Secretary of War, 1878,* 45th Cong., 3rd sess., *House Executive Document No. 1* (Serial 1843), pt. 2, p. 34.

21. Annual Report of Gen. Pope, *Annual Report of the Secretary of War, 1877* (Serial 1794), p. 60.

22. Annual Report of Gen. Pope, *Annual Report of the Secretary of War, 1876,* 44th Cong., 2nd sess., *House Executive Document No. 1* (Serial 1742), pt. 2, p. 450.

23. Annual Report of James Haworth, *Annual Report of the Secretary of the Interior, 1877,* 45th Cong., 2nd sess., *House Executive Document No. 1* (Serial 1800), pt. 5, p. 483. Annual Report of John Miles, *Annual Report of the Secretary of the Interior, 1881* (Serial 2018), p. 126. Annual Report of P. B. Hunt, *Annual Report of the Secretary of the Interior, 1880,* 46th Cong., 3rd sess., *House Executive Document No. 1* (Serial 1959), pt. 5, p. 195.

24. Annual Report of V. T. McGillycuddy, *Annual Report of the Secretary of the Interior, 1881* (Serial 2018), p. 105.

25. Pope to Williams, June 22, 1883, L. S., D.Mo. This letter lists the property taken from the Indians since 1870. Annual Report of James Haworth, *Annual Report of the Secretary of the Interior, 1877* (Serial 1800), p. 483.

CHAPTER ELEVEN

1. *Daily New Mexican* (Santa Fe), Feb. 21 and May 5, 1871.

2. Ibid., June 4, 1870.

3. Ibid., Sept. 22 and Oct. 29, 1870.

4. Ibid., June 9 and Aug. 27, 1870.

5. Ibid., Dec. 2, 1870; Feb. 22, 1871. *The Borderer* (Las Cruces), Nov. 11 and Dec. 13, 1871.

6. *Daily New Mexican* (Santa Fe), May 6 and Aug. 27, 1871.

7. Annual Report of Agent Piper, *Annual Report of the Secretary of the Interior, 1872,* 42nd Cong., 3rd sess., *House Executive Document No. 1* (Serial 1560), pt. 5, p. 690. Colyer Report in Annual Report of the Board of Indian Commissioners, *Annual Report of the Secretary of the Interior, 1871,* 42nd Cong., 2nd sess., *House Executive Document No. 1* (Series 1505), pt. 5, pp. 457-511.

8. Report of Gen. Howard, *Annual Report of the Secretary of the Interior, 1872* (Serial 1560), pp. 558-61. Pope to Sheridan, Dec. 11, 1872 and Jan. 10,

1873, Dept. of the Missouri, Letters Sent, Records of the War Department, U.S. Army Commands, National Archives, Washington, D.C. Hereafter cited as L.S., D.Mo.

9. Annual Report of Benjamin Thomas, *Annual Report of the Secretary of the Interior, 1873,* 43rd Cong., 1st sess., *House Executive Document No. 1* (Serial 1601), pt. 5, p. 644. Annual Report of Benjamin Thomas, *Annual Report of the Secretary of the Interior, 1874,* 43rd Cong., 2nd sess., *House Executive Document No. 1* (Serial 1639), pt. 5, pp. 618-19.

10. Annual Report of Gen. Pope, *Annual Report of the Secretary of War, 1876,* 44th Cong., 2nd sess., *House Executive Document No. 1* (Serial 1742), pt. 2, p. 449. Annual Report of Gen. Pope, *Annual Report of the Secretary of War, 1877,* 45th Cong., 2nd sess., *House Executive Document No. 1* (Serial 1794), pt. 2, p. 61. Pope to Drum, Nov. 5, 1877, L.S., D.Mo.

11. Annual Report of Gen. Pope, *Annual Report of the Secretary of War, 1880,* 46th Cong., 3rd sess., *House Executive Document No. 1* (Serial 1952), pt. 2, pp. 87-88. Pope was also concerned about future relationships with the Apache and recommended that the Mescalero and San Carlos reservations be moved farther from the sanctuary offered by the proximity of Mexico. Pope to Whipple, Oct. 23, 1880: L.S., D.Mo. It is also worth noting that troops under Pope's command did take advantage of a temporary agreement and crossed into Mexico briefly.

12. Annual Report of Gen. Pope, *Annual Report of the Secretary of War, 1871,* 42nd Cong., 2nd sess., *House Executive Document No. 1* (Serial 1503), pt. 2, pp. 41-42.

13. Sherman to Sheridan, May 2, 6, and 7, 1879, 46th Cong., 1st sess., *Senate Executive Document No. 20* (Serial 1869), pp. 25, 28, 29.

14. Annual Report of Gen. Pope, *Annual Report of the Secretary of War, 1881,* 47th Cong., 1st sess., *House Executive Document No. 1* (Serial 2010), pt. 2, pp. 114-15. Annual Report of Gen. Pope, *Annual Report of the Secretary of War, 1883,* 48th Cong., 1st sess., *House Executive Document No. 1* (Serial 2182), p. 130. Carl C. Rister, *Land of Hunger: David L. Payne and the Oklahoma Boomers* (Norman: University of Oklahoma Press, 1942), pp. 47-48.

15. Annual Report of Edward McCook, *Annual Report of the Secretary of the Interior, 1870,* 41st Cong., 3rd sess., *House Executive Document No. 1* (Serial 1449), pt. 4, p. 629.

16. *Boulder County News* (Colo.), July 26 and Sept. 13, 1872.

17. Pope to Hartsuff, May 24, 1870; Pope to Superintendent of Indian Affairs for Colorado and New Mexico, June 22, 1873: L.S., D.Mo.

18. Pope to Drum, Nov. 14, 1877, L.S., D.Mo. Pope to Townsend, Feb. 21, 1878, "Protection of the Citizens of Colorado Against the Indians," 45th Cong., 2nd sess., *House Executive Document No. 91* (Serial 1809), pp. 3-4. Annual Report of Gen. Pope, *Annual Report of the Secretary of War, 1879,*

45th Cong., 2nd sess., *House Executive Document No. 1* (Serial 1903), pt. 2, p. 81.

19. Pope to Sheridan, Sept. 7, 1878, L.S., D.Mo.

20. Pope to Sheridan, Sept. 7, 1878, L.S., D.Mo. Annual Report of E. A. Hayt, *Annual Report of the Secretary of the Interior, 1878,* 45th Cong., 3rd sess., *House Executive Document No. 1* (Serial 1850), pt. 5, p. 471.

21. Pope to Mackenzie, Sept. 20, 1879, L.S., D.Mo.

22. Pope to Whipple, May 24, 1880, L.S., D.Mo. Annual Report of Gen. Pope, *Annual Report of the Secretary of War, 1880* (Serial 1952), p. 85.

23. Pope to Adjt. Gen. of the U.S., July 15, 1881, L.S., D.Mo. Annual Report of Gen. Pope, *Annual Report of the Secretary of War, 1881* (Serial 2010), pp. 119, 121. Political connections allowed Eastman to recover his position; he was the brother-in-law of Senator T. W. Ferry of Michigan. Frank McNitt, *The Indian Traders* (Norman: University of Oklahoma Press, 1962), p. 168.

24. William Folwell, *A History of Minnesota* (St. Paul: Minnesota Historical Society, 1924), vol. 2, pp. 374-76.

25. Report of Special Agent G. F. Jocknick, *Annual Report of the Secretary of the Interior, 1871* (Serial 1505), pp. 676-80.

26. Major D. R. Clendenin to Asst. Adjt. Gen., Dist. of New Mexico, Jan. 5, 1875 enclosed in Lt. Col. Thomas Devin, Commanding Officer, Dist. of New Mexico, to Asst. Adjt. Gen., Dept. of the Missouri, Jan. 15, 1875, Office of Indian Affairs, Letters Received, New Mexico Superintendency, Records of the Bureau of Indian Affairs, National Archives, Washington, D.C. Clendenin to Asst. Adjt. Gen., Dist. of New Mexico, Jan. 13, 1875, enclosed in Devin to Asst. Adjt. Gen., Dept. of the Missouri, Jan. 29, 1875, Dept. of the Missouri, Letters Received, File N54, Records of the War Department, U.S. Army Commands, National Archives, Washington, D.C.

27. Capt. J. MacMurray to Asst. Adjt. Gen., Dept. of the Columbia, Sept. 19, 1884; Major W. F. Drumm to Asst. Adjt. Gen., Dept. of the Columbia, Adj. Gen.'s Office: Letters Received, File 5474/1884, filed with 6067/1881, Records of the War Department, National Archives, Washington, D.C.

CHAPTER TWELVE

1. Sherman to Sheridan, Mar. 9, 1879, Sheridan Papers (Sherman-Sheridan Correspondence), Division of Manuscripts, Library of Congress, Washington, D.C. Sherman to Pope, Oct. 10, 1881, Headquarters of the Army, Letters Sent, Records of the War Dept., National Archives, Washington, D.C.

2. Loring B. Priest, *Uncle Sam's Stepchildren: The Reformation of the United States Indian Policy, 1865-1887* (New Brunswick: Rutgers University Press, 1942), pp. 64-65.

3. Annual Report of John Cromsie, *Annual Report of the Secretary of the*

Interior, 1886, 49th Cong., 2nd sess., *House Executive Document No. 1* (Serial 2467), pt. 5, p. 280.

4. Miles to Commissioner Hayt, Nov. 30, 1877, Field Office Files, Cheyenne-Arapaho Agency, Records of the Bureau of Indian Affairs, National Archives, Washington, D.C.

5. Sherman to John Rawlins, Sept. 21, 1866, 39th Cong., 2nd sess., *House Executive Document No. 23* (Serial 1288), p. 15.

6. Testimony of General Crook, "Transfer of the Indian Bureau to the War Department," 45th Cong., 3rd sess., *Senate Miscellaneous Document No. 53* (Serial 1835), p. 113.

7. Lee and Bennett are good examples of the type of officer who served briefly as Indian agents. Jesse Lee became a 2nd lieutenant in 1863, a 1st lieutenant in 1866, a captain in 1879, a major in 1898, and a brigadier general in 1902.

8. Sherman to Sheridan, Mar. 5, 1870, 41st Cong., 2nd sess., *House Executive Document No. 269* (Serial 1426), p. 10.

9. *Daily New Mexican* (Santa Fe), May 28, 1877.

10. Ibid., Oct. 24, 1877.

11. *Omaha Republican* (Nebr.), Oct. 27, 1875.

12. *Boulder County News* (Colo.), May 9, 1873. *Sentinel* (Monroe, Wis.), quoted in the *Boulder County News* (Colo.), June 15, 1870.

Bibliography

MANUSCRIPTS

1. *Library of Congress, Washington, D.C.*
   Ulysses S. Grant Papers
   Abraham Lincoln Papers
   Philip H. Sheridan Papers
   William T. Sherman Papers

2. *National Archives, Washington, D.C.*
   a. *Records of Bureau of Indian Affairs, Record Group 75*
      Board of Indian Commissioners, Letters Received
      Board of Indian Commissioners, Letters Sent
      Board of Indian Commissioners, Minutes of Board Meetings
      Office of Indian Affairs, Letters Received
      Central Superintendency, Letters Sent to Commissioner of Indian Affairs
      Field Office Files, Cheyenne-Arapaho Agency, 1870-78
      Field Office Files, Kiowa-Comanche Agency, 1870-78
      Field Office Files, Southern Apache Agency, 1873-78
      Indian Office Report Books
   b. *Army-Navy Branch, Record Group 94*
      Office of the Adjutant General, Letters Received, 1883-86
      Record Group 98
      Department of Arizona, Letters Received, 1883-86
      Department of the Missouri, General Orders, 1870-83
      Department of the Missouri, Letters Received, 1865-66
      Department of the Missouri, Letters Received, 1870-83
      Department of the Missouri, Letters and Telegrams Sent, 1870-83
      Division of the Mississippi, Letters and Telegrams Sent, 1863-65
      Division of the Mississippi, Letters Sent, 1865-66
      Division of the Missouri, General Orders, 1865-82

Division of the Missouri, Letters Received, 1866-69, Special File
Division of the Missouri, Letters Received, 1877-79
Division of the Missouri, Letters Sent and Received, 1865
Division of the Missouri, Letters Sent, 1868-71
Division of the Missouri, Letters Sent, 1874-76
Division of the Missouri, Special Orders, 1865
Division of the Missouri, Telegrams Sent and Received, 1865
Record Group 108
Headquarters of the Army, Letters Sent, 1873-83

3. *Other Depositories*

Frank D. Baldwin Papers, Henry E. Huntington Library, San Marino, Calif.
William Carey Brown Papers, University of Colorado Library, Boulder, Colo.
Cobb Collection, University of Colorado Library, Boulder, Colo.
Charles A. R. Dimon Papers, Yale University Library, New Haven, Conn.
Henry H. Sibley Papers, Minnesota Historical Society, St. Paul, Minn.
Lawrie Tatum Papers, William Penn College, Oskaloosa, Iowa

4. *Dissertations and Theses*

Cox, Merlin G. "John Pope, Fighting General from Illinois," unpublished doctoral dissertation, University of Florida, 1956.

Jorstad, Erling T. "The Life of Henry Hastings Sibley," unpublished doctoral dissertation, University of Wisconsin, 1957.

Mardock, Robert W. "The Humanitarians and Post-Civil War Indian Policy," unpublished doctoral dissertation, University of Colorado, 1958.

Unrau, William. "The Role of the Indian Agent in the Settlement of the South-Central Plains, 1861-1868," unpublished doctoral dissertation, University of Colorado, 1963.

Waddel, William S. "The Military Relations between the Sioux Indians and the United States Government in Dakota Territory, 1860-1891," unpublished master's thesis, University of South Dakota, 1931.

Waltmann, Henry G. "The Interior Department, War Department and Indian Policy, 1865-1887," unpublished doctoral dissertation, University of Nebraska, 1962.

DOCUMENTS

1. *Congressional Documents*

Annual Report of the Board of Indian Commissioners.
Annual Report of the Secretary of the Interior.
Annual Report of the Secretary of War.
"Condition of the Indian Tribes," 39th Cong., 2nd sess., *Senate Report No. 156* (Serial 1279).
Letter from the Secretary of the Interior in answer to a Senate resolution of

Mar. 19, 1874, communicating information in relation to the number of Indians captured or killed by U.S. troops during the year 1873, 43rd Cong., 2nd sess., *Senate Executive Document No. 22* (Serial 1629).

Letter from the Secretary of the Interior in answer to a resolution of the House of 23rd of May, in regard to the conduct of Indian affairs in Dakota Territory, 39th Cong., 1st sess., *House Executive Document No. 147* (Serial 1267).

Letter from the Secretary of War in answer to a resolution of the House of 19th instant, transmitting report of Captain J. L. Fisk, of the expedition to escort emigrants from Fort Abercrombie to Fort Benton, etc., 37th Cong., 3rd sess., *House Executive Document No. 80* (Serial 1164).

Letter from the Secretary of War in answer to a resolution of the House of Feb. 26, transmitting report of Captain Fisk, of his late expedition to the Rocky Mountains and Idaho, 39th Cong., 1st sess., *House Executive Document No. 45* (Serial 1189).

Letter from the Secretary of War in answer to a resolution of the House, of Mar. 3, 1870, in relation to the late expedition against the Piegan Indians in the Territory of Montana, 41st Cong., 2nd sess., *House Executive Document No. 269* (Serial 1426).

Letter from the Secretary of War, transmitting a communication from Colonel Mackenzie relative to matters at Fort Sill, 44th Cong., 1st sess., *House Executive Document No. 175* (Serial 1691).

Message of the President of the U.S., communicating a report from the Secretary of State in answer to a resolution of the Senate of the 26th of Jan., respecting the correspondence with the authorities of Great Britain in relation to the proposed pursuit of hostile bands of the Sioux Indians into the Hudson's Bay territories, 38th Cong., 1st sess., *Senate Executive Document No. 13* (Serial 1176).

Message of the President of the U.S. in answer to a resolution of the Senate of the 5th instant in relation to the Indian barbarities in Minnesota, 37th Cong., 3rd sess., *Senate Executive Document No. 7* (Serial 1149).

Message from the President of the U.S. in answer to Senate resolution of May 7, 1879, for information on alleged occupation of a portion of the Indian Territory, 46th Cong., 1st sess., *Senate Executive Document No. 20* (Serial 1869).

"Papers in Relation to the Reorganization of the Army," 46th Cong., 1st sess., *Senate Misc. Document No. 14* (Serial 1873).

"Protection Across the Continent," 39th Cong., 2nd sess., *House Executive Document No. 23* (Serial 1288).

"Protection of the Citizens of Colorado Against the Indians," 45th Cong., 2nd sess., *House Executive Document No. 91* (Serial 1809).

Report of the Committee of Indian Affairs on Removal of Dakota and Winnebago Indians, 37th Cong., 3rd sess., *House Report No. 13* (Serial 1173).

Testimony taken by the Joint Committee appointed to take into consideration the expediency of transferring the Indian Bureau to the War Department, 45th Cong., 3rd sess., *Senate Misc. Document No. 53* (Serial 1835).

2. *General Government Documents*

Hodge, Federick Webb, ed. *Handbook of American Indians North of Mexico.* Bureau of American Ethnology *Bulletin No. 30,* 2 vols., 1907.

Kappler, Charles J., ed. *Indian Affairs: Laws and Treaties,* 4 vols., Washington, D.C.: 1904, 1913, 1927.

Mooney, James. *Calender History of the Kiowa Indians.* Bureau of American Ethnology, *17th Annual Report,* vol. 2, 1898.

The War of the Rebellion: A Compilation of the Official Records of the Union and Confederate Armies. Four series, 128 vols. Washington D.C.: Government Printing Office, 1880-1901.

3. *State Documents*

Board of Commissioners (Minn.). *Minnesota in the Civil and Indian Wars, 1861-1865.* St. Paul: The Pioneer Press Co., 1890.

NEWSPAPERS

Borderer, Las Cruces, N.M.
Boulder County News, Colo.
Colorado Chieftain, Pueblo, Colo.
Daily Mining Journal, Blackhawk, Colo.
Daily New Mexican, Santa Fe, N.M.
Daily Optic, Las Vegas, N.M.
Daily Southwest, Silver City, N.M.
Denver *Tribune*
Frontier Scout, Fort Rice, Dakota Territory
Frontier Scout, Fort Union, Dakota Territory
Grant County Herald, Silver City, N.M.
Junction City Union, Kan.
Leavenworth Daily Times, Kan.
Missouri Republican, St. Louis, Mo.
New York *Herald*
New York *Times*
Omaha Republican, Neb.
Rocky Mountain News, Denver, Colo.
Thirty-Four, Las Cruces, N.M.
Yankton Dakotian, Dakota Territory
Union and Dakotaian, Yankton, Dakota Territory

BOOKS

Athearn, Robert G. *William Tecumseh Sherman and the Settlement of the West.* Norman: University of Oklahoma Press, 1956.

270

————. *Forts of the Upper Missouri.* Englewood Cliffs, N.J.: Prentice-Hall, Inc. 1967.

Bailey, Lynn R. *The Long Walk.* Los Angeles: Westernlore Press, 1964.

Barrows, William. *The Indian's Side of the Indian Question.* Boston: C. Lothrop Co., 1887.

Battey, Thomas C. *Life and Adventures of a Quaker Among the Indians.* Norman: University of Oklahoma Press, 1968. First published 1875.

Beaver, R. Pierce. *Church, State, and the American Indians.* St. Louis: Concordia Publishing House, 1966.

Berkhofer, Robert F. *Salvation and the Savage: An Analysis of Protestant Missions and American Indian Response, 1787-1862.* Lexington: University of Kentucky Press, 1965.

Berthrong, Donald J. *The Southern Cheyennes.* Norman: University of Oklahoma Press, 1963.

Blegen, Theodore C. *Minnesota: A History of the State.* Minneapolis: University of Minnesota Press, 1963.

Boller, Henry A. *Among the Indians, Eight Years in the Far West, 1858-1866.* Edited by Milo M. Quaife. Chicago: R. R. Donnelley & Sons, Co., 1959.

Bowles, Samuel. *Across the Continent: A Summer's Journey to the Rocky Mountains, the Mormons, and the Pacific States with Speaker Colfax.* Springfield, Mass.: Samuel Bowles & Co., 1866.

Brophy, William A. and Sophie D. Aberle, *The Indian: America's Unfinished Business.* Norman: University of Oklahoma Press, 1966.

Brown, D. Alexander. *The Galvanized Yankees.* Urbana: University of Illinois Press, 1963.

Brown, Dee. *Fort Phil Kearny.* New York: G. P. Putman's Sons, 1962.

Carley, Kenneth. *The Sioux Uprising of 1862.* St. Paul: Minnesota Historical Society, 1961.

Carter, Robert G. *The Old Sergeant's Story: Winning the West from the Indians and Bad Men in 1870 to 1876.* New York: Frederick H. Hitchcock, 1926.

Carter, Robert G., *On the Border with Mackenzie,* New York: Antiquarian Press, Ltd., 1961. First published 1935.

Crawford, Samuel. *Kansas in the Sixties.* Chicago: A. C. McClurg and Co., 1911.

Crook, George. *General George Crook, His Autobiography.* Edited by Martin Schmitt. Norman: University of Oklahoma Press, 1946.

Custer, George A. *My Life on the Plains or, Personal Experiences with Indians.* Norman: University of Oklahoma Press, 1962.

Dale, Edward E. *The Indians of the Southwest.* Norman: University of Oklahoma Press, 1949.

Dodge, Grenville M. *The Battle of Atlanta, and other Campaigns, Addresses, etc.* Denver: Sage Books, 1965.

Dodge, Richard I. *Our Wild Indians; Thirty-three Years' Personal Experiences*

271

Among the Red Men of the Great West. Hartford: A. D. Worthington, 1882.
————. *The Plains of the Great West and their Inhabitants.* New York: Putnam, 1877.

Drips, Joseph. *Three Years Among the Indians in Dakota.* Kimball, S. Dak.: Brulé Index, 1894.

Emmitt, Chris. *Fort Union and the Winning of the Southwest.* Norman: University of Oklahoma Press, 1965.

Eposito, Vincent J., *The West Point Atlas of American Wars.* New York: Frederick A. Praeger, Inc., 1959.

Faulk, Odie B. *The Geronimo Campaign.* New York: Oxford University Press, 1969.

Flandrau, Charles E. *The History of Minnesota and Tales of the Frontier.* St. Paul: E. W. Porter, 1900.

Folwell, William W. *A History of Minnesota.* 4 vols. St. Paul: Minnesota Historical Society, 1911.

Frazer, Robert W. *Forts of the West.* Norman: University of Oklahoma Press, 1965.

Fritz, Henry E. *The Movement for Indian Assimilation, 1860-1890.* Philadelphia: University of Pennsylvania Press, 1963.

Gard, Wayne, *The Great Buffalo Hunt.* New York: Alfred A. Knopf, 1959.

Glass, Major E. L. N. *The History of the Tenth Cavalry, 1866-1921.* Tucson: Acme Printing Co., 1921.

Goetzmann, William. *Army Exploration in the American West, 1803-1863.* New Haven: Yale University Press, 1959.

Grinnell, George, Bird. *The Fighting Cheyennes.* Norman: University of Oklahoma Press, 1956.

Hafen, LeRoy R. and Ann W. Hafen (eds.). *Powder River Campaigns and Sawyer's Expedition of 1865.* Glendale, Calif.: Arthur H. Clark Co., 1961.

Hafen, LeRoy R. and Francis M. Young (eds.). *Fort Laramie and the Pageant of the West, 1834-1890.* Glendale, Calif.: Arthur H. Clark Co., 1938.

Hagan, William T. *American Indians.* Chicago: University of Chicago Press, 1961.

————. *Indian Police and Judges: Experiments in Acculturation and Control.* New Haven: Yale University Press, 1966.

Harmon, George D. *Sixty Years of Indian Affairs: Political, Economic, and Diplomatic, 1789-1850.* Chapel Hill: University of North Carolina Press, 1941.

Heard, Issac V. D. *History of the Sioux War and Massacres of 1862 and 1863.* New York: Harper and Brothers, 1864.

Hirshson, Stanley P. *Grenville M. Dodge: Soldier, Politician, Railroad Pioneer.* Bloomington: Indiana University Press, 1967.

Hoig, Stan. *The Sand Creek Massacre.* Norman: University of Oklahoma Press, 1961.

Hoopes, Alban W. *Indian Affairs and their Administration: With Special Refer-*

ence to the Far West, 1849-1860. Philadelphia: University of Pennsylvania Press, 1932.

Howard, Oliver O. *My Life and Experiences Among our Hostile Indians.* Hartford: A. D. Worthington, 1907.

Hunt, Aurora. *James H. Carleton, Frontier Dragoon.* Glendale, Calif.: Arthur H. Clark Co., 1958.

Hyde, George E. *Red Cloud's Folk.* Norman: University of Oklahoma Press, 1937.

————. *A Sioux Chronicle.* Norman: University of Oklahoma Press, 1956.

————. *Spotted Tail's Folk: A History of the Brulé Sioux.* Norman: University of Oklahoma Press, 1961.

————. *Life of George Bent Written From His Letters.* Edited by Savoie Lottinville. Norman: University of Oklahoma Press, 1968.

Jackson, Helen Hunt. *Century of Dishonor.* New York: Harper and Brothers, 1881.

Jackson, William T. *Wagon Roads West; A Study of Federal Road Surveys and Construction in the Trans-Mississippi West, 1846-1869.* Berkeley: University of California Press, 1952.

Johnson, Virginia W. *The Unregimented General: A Biography of Nelson A. Miles.* Boston: Houghton Mifflin Co., 1962.

Jones, Douglas C. *The Treaty of Medicine Lodge.* Norman: University of Oklahoma Press, 1966.

Jones, Robert H. *The Civil War in the Northwest.* Norman: University of Oklahoma Press, 1960.

Kelsey, Rayner W. *Friends and the Indians, 1655-1917.* Philadelphia: The Associated Executive Committee of Friends on Indian Affairs, 1917.

Kenner, Charles L. *A History of New Mexican-Plains Indian Relations.* Norman: University of Oklahoma Press, 1969.

King, James. T. *War Eagle: A Life of General Eugene A. Carr.* Lincoln: University of Nebraska Press, 1963.

Lamar, Howard R. *Dakota Territory, 1861-1889.* New Haven: Yale University Press, 1956.

Larpenteur, Charles. *Forty Years a Fur Trader on the Upper Missouri: The Personal Narrative of Charles Larpenteur, 1833-1872.* 2 vols. Edited by Elliott Coues. New York: Francis P. Harper, 1898.

Lass, William. *A History of Steamboating on the Upper Missouri River.* Lincoln: University of Nebraska Press, 1962.

Lavender, David. *Bent's Fort.* Garden City: Doubleday and Co., Inc., 1954.

Leckie, William H. *The Buffalo Soldiers: A Narrative of the Negro Cavalry in the West.* Norman: University of Oklahoma Press, 1967.

————. *The Military Conquest of the Southern Plains.* Norman: University of Oklahoma Press, 1963.

Lockwood, Frank C. *The Apache Indians.* New York: The Macmillan Co., 1938.

McNitt, Frank. *The Indian Traders.* Norman: University of Oklahoma Press, 1962.

Malin, James C. *Indian Policy and Westward Expansion.* Lawrence: University of Kansas Humanistic Studies, vol. 2, no. 3, November 1921.

Mayhall, Mildred. *The Kiowas.* Norman: University of Oklahoma Press, 1962.

Meyer, Roy W. *History of the Santee Sioux: United States Indian Policy on Trial.* Lincoln: University of Nebraska Press, 1967.

Miles, Nelson A. *Personal Recollections and Observations of General Nelson A. Miles.* Chicago: The Werner Co., 1897.

————. *Serving the Republic.* New York: Harper and Brothers, 1911.

Mishkin, Bernard. *Rank and Warfare among the Plains Indians.* Monographs of the American Ethnological Society, III. New York: J. J. Augustin, 1940.

Nadeau, Remi. *Fort Laramie and the Sioux Indians.* Englewood Cliffs, N.J.: Prentice-Hall, Inc., 1967.

Nankivell, Major John H. *History of the Military Organizations of the State of Colorado, 1860-1935.* Denver: The W. H. Kistler Stationary Co., 1935.

Night, Oliver. *Following the Indian Wars: The Story of the Newspaper Correspondents among the Indian Campaigners.* Norman: University of Oklahoma Press, 1960.

Nye, Wilbur S. *Bad Medicine & Good: Tales of the Kiowas.* Norman: University of Oklahoma Press, 1962.

————. *Carbine and Lance: The Story of Old Fort Sill.* Norman: University of Oklahoma Press, 1943.

Oehler, C. M. *The Great Sioux Uprising.* New York: Oxford University Press, 1959.

Ogle, Ralph H. *Federal Control of the Western Apaches: 1848-1886.* Albuquerque: University of New Mexico Press, 1940. New edition 1970.

Olson, James C. *Red Cloud and the Sioux Problem.* Lincoln: University of Nebraska Press, 1965.

Opler, Marvin K. *The Southern Ute of Colorado.* Reprinted from *Acculturation in Seven American Indian Tribes.* New York: D. Appleton-Century Co., 1949.

Parker, James. *The Old Army, Memories, 1872-1918.* Philadelphia: Dorrance and Co., 1929.

Pearce, Roy H. *The Savages of America: A Study of the Indian and the Idea of Civilization.* Baltimore: Johns Hopkins Press, 1953.

Pope, John. *General Pope's Reports and Letters on Indian Affairs.* n.p. n.d.

————. *The Indian Question.* Address by General Pope before the Social Science Association at Cincinnati, Ohio, May 20, 1878. n.p., n.d.

Price, George F. *Across the Continent with the Fifth Cavalry.* New York: Antiquarian Press, Ltd., 1959.

Priest, B. Loring. *Uncle Sam's Stepchildren: The Reformation of the United States Indian Policy, 1865-1887.* New Brunswick, N.J.: Rutgers University Press, 1942.

————. *American Indian Policy in the Formative Years: The Indian Trade and Intercourse Acts, 1790-1834.* Cambridge, Mass.: Harvard University Press, 1962.

Prucha, Francis P. *A Guide to the Military Posts of the United States, 1789-1895.* Madison: State Historical Society of Wisconsin, 1964.

Rahill, Peter. *The Catholic Indian Missions and Grant's Peace Policy, 1870-1884.* Washington, D.C.: The Catholic University of America Press, 1953.

Richardson, James. *A Compilation of the Messages and Papers of the Presidents.* New York: Bureau of National Literature and Art, 1910.

Richardson, Rupert. *The Comanche Barrier to the South Plains Settlement.* Glendale, Calif.: Arthur H. Clark Co., 1934.

————. *The Frontier of Northwest Texas, 1846-1876.* Glendale, Calif.: Arthur H. Clark Co., 1963.

Riggs, Stephen R. *Mary and I, Forty Years with the Sioux.* Chicago: W. G. Holmes, 1880.

————. *Tah-koo- Wah-kan, or, The Gospel Among the Dakotas.* Boston: Congregational Sabbath-School and Publishing Society, 1869.

Rister, Carl Coke. *Border Command: General Phil Sheridan in the West.* Norman: University of Oklahoma Press, 1944.

————. *Fort Griffin on the Texas Frontier.* Norman: University of Oklahoma Press, 1956.

————. *Land Hunger: David L. Payne and the Oklahoma Boomers.* Norman: University of Oklahoma Press, 1942.

————. *The Southwestern Frontier.* Cleveland: Arthur H. Clark Co., 1928.

Robinson, Elwyn B. *History of North Dakota.* Lincoln: University of Nebraska Press, 1966.

Rockwell, Wilson. *The Utes, A Forgotten People.* Denver: Sage Books, 1956.

Roddis, Louis H. *The Indian Wars of Minnesota.* Cedar Rapids, Iowa: The Torch Press, 1956.

Rogers, Fred B. *Soldiers of the Overland.* San Francisco: The Grabhorn Press, 1930.

Rushmore, Elsie M. *The Indian Policy during Grant's Administration.* Jamaica, N.Y.: Marion Press, 1914.

Schell, Herbert S. *History of South Dakota.* Lincoln: University of Nebraska Press, 1961.

Schmeckebier, Laurence. *The Office of Indian Affairs, Its History, Activities, and Organization.* Baltimore: Johns Hopkins Press, 1927.

Seger, John H. *Early Days Among the Cheyenne and Arapahoe Indians.* Edited by Stanley Vestal. Norman: University of Oklahoma Press, 1934.

Sheftan, James E. *The United States Army and Reconstruction, 1865-1877.* Baton Rouge, Louisiana State University Press, 1967.

Sheridan, Philip. *Personal Memoirs of P. H. Sheridan.* 2 vols. New York: Charles L. Webster & Co., 1888.

Sherman, William T. *Memoirs of Gen. W. T. Sherman.* 2 vols., 4th ed. New York: Charles L. Webster & Co., 1891.

Slattery, Charles L. *Felix Reville Brunot, 1820-1898.* New York: Longmans, Green, and Co., 1901.

Sonnichsen, C. L. *The Mescalero Apaches.* Norman: University of Oklahoma Press, 1958.

Spicer, Edward H. *Cycles of Conquest: The Impact of Spain, Mexico, and the United States on the Indians of the Southwest, 1533-1960.* Tucson: University of Arizona Press, 1962.

Sprague, Marshall. *Massacre: The Tragedy at White River.* Boston: Little, Brown and Co., 1957.

Stanley F. *The Apaches of New Mexico, 1540-1940.* Pampa, Texas: Pampa Print Shop, 1962.

Stratton, Porter. *The Territorial Press of New Mexico, 1834-1912.* Albuquerque: University of New Mexico Press, 1969.

Sunder, John E. *The Fur Trade on the Upper Missouri, 1840-1865.* Norman, University of Oklahoma Press, 1965.

Tatum, Lawrie. *Our Red Brothers and the Peace Policy of President Ulysses S. Grant.* Philadelphia: John C. Winston & Co., 1899. New edition, Lincoln: University of Nebraska Press, 1970.

Thrapp, Dan L. *The Conquest of Apacheria.* Norman: University of Oklahoma Press, 1967.

Underhill, Ruth M. *The Navajos.* Norman: University of Oklahoma Press, 1956.

Utley, Robert M. *The Last Days of the Sioux Nation.* New Haven: Yale University Press, 1963.

————. *Frontiersmen in Blue: The United States Army and the Indian, 1840-1865.* New York: The Macmillan Co., 1967.

Vaughn, J. W. *The Battle of Platte Bridge.* Norman: University of Oklahoma Press, 1963.

Walker Francis A. *The Indian Question.* Boston: James R. Osgood and Co., 1874.

Wallace, Ernest. *Ranald S. Mackenzie on the Texas Frontier.* Lubbock: West Texas Museum Association, 1964.

Wallace, Ernest and E. Adamson Hoebel. *The Comanches: Lords of the South Plains.* Norman: University of Oklahoma Press, 1952.

Ware, Eugene F. *The Indian War of 1864.* Edited by Clyde Walton. New York: St. Martin's Press, 1960.

West, Nathaniel. *The Ancestry, Life, and Times of Hon. Henry Hastings Sibley. L.L.D.* St. Paul: Pioneer Press Publishing Co., 1889.

Whipple, Henry B. *Lights and Shadows of a Long Episcopate.* New York: The Macmillan Co., 1912.

White, Helen M. (ed.). *Ho! For the Gold Fields: Northern Overland Wagon Trains of the 1860's.* St. Paul: Minnesota Historical Society, 1966.

Williams, Kenneth. *Lincoln Finds a General.* 5 vols. New York: The Macmillan Co., 1949.
Williams, T. Harry. *Lincoln and the Radicals.* Madison: University of Wisconsin Press, 1941.
————. *Lincoln and His Generals.* New York: Alfred A. Knopf, 1952.

PERIODICALS

Athearn, Robert G. "Frontier Critics of the Western Army," *Montana, the Magazine of Western History,* vol. 5 (spring 1955), pp. 16-28.
————. "War Paint Against Brass: The Army and the Plains Indian," *Montana, the Magazine of Western History,* vol. 6 (July 1956), pp. 11-22.
Babcock, Willoughby M. "Minnesota's Indian War," *Minnesota History,* vol. 38 (September 1962), pp. 93-98.
————. "Minnesota's Frontier: A Neglected Sector of the Civil War," *Minnesota History* 38 (June 1963), pp. 274-86.
Buntin, Martha. "The Quaker Indian Agents of the Kiowa, Comanche, and Wichita Indian Reservations," *Chronicles of Oklahoma,* vol. 10 (June 1932), pp. 204-18.
Campbell, C. E., "Down Among the Red Men," *Collections of the Kansas State Historical Society,* vol. 17 (1928), pp. 623-91.
Campbell, Walter S. "The Cheyenne Dog Soldiers," *Chronicles of Oklahoma,* vol. 1 (January 1923), pp. 90-97.
Carley, Kenneth, "As Red Men Viewed It: Three Indian Accounts of the Uprising," *Minnesota History,* vol. 38 (September 1962), pp. 126-49.
————. The Sioux Campaign of 1862: Sibley's Letters to His Wife," *Minnesota History,* vol. 38 (September 1962), pp. 99-114.
Clark, Dan E. "Frontier Defense in Iowa, 1850-1865," *Iowa Journal of History and Politics,* vol. 16 (July 1918), pp. 315-86.
Connelley, William. "The Treaty Held at Medicine Lodge," *Collections of the Kansas State Historical Society,* vol. 7 (1928), pp. 601-06.
Connolly, James B. "Father DeSmet in North Dakota," *North Dakota History,* vol. 27 (winter 1960), pp. 5-24.
Covington, James W. "Causes of the Dull Knife Raid," *Chronicles of Oklahoma,* vol. 16 (spring 1948), pp. 13-22.
Crane, R. C. "Settlement of Indian Troubles in West Texas, 1874-1875," *West Texas Historical Association Yearbook,* vol. 1 (June 1925), pp. 3-14.
DeLand, Charles E. "The Sioux Wars," *South Dakota Historical Collections,* vol. 15 (1930), pp. 9-724.
Dunne, Adrian R. "A History of Old Fort Berthold," *North Dakota History,* vol. 30 (October 1963), pp. 157-240.
Ellis, Richard N. "Copper-Skinned Soldiers: The Apache Scouts," *Great Plains Journal,* vol. 5 (spring 1966), pp. 51-67.
————. "General John Pope and the Southern Plains Indians, 1875-1883," *Southwestern Historical Quarterly,* vol. 72 (October 1968), pp. 152-69.

————. (ed.). "Carson, Bent and the Indian Problem," *Colorado Magazine,* vol. 46 (winter 1969), pp. 55-68.

————. (ed.). "General Pope's Report on the West, 1866," *Kansas Historical Quarterly,* vol. 35 (winter 1969), pp. 345-72.

————. "The Humanitarian Soldiers," *Journal of Arizona History,* vol. 10 (summer 1969), pp. 53-66.

————. "After Bull Run: The Later Career of General John Pope," *Montana, the Magazine of Western History,* vol. 19 (autumn 1969), pp. 46-57.

————. "Volunteer Soldiers in the West, 1865," *Military Affairs,* vol. 34 (April 1970), pp. 53-56.

————. "Civilians, the Army, and the Indian Problem on the Northern Plains, 1862-1865," *North Dakota History,* vol. 37 (winter 1970) pp. 20-39.

————. "Political Pressures and Army Policies on The Northern Plains," *Minnesota History,* vol. 42 (summer 1970), pp. 43-53.

"Ending the Outbreak," *South Dakota Historical Collections,* vol. 9 (1918), pp. 409-69.

English, A. M. "Dakota's First Soldiers, History of the First Dakota Cavalry, 1862-1865," *South Dakota Historical Collections,* vol. 9 (1918), pp. 204-307.

Ferril, Will C. "The Sixteenth Kansas Cavalry in the Black Hills in 1865," *Rocky Mountain Herald* (Denver), July 2, 1927, in *Collection of the Kansas Historical Society,* vol. 17 (1928), pp. 855-58.

Foreman, Carolyn T. "General Benjamin Grierson," *Chronicles of Oklahoma,* vol. 14 (summer 1946), pp. 195-218.

————. "Colonel Jesse Henry Leavenworth," *Chronicles of Oklahoma,* vol. 5 (March 1935), pp. 14-29.

Foreman, Grant, "Historical Background of the Kiowa-Comanche Reservation," *Chronicles of Oklahoma,* vol. 19 (June 1941), pp. 129-40.

Garfield, Marvin. "The Military Post as a Factor in the Frontier Defense of Kansas, 1865-1869," *Kansas Historical Quarterly* vol. 1 (November 1931), pp. 50-62.

————. "Defense of the Kansas Frontier, 1864-1865," *Kansas Historical Quarterly,* vol. 1 (February 1932), pp. 140-52.

————. "Defense of the Kansas Frontier, 1866-1867," *Kansas Historical Quarterly,* vol. 1 (August 1932), pp. 326-44.

————. "Defense of the Kansas Frontier, 1868-1869," *Kansas Historical Quarterly,* vol. 1 (November 1932), pp. 451-74.

————. "The Indian Question in Congress and in Kansas," *Kansas Historical Quarterly,* vol. 2 (February 1933), pp. 29-44.

Gluek, Albin C., Jr. "The Sioux Uprising: A Problem in International Relations," *Minnesota History,* vol. 34 (winter 1955), pp. 317-24.

Hagerty, Leroy W. "Indian Raids Along the Platte and Little Blue Rivers, 1864-1865," *Nebraska History,* vol. 28 (July-September 1947), pp. 239-60.

Haley, J. Evetts. "The Comanchero Trade," *Southwestern Historical Quarterly*, vol. 38 (January 1935), pp. 157-76.

Hampton, H. D. "The Powder River Indian Expedition of 1865," *Montana, the Magazine of Western History*, vol. 14 (October 1964), pp. 2-15.

Haugland, John C. "Alexander Ramsey and the Birth of Party Politics in Minnesota," *Minnesota History*, vol. 39 (summer 1964), pp. 37-48.

"The Indian Bureau Transfer," *The Nation*, vol. 28 (January 1879), pp. 7-8.

"The Indian Problem," *North American Review*, vol. 128 (March 1879), pp. 304-14.

"The Indian System," *North American Review*, vol. 89 (October 1864), pp. 449-64.

Jackson, W. Turrentine. "The Fisk Expeditions to the Montana Gold Fields," *The Pacific Northwest Quarterly*, vol. 33 (July 1942), pp. 265-82.

King, James T. "George Crook: Indian Fighter and Humanitarian," *Arizona and the West*, vol. 9 (winter 1967), pp. 333-48.

Kingman, Samuel A. "Diary of Samuel A. Kingman at the Indian Treaty in 1865," *Kansas Historical Quarterly*, vol. 1 (November 1932), pp. 442-50.

Kingsbury, David L. "Sully's Expedition Against the Sioux in 1864," *Collections of the Minnesota Historical Society*, vol. 8 (1898), pp. 449-62.

Lass, William. "The Removal from Minnesota of the Sioux and Winnebago Indians," *Minnesota History*, vol. 38 (December 1963), pp. 353-64.

————. "The 'Moscow Expedition,'" *Minnesota History*, vol. 39 (summer 1965), pp. 227-40.

Lingk, Ray, "The Northwest Indian Expedition—The Sully Trail of 1864," *North Dakota History*, vol. 24 (October 1957), pp. 181-200.

Lubers, H. L. "William Bent's Family and the Indians of the Plains," *Colorado Magazine*, vol. 12 (January 1936), pp. 19-22.

Mattison, Ray. "The Army Post on the Northern Plains, 1865-1885," *Nebraska History*, vol. 35 (March 1954), pp. 17-43.

————. "The Military Frontier on the Upper Missouri," *Nebraska History*, vol. 38 (September 1959), pp. 159-82.

Mantor, Lyle E. "Fort Kearny and the Westward Movement," *Nebraska History*, vol. 29 (September 1948), pp. 175-207.

Meyer, Roy W. "The Establishment of the Santee Reservation, 1866-1869," *Nebraska History*, vol. 45 (March 1964), pp. 59-97.

————. "The Canadian Sioux: Refugees from Minnesota," *Minnesota History*, vol. 41 (spring 1968), pp. 13-28.

Mitchell, Michael D. "Acculturation Problems Among the Plains Tribes of the Government Agencies in Western Indian Territory," *Chronicles of Oklahoma*, vol. 44 (autumn 1966), pp. 281-89.

Neil, William M. "The Territorial Governor as Indian Superintendent in the Trans-Mississippi West," *Mississippi Valley Historical Review*, vol. 43 (September 1956), pp. 213-37.

Nichols, Colonel G. W. "The Indian: What We Should Do with Him," *Harper's Monthly Magazine,* vol. 40 (April 1870), pp. 732-39.

Perry, Dan W. "The Kiowa's Defiance," *Chronicles of Oklahoma,* vol. 5 (March 1935), pp. 30-36.

Pfaller, Rev. Louis. "Sully's Expedition of 1864," *North Dakota History,* vol. 31 (January 1964), pp. 25-77.

"The Recent Change in the Indian Bureau," *The Nation,* vol. 13 (August 17, 1871), pp. 100-01.

Reckmeyer, Clarence. "The Battle of Summit Springs," *Colorado Magazine,* vol. 6 (November 1929), pp. 211-20.

Reeve, Frank D. "Federal Indian Policy in New Mexico, 1858-1880," *New Mexico Historical Review,* vol. 12 (July 1937), pp. 218-69; and vol. 13 (January, April, and July 1938), pp. 14-62, 146-91, 261-313.

––––. "The Government and the Navajo," *New Mexico Historical Review,* vol. 16 (July 1941), pp. 275-312; and vol. 18 (January 1943), pp. 17-51.

Renville, Gabriel. "A Sioux Narrative of the Outbreak in 1862, and of Sibley's Expedition in 1863," *Collections of the Minnesota Historical Society,* vol. 10 (1905), pp. 595-618.

Riggs, Alfred. "What Shall We Do with the Indian?" *The Nation,* vol. 5 (October 31, 1867), p. 356.

Rister, Carl Coke. "Documents Relating to General W. T. Sherman's Southern Plains Indian Policy, 1871-1875," *Panhandle-Plains Historical Review,* vol. 9 (1936), pp. 7-8; and vol. 10 (1937), pp. 50-60.

––––. "Harmful Practices of Indian Traders of the Southwest, 1865-1876," *New Mexico Historical Review,* vol. 6 (July 1931), pp. 231-48.

––––. "Significance of the Jacksboro Affair of 1871," *Southwestern Historical Quarterly,* vol. 29 (January 1926), pp. 181-200.

––––. "The Significance of the Destruction of the Buffalo in the Southwest," *Southwestern Historical Quarterly,* vol. 33 (July 1929), pp. 34-49.

Schurz, Carl. "Present Aspects of the Indian Problem," *North American Review,* vol. 133 (July 1881), pp. 1-24.

Taylor, A. A. "Medicine Lodge Peace Council," *Chronicles of Oklahoma,* vol. 2 (June 1924), pp. 98-118.

Taylor, Joe F. "The Indian Campaign on the Staked Plains, 1874-1875: Military Correspondence from the War Department, Adjutant General's Office, File 2815-1874," *Panhandle-Plains Historical Review,* vol. 34 (1961), pp. 1-156.

Unrau, William. "Investigation or Probity?–Kiowa-Comanche Agency," *Chronicles of Oklahoma,* vol. 42 (autumn 1964), pp. 300-19.

Utley, Robert M. "The Celebrated Peace Policy of General Grant," *North Dakota History,* vol. 20 (July 1953), pp. 121-42.

––––. "Captain John Pope's Plan of 1853 for the Frontier Defense of New Mexico," *Arizona and the West,* vol. 5 (summer 1963), pp. 149-63.

Walker, Francis, "The Indian Question," *North American Review,* vol. 116 (April 1873), pp. 329-88.

Welty, Raymond L. "The Frontier Army on the Missouri River, 1860-1870," *North Dakota Historical Quarterly,* vol. 2 (January 1928), pp. 85-99.

————. "The Frontier Army on the Missouri River, 1860-1870," *North Dakota Historical Quarterly,* vol. 2 (January 1928), pp. 85-99.

White, Helen M. "Minnesota, Montana, and Manifest Destiny," *Minnesota History,* vol. 38 (June 1962), pp. 53-62.

Index